EMPTY CLOUD

THE AUTOBIOGRAPHY OF THE CHINESE ZEN MASTER

XU-YUN

The Timeless Mind . . . Undated picture of Xu-yun.

EMPTY CLOUD

THE AUTOBIOGRAPHY OF THE CHINESE ZEN MASTER

XU-YUN

Translated by Charles Luk

Revised and edited by Richard Hunn

ELEMENT BOOKS

This edition first published 1988 by
Element Books Limited
Longmead, Shaftesbury, Dorset

Printed and bound in Great Britain by
Billings, Hylton Road, Worcester

Designed by Max Fairbrother

British Library Cataloguing in Publication Data
Xu-yun, d. 1959
Empty Cloud.
1. Zen Buddhism. Xu-yun, d. 1959
I. Title   II. Hunn, Richard
294.3'927'0924
ISBN 1-85230-031-0

CONTENTS

ACKNOWLEDGEMENTS

For the 1980 edition, I would like to mention and thank: W. M. Wong, C. Y. Moi, Erick and Grace Chong, Vinaya Chandra, Maureen Corcoron, Simon Torrens and John Alexander, all of whom encouraged interest for the text.

Now, with the Element edition, I would like to remember my Kalyanamitra and kind friend, Charles Luk, who worked so hard to present many fine translations of Chinese Buddhist texts, besides which I must thank Irene Luk, his daughter, for continuing to take an interest in her father's work and allowing this text to become available again, albeit in modified form. Thanks also to Hugh Clift of Tharpa Publications and Gill; I must thank Stephen Batchelor, who kindly read through an earlier draft and made interesting suggestions, besides offering some photographs from his collection. Also on the photographic front, I must thank James Tsai of Taiwan for the picture of Yin-guang; Dharma-Master Hin-lik for a plate of Xu-yun and sending a copy of the Master's biography. Michael McCracken of Double Visions was a real boon with his photographic skills. I must thank the Buddhist Library of China in Hong Kong for a rare copy of Xu-yun's biography; Oliver Caldecott for permission to quote from Xu-yun's *Dharma Discourses* (pages 49–83/110–17 of a work on Rider's lists). For general encouragement, I must thank Paul and Graham, Tang Hung Tao in Taiwan, Peter and Connie – and finally, I must thank Michael Mann, Simon Franklin and staff at Element Books for their warm welcome, patience and professionalism.

INTRODUCTION

Long before the time of his death in 1959 at the venerable age of 120 on Mount Yun-ju, Jiangxi Province, Master Xu-yun's name was known and revered in every Chinese Buddhist temple and house-hold, having become something of a living legend in his own time. His life and example has aroused the same mixture of awe and inspiration in the minds of Chinese Buddhists as does a Milarepa for the Tibetan Buddhist tradition, remarkable in view of the fact that Xu-yun lived well into our own era, tangibly displaying those spiritual powers that we must otherwise divine by looking back through the mists of time to the great Chan adepts of the Tang, Song and Ming Dynasties. They were great men whose example still inspires many today, but in many cases, we have scant details as to their lives as individuals, outside their recorded dialogues or talks of instruction.

The compelling thing about Xu-yun's story which follows is that it paints a vivid portrait of one of China's greatest Buddhist figures complete with all the chiaroscuro of human and spiritual exper-ience. It is not a modern biography in the Western sense, it is true, but it does lay bare the innermost thoughts and feelings of Master Xu-yun, making him seem that much more real to us. No doubt, the main thing for a Buddhist is the instructional talks, and Xu-yun's are rich in insight, but it is only natural that we should wonder about the individual, human factors, asking what life was like for these fascinating figures. After all, holy men are like mountains, while their 'peaks of attainment' may thrust into unbounded space, they must rest on the broad earth like the rest of us. That part of their experience – how they relate to temporal conditions – is an intrinsic part of their development, even if the ultimate goal be to 'pass beyond' the pale of this world. In Xu-yun's account we are given a fascinating glimpse into the inner life of a great Chinese Buddhist Master.

By the time of his passing, Xu-yun was justifiably recognised as the most eminent Han Chinese Buddhist in the 'Middle Kingdom'. When he gave his talks of instruction at meditation meetings and transmitted the precepts in his final decades, literally hundreds of disciples converged upon the various temples where he met and received his followers and, on some occasions, this number swelled to thousands. Such a wave of renewed enthusiasm had not been witnessed in the Chinese monasteries since the Ming Dynasty when Master Han-shan (1546–1623) appeared. This eminent Master had also found the Dharma in decline and set about reconstructing the temples and reviving the teachings, as would Master Xu-yun some three hundred years or so later. Only years before these great gatherings around Master Xu-yun, many of the temples which he was subsequently to use had been little more than ruined shells, decrepit shadows of their former grandeur and vitality, but the Master revived these along with the teachings that were their very *raison d'être*.

Not surprisingly, Xu-yun soon acquired the nickname 'Han-shan come again' or 'Han-shan returned', for their careers were in many respects similar. Both had shared the ordination name of 'De-qing' and both had restored the Monastery of Hui-neng at Cao-xi among others in their times. However, unlike his eminent predecessors in the Tang, Song and Ming Dynasties who had frequently enjoyed official patronage and support from Emperor and State, Xu-yun's long life of 120 years spanned a most troublesome time both for China and Chinese Buddhism. It was a period continually punctuated by both civil and international conflict, with almost perpetual doubt and confusion as to China's future and security, one in which general want and straitened circumstances were the order of the day.

Xu-yun was born in 1840 around the time of the Opium Wars and by 1843 the Treaty of Nanjing had been signed with the ceding of Hong Kong to Great Britain, the thin end of a wedge of foreign intervention in China's affairs that was to have fateful and long-lasting repercussions. Xu-yun lived to see the last five reigns of the Manchu Dynasty and its eventual collapse in 1911, the formation of the new Republican era taking place in the following year. With the passing of the old order, much was to change in China. China's new leaders were not that concerned about the fate of Buddhism and indeed, many of them were inclined to regard it as a medieval superstition standing in the way of all social and economic progress. The waves of modernism sweeping China at this time were not at all sympathetic towards Buddhism nor any other traditional teachings. Needless to say, many of the monasteries found themselves falling on hard times and many others had already been in ruins before the fall of the dynasty. Government support for the Buddhist temples was scanty when not altogether absent. Of course, China's new leaders had other things on their minds, for besides the frequent famines, droughts and epidemics which ravaged China during these years, there was also the growing threat of Japanese invasion. The Communist Chinese were rising in the countryside, soon to find sufficient strength to take on the Nationalist armies. By the late 1930s, Japanese troops occupied large areas of northern China. It goes without saying that this unfortunate social and political climate hardly offered the best of circumstances in which to embark upon large-scale renewal of the Chinese Buddhist tradition.

However, despite the odds stacked against him by dint of all this chaos, Xu-yun succeeded in retrieving Chinese Buddhism from abysmal decline and actually injected fresh vigour into it. In many ways, the story of Xu-yun is the story of the modern Chinese Buddhist revival, for by the end of his career, he had succeeded in rebuilding or restoring at least a score of the major Buddhist sites, including such famous places as the Yun-xi, Nan-hua, Yun-men and Zhen-ru monasteries, besides countless smaller temples, also founding numerous Buddhist schools and hospitals. His followers were scattered throughout the length and breadth of China, as well as in Malaysia and other outposts where Chinese Buddhism had taken root. During the Master's visit to Thailand, the King became a personal disciple of Xu-yun, so impressed was he by the Master's example. Xu-yun's life-work would have been an achievement of note even during more auspicious days when official patronage had been freely given, but that this tenacious and devoted spirit succeeded in his aims amid the general want and turmoil of his times was even more remarkable and nothing short of miraculous. This was possible only because of the Master's deep spiritual life, which alone could provide the energy for renewal amid confusion and decay. His external works were a reflection of the inner life he cultivated and one of a piece.

To many Chinese Buddhists, Xu-yun appeared like an incarnation and personal embodiment of all that was great about the

Chinese Sangha in the halcyon days of the Tang and Song, and as a modern scholar in the West put it, Xu-yun 'lived hagiography', his life strangely infused with the spirit of greater times. The Master's restoration work was often bidden in strange ways, as if a hidden reservoir of the whole Chinese Buddhist tradition wished to speak anew through his very being. When serving as Abbot of Gu-shan Monastery, Fujian, in 1934, the Master beheld the Sixth Chan Patriarch (d. 713) in his evening meditation. The Patriarch said, 'It is time for you to go back.' Thinking that this betokened the end of his earthly career, the Master said a few words about it to his attendant in the morning and then put it out of mind. In the fourth month of that same year, he again beheld the Patriarch in a dream, who this time thrice urged him to 'go back'. Shortly afterwards, the Master received a telegram from the provincial authorities in Guangdong, inviting him to take over and restore the Sixth Patriarch's monastery at Cao-xi, then in just the same dilapidated condition as Han-shan had found it back in the Ming Dynasty before his own restoration work. Thus, Xu-yun handed over Gu-shan Monastery to another Abbot and proceeded to Cao-xi to set about restoring the famous Nan-hua Monastery, formerly known as 'Bao-lin' or 'Precious Wood', and from which the Chan Schools of yore had received their impetus and inspiration.

Throughout the Master's long career, whether in good fortune or bad, he remained a simple and humble monk. Those who met him, including the usually more critical Western observers, found him to be thoroughly detached from his considerable achievements, unlike one or two other Chinese Buddhists who had welcomed publicity and self-glorification as instruments behind the Chinese Buddhist renaissance. While many talked, Xu-yun quietly went his way, as unaffected as the 'uncarved block' so dear to a wise Chinese heart. Again, despite the munificence of the temples he helped to restore, his noble simplicity remained entire. When the Master approached a holy site for restoration, he took a staff with him as his only possession; when he had seen his task completed, he left with that same staff as his sole possession. When he arrived at the Yun-ju mountain to restore the Zhen-ru Monastery, then a shambles, he took up residence in a cowshed. Despite the large sums of money which came in from devotees during restoration, the Master remained content with his simple cowshed and still preferred it, even after the Zhen-ru Monastery had risen, phoenix-like, from its ashes. But this was to be expected from a monk who had once lived on nothing but pine needles and water while on retreat in the mountain fastness of Gu-shan.

Famous, too, were the Master's long pilgrimages on foot to holy sites at home and abroad, totally at the mercy of the elements and often with little more than his faith to support him. His greatest pilgrimage began in his 43rd year when he set out for the isle of Pu-tuo in Zhejiang, sacred to Avalokitesvara Bodhisattva. Carrying incense in hand, he prostrated every third step of the way to pay reverence to the 'three gems'. Thence in a similar fashion, he headed for Mount Wu-tai in Shansi, sacred to Manjusri Bodhi-sattva, one point of his pilgrimage being to pay back the debt of gratitude he felt towards his parents; the strength of his determina-tion can well be measured by the fact that he nearly perished twice in the bitter cold of Wu-tai's snowy peaks but never gave up. He was saved by a beggar named Wen-ji, regarded by Chinese Buddhists as a 'transformation-body' of Manjusri. From Mount Wu-tai, the Master headed towards Tibet, which he visited, going on to Bhutan, India, Ceylon and Burma before returning to China via Yunnan, calling at holy sites *en route*.

During his travels the Master succeeded in realising 'singleness of mind' throughout day and night, so that by the time of his return to China, conditions were ripe for his final or complete enlighten-ment, which took place in his 56th year while at the Gao-min Monastery in Yangzhou. He was, as the Chinese say, one who had 'ancient bones', for as regards his later career of restoration which included reviving the teaching of the Five Chan Schools (Wu-jia), the Master was very much a 'self-made man' who had re-estab-lished these teachings on the strength of this own insight without teachers. A flash of the old insight was to be found here and there in the temples as Xu-yun had known them in his youth, but the Chan tradition had been in decline by and large. His first teachers had been either Dharma-Masters or Tian-tai Masters, though indeed his Tian-tai teacher had given him his first *gong-an* [Jap. *koan*] ('Who is dragging this corpse about?') and it would not be true to say that the Chinese temples had been totally lacking in enlightened individuals. The marked revival of the Chan tradition in the period extending from the mid-1930s through to the 1950s was largely attributable to Xu-yun's endeavours.

The Master cared greatly for lay-Buddhists, too, and he was

progressive for the way in which he opened up the temple doors to layfolk, teaching them alongside Sangha members. He made much of the *pu-shuo* or 'free sermon' and addressed all who came to him. Though a monk for 101 years, he never pretended that the Dharma was beyond the reach of layfolk. While his *gathas* and verses of instruction reveal the insight of one who saw beyond the pale of this world, he never failed to remind his disciples that the great *bodhi* is ever-present, always there in our daily acts and seemingly mundane circumstances. Like all the great Masters of Chan before him, he laid stress on the non-abiding mind which is beyond reach of all conditioned relativities, even as they arise within it, a paradox that only the enlightened truly understand.

Though the Master became famous as a Chan adept, he also taught Pure Land Buddhism, which he considered to be equally effective as a method of self-cultivation, for like the *hua-tou* technique, the single-minded recitation of the Pure Land mantra stills the dualistic surface activity of the mind, enabling practitioners to perceive their inherent wisdom. This will surprise some Western people who tuned in to the 'Zen craze' a few years back, in which it was often said that Chan or Zen Masters eschewed use of the Pure Land practice. Also, contrary to what has been said on occasions, Xu-yun gave regular talks of instruction on the *sutras* and *shastras*, which he knew thoroughly after many decades of careful study and which he understood experientially, in a way which went beyond the grasp of mere words, names and terms in their literal sense.

By the time Xu-yun had rebuilt the physical and moral fabric of Chinese Buddhism, few of the disciples who gathered round the Master or attended the other temples he rebuilt had to suffer the same indignities and privations that he had experienced himself when calling at monasteries in his youth. He had often been turned away from temples that had fallen into the degenerate system of hereditary ownership, not even allowed a night's lodging. When he had called at some temples, only a handful of monks were to be found because of the general decline. In one instance, famine had reduced the whole population of locals and monks at one site to just a single person who used to put on a 'brave face' if callers happened by. Given that kind of background, it is hardly surprising that Xu-yun recognised the need to recreate that self-sufficiency extolled by the ancient Master Bai-zhang Hui-hai (d. 814) in his famous dictum, 'A day without work, a day without food'. Thus, wherever possible, Xu-yun revived the monastic agricultural system to live up to this tradition of self-sufficiency.

Thus far, all the necessary ingredients were present to sustain a revival which had borne fruit through decades of devoted effort. But we now come to a most tragic interlude in the life of Xu-yun which might well be called a 'twilight of the gods' were it the finale, though thankfully it was not. As is well known, the Communist Government took effective control of China in 1949 about the time that Xu-yun had set his aim on restoring the Yun-men Monastery in Guangdong. By 1951–52 the first tremors of what was to follow in the Cultural Revolution were beginning to make themselves felt. The restoration of the Yun-men Monastery was more or less complete, but misfortune struck from without with a purge of so-called 'rightist elements' in Guangdong Province. Being very much a 'traditionalist' in outlook, Master Xu-yun was an obvious target. Fears that Xu-yun might not be safe in the volatile atmosphere of these times had been voiced, the Master's overseas disciples urging him to leave the mainland until things settled down. He refused to leave, however, expressly because he felt that it was his duty to look after the welfare of the monasteries. What happened next was almost inevitable; a horde of Communist cadres descended on the Yun-men Monastery which they surrounded. They locked the Master up in a room for several days, where he was interrogated and ruthlessly beaten, left for dead. Perhaps the less said about this episode, the better. Suffice it to say that the Master had broken ribs and bled profusely, being for a while most seriously ill. Remarkably enough though, while then in his 112th year, Xu-yun recovered from a beating severe enough to have killed someone less than half his age. This was not the first time that he had been beaten, for the police in Singapore had roughed him up back in 1916, ironically enough on the suspicion of being a 'leftist' from the mainland. But the beating he suffered in his 112th year was infinitely worse. Even so, without trying to make too little out of the violence he suffered, the old Master bounced back with all the properties of a proverbial 'Da-ruma doll' and lived to carry on teaching not only at the Yun-men Monastery but many others besides, also finding time and energy for one more round of restoration work at the Zhen-ru Monastery on Mount Yun-ju, Jiangxi Province, where he eventually departed from this world on 13 October 1959. He had been in the Sangha for 101 years.

With the Master's passing in 1959, the Cultural Revolution was just around the corner. As we know, the monasteries had to suffer bitterly during that period. For many monks, nuns and lay devotees, it must have seemed that everything the Master had striven for was about to sink into oblivion. That draconian measures were already evident in Xu-yun's last years must have caused him some concern; as it was, the episode at Yun-men cost him his most able disciple, Miao-yuan, who was executed. Other disciples had been harmed too. Things did look bleak, and even the news of events at Yun-men had to be smuggled out of mainland China by inserting records in the blank innerfolds of traditionally bound Chinese books. But as many on the mainland today are prepared to admit, the excesses of the Cultural Revolution were wrong; few would disagree.

Whether the long-term effects of ideological reform have been as catastrophic for Chinese Buddhism as once predicted is a good question. We should not deceive ourselves into thinking that Buddhism had been immune from persecution under the ancient regime. In the Hui-chang period (842–5) of the Tang Dynasty, a massive purge of Chinese Buddhism took place with the near destruction of some 4,600 monasteries, with 260,000 monks and nuns being forced back into lay life, the confiscation of monastic property and land being widespread. The monasteries managed to recover from that and by way of contrast, the modern picture is not entirely pessimistic. It is some consolation to learn that the temples which Xu-yun restored are not only being patched up after the ravages of the revolution, but that many are being restored to their proper use and once more assuming an air of normality, though the complement of monks and nuns is much smaller these days. At any rate, these are not the 'actor monks' shuffled around China by the authorities twenty years ago, who fooled nobody, but *bona fide* occupants. Of this I have been given reliable assurance from two sources, my friends Dharma-Master Hin-lik and Stephen Batchelor (Gelong Jhampa Thabkay), both of whom made recent visits to the monasteries in southern China.

Thus, rather than ending on a pessimistic note, we should rejoice in the fact that Xu-yun's endeavours did not fall entirely on stony ground. Without the energies he released into Chinese Buddhism, it is quite likely that the Chinese Sangha would have suffered far greater setbacks than it did during the revolution. In this sense, Master Xu-yun lived out the mythical role of the 'poison-eating peacock' in Buddhist lore; from the bitterness of that poison something spiritual sprang forth. In the long run it seems that, as with the suppression of Buddhism in Tibet, the suppression of Chinese Buddhism has had the precise opposite effect to that intended by the suppressors. Not only has the Asian Buddhist had to reappraise the worth of the Dharma in his own context, but its merits have also struck the attention of the whole world.

Was it merely coincidence that at the height of the Cultural Revolution in China, copies of Lao-zi and Chan (Zen) texts went into record numbers of reprints in the West? Anyone at all familiar with the Jungian theory of synchronicity would find it hard not to see this phenomenon as a profound act of compensation in the collective psyche. Some things are meant to be and cannot be destroyed. Though all outward signs and symbols may be denied for a while, their inner archetypes always remain and, like seeds, they reassert themselves. It is salutary to note in this respect that no lesser person than the late C. G. Jung was reading Xu-yun's *Dharma-discourses* while on his death-bed.

Over the years, the editor has received a number of letters from home and abroad inquiring about Xu-yun, his life and teachings. Such interest has sprung from a variety of sources and lands, ranging from Europe, Australia and the USA, to Scandinavia and even a small South American state. In view of such wide interest, the story of Xu-yun's life will appeal to many, for while his teachings have been available for years, the autobiography has so far appeared only in limited editions.

In America, Roshi Philip Kapleau has read from Xu-yun's account to inspire his students at the Rochester Zen Center. This could only be because Xu-yun's story is a testimony to the deep human need for spiritual nourishment. When reading the story of the Master's quest, we see a reflection of our own therein. He symbolises the 'great man' hidden in ourselves and his name 'Empty Cloud' reminds us of that greater, 'undiscovered Self' that we are all fated to explore.

So much then for the great man with whom our text deals; a brief word must now be said about the text itself. It is a cause for rejoicing that a new edition of *Empty Cloud* is to become available under the banner of Element Books. Though Xu-yun's teachings are quite widely known via the *Discourses and Dharma Words* translated by Upasaka Lu K'uan Yu (Charles Luk) in his *Chan and Zen Teaching* series (see Bibliography), Lu's translation of the Master's biography never saw regular publication, though limited editions have indeed appeared, once in the USA, through the inspired initiative of Roshi Philip Kapleau and friends at the Rochester Zen Center (1974), and an English edition (1980), thanks to the editor's friends who helped finance that version.

In anticipation of further reprints, it seemed advisable to incorporate a number of corrections, revisions and additions to bring the text up to date. Some of these errors had been drawn to my notice by Upasaka Lu back in 1975 and vice versa, but as Lu sadly passed away in 1978 he was unable to make further revisions. To compensate, I have checked the translation several times against the *Xu-yun He-shang Nian-pu* from which Lu worked, incorporating whatever changes seemed to be required, including extra notes, minor additions, a glossary, etc. although the translation is still basically Luk's original which first appeared in serialised form in *World Buddhism* back in the 1960s, several passages have either been rewritten or added, and to that extent constitute new translations.

Another modification has been to substitute the *pinyin* form of romanisation; this is rapidly becoming the standard form in the West and it is also the form that visitors will find used in China in guidebooks and publications. I have departed from this in two or three instances, as in the retention of Canton for Guangzhou, the old form still being used in guidebooks; I have kept Amoy for Xiamen, and in order to avoid an apparent ambiguity likely to ensnare the general reader, I have kept the old spellings of Shensi and Shansi (*pinyin*: Shaanxi and Shanxi). Again, while not quite orthodox, I have hyphenated some *pinyin* names more than usual so as to recall the older spellings. Readers with *pinyin* should have no trouble with 'Bao-lin' and those familiar with Wade-Giles will readily spot the transition from 'Pao-lin'. Written as 'Baolin', however, the name is not identifiable in the same way. I have retained the Chinese *li* as a measurement of distance, for it is much shorter than the English mile (about ⅓ mile) and should pose no more problems than the kilometre in Continental writings. As a final note, it is worth reminding readers that Luk's translation was made from the early edition of Xu-yun's biography; in recent years this has been expanded to include collections of the recorded teachings and lectures given at many monasteries, in fact extra books. To translate all of this material would be interesting, but something of a magnum opus for the would-be translator. However, a couple of supplementary records have been added in this edition. Extra sources of Xu-yun's teaching, both English translations and Chinese originals, are listed in the bibliographical section.

May all beings attain release!

UPASAKA WEN-SHU (RICHARD HUNN)
Thorpe Hamlet, Norwich.

13 October 1987.
The Anniversary of Xu-yun's Nirvana.

Master Xu-yun at the Guang-ji Monastery, Beijing, 1952.

EARLY YEARS

MY 1ST YEAR
(1840/41)

I was born at the headquarters of Quanzhou Prefecture on the last day of the seventh month in the year Geng-zi, the twentieth of the Dao-guang reign [26 August 1840]. When my mother saw that she had given birth to a fleshy bag [presumably she had suffered a prolapse of the womb] she was frightened and thinking that there was no hope of bearing child again, she succumbed to her desperation and passed away. The following day an old man selling medicine came to our house and cut open the bag, taking out a male child which was reared by my stepmother.

MY 11TH YEAR
(1850/51)

My grandmother was ageing and since I had also been adopted by my uncle as his heir, she decided that I should take two girls as wives from the Tian and Tan families. Both were Hunanese mandarin families living in Fujian and we had been friends of theirs for many generations. That winter, my grandmother passed away.

MY 13TH YEAR
(1852/53)

That year, I accompanied my father while taking my grandmother's coffin to Xiangxiang where she was buried. Monks were invited to perform Buddhist rites so I had my first chance to see sacred articles and was very pleased at this sight. There were many Buddhist *sutras* [scriptures] in our home library and I thus read the story of the 'Fragrant Mountain' and Avalokitesvara Bodhisattva's attainment of enlightenment which had a great influence upon my mind. In the eighth month, I followed my uncle to Nan-yue, where we visited monasteries. I felt as if some former karmic cause made me unwilling to return home but as my uncle was very stern, I dared not tell him my feelings.

MY 14TH YEAR
(1853/54)

My father discovered that I wanted to leave home to join the Sangha and in order to keep me, he engaged a Daoist called Wang to teach me Daoist practices at home. The teacher gave me Daoist books to read and also taught me the Daoist 'inner' and 'outer' yogas [Nei-gong and Wai-gong in Daoism]. I did not like the teaching but dared not reveal my unfavourable opinion of it. That winter the period of mourning for my grandmother ended and after entrusting my uncle with the care of my education, my father returned alone to Fujian.[1]

Notes
1. The period of mourning for close relatives set by Confucianism is three years. This is why Xu-yun's father had not returned to Fujian earlier.

MY 17TH YEAR
(1856/57)

I had been studying Daoism at home for the last three years but realised that the teaching I had been given failed to reach the ultimate pattern. Although I felt as if I were sitting on a mat of needles, I kept up a pretence of doing everything to make my uncle happy, working in the house to escape his watchful eye. One day, as he went out, I thought it an opportune moment to take my leave, packed my things and headed for Nan-yue. There were many difficult and divergent roads *en route* and when but halfway, I was found by a man sent out in pursuit of me and brought back. Along with my cousin Fu-guo, I was sent to Quanzhou and shortly afterwards, my father sent for the two girls from the Tian and Tan families and my marriage to them was celebrated whether I liked it or not. Thus, I was placed under 'house arrest'. I lived with the two girls but had no intercourse with them. I expounded the Buddhadharma to them, which they understood. My cousin Fu-guo noticed that they were above worldly things and also expounded the Dharma to them from time to time. Thus, either in our private quarters or in the reception hall, we were merely pure-minded companions.

MY 19TH YEAR
(1858/59)

I vowed to retire from the world and my cousin also shared this aspiration. In secret, I inquired about the way to Mount Gu in Fuzhou. I wrote the 'Song of the Skin Bag' [see Appendix], which was left behind for the two girls to read. With Fu-guo, I fled to the Yung-quan (Bubbling Spring) Monastery on Mount Gu in Fuzhou, where my head was shaved by the elderly Master Chang-kai.

MY 20TH YEAR
(1859/60)

I followed Master Miao-lian on Mount Gu and received full ordination from him. I was given the Dharma-name Gu-yan, plus the aliases Yan-che and De-qing. My father, who was then at Quanzhou Prefecture, sent out servants in search of me. My cousin, Fu-guo, left on a journey in search of enlightened Masters after his full ordination and I never heard from him again. I hid myself in a grotto behind the mountain where I made penitential offerings to myriads of Buddhas in observance of the rules for repentance and reform. I dared not come out of hiding (for fear of being found by the scouts sent out by my father). Though I was occasionally visited by tigers and wolves, I was not in the least scared.

3

MY 23RD YEAR
(1862/63)

I had by now completed the three years' observance of the rules for repentance and reform. One day, a monk came from Mount Gu and said, 'There is no need for you to hide now as your old father has retired on account of his age and he has left for home. The elderly Master Miao-lian has praised your long austerities but said that, in addition to wisdom, you should cultivate the blessing that arises from altruistic activities. You can return to the mountain temple, take up a post and serve others. Thereupon I returned to the mountain temple where I was given work.

MY 25TH YEAR
(1964/65)

Still holding the post on Mount Gu. That winter in the twelfth month, I heard that my father had passed away at home in Xiangxiang. Since then I no longer inquired about my family and heard nothing more about them.

MY 27TH YEAR
(1866/67)

A man came from Xiangxiang and informed me that after my father's death, my stepmother Wang and her two daughters-in-law had left home to become nuns. My stepmother Wang took the Dharma-name of Miao-jing (Profound Purity), my wife Tian, that of Zhen-jie (True Cleanness) and my wife Tan, that of Qing-jie (Clear Chastity). For four years I had held various jobs in the temple on Mount Gu, serving as its water-man, gardener, hall-keeper and verger and they were all but austerities. Occasionally I was given a sinecure which I turned down. In the monastery, they were times when donations were divided out between the monks, but I always declined my share. Each day, I took a mug of rice-gruel but my health was never so robust.

At the time, Chan Master Gu-yue surpassed all those who were engaged in austerities at the temple and as I had many long chats with him when occasion allowed, I since thought 'The jobs I have held these years have in some way hindered my practice,' and I recalled Dharma-Master Xuan-zang who had wanted to visit India in search of sutras and who, ten years before his travels, learned Sanskrit and trained by walking a hundred *li* per day.[1] He also tried to abstain from cereals first for one full day and then gradually for a certain number of days so as to accustom himself to desert travel conditions where even water and grass might not be available. If an ancient could engage in such austerities to reach his goal, who am I that I should not follow his example?[2]

Afterwards, I gave up all my jobs at the monastery, distributed my garments to the monks and, equipped with a robe, a pair of trousers, shoes, a straw raincoat and hassock, I returned to the mountain grotto and resumed my life there.

Notes
1. The Chinese *li* is a unit of length, approximately $\frac{1}{2}$ kilometre. In ancient times, it varied slightly for different purposes.
2. Xuan-zang (600-64) was a famous Dharma-Master who went to India to collect sutras and subsequently translated them into Chinese.

MY 28TH, 29TH AND 30TH YEARS
(1867/70)

I stayed in the grotto for three years. During those years, my food consisted of pine needles and green blades of grass, my drink the water of the mountain streams. As time went by, my trousers and shoes wore out and I had only my robe to cover my body. My hair and beard grew to over a foot in length so I wore a top-knot on my head. My eyes became bright and piercing so that those who saw me took me for a mountain spirit and ran off. Thus I avoided speaking to others.

In the first and second years of my seclusion I had many unusual experiences, but I refrained from discriminating about them, turning back in singleness of mind to look into them whilst reciting the Buddha's name. Deep in the mountains and marshy land, I was not attacked by tigers or wolves, nor was I bitten by snakes or insects. I neither craved for human sympathy nor took the cooked food normally eaten by people. Lying on the ground with the sky above me, I felt that the myriad things were complete in myself; I experienced a great joy as if I were a deva [god] of the fourth *dhyana*-heaven.[1] I thought that the worst calamity for worldly men was having a mouth and body and remembered an ancient who once said that his begging bowl could 'slight the sound of ten thousand bells'.[2] Since I had not even a bowl myself, I experienced boundless freedom from all impediments. Thus my mind was clear and at ease and my strength grew with each passing day. My eyes and ears became sharp and penetrating and I walked with rapid steps as if I were flying. It seemed inexplicable how I came to be in such a condition. In the third year I was able to make my heart content moving freshly as I wished. As there were mountains to stay on and wild herbs to eat, I started wandering from place to place and thus passed the year oblivious of time.

Notes

1. Devas have only the organ of mind.
2. Chan Master Han-shan (1546-1623) said of his begging bowl that it was 'a utensil that slights [or can be heard above] ten thousand bells', meaning that even attachment to a begging bowl can seriously distract the mind of the practitioner just as effectively as the din of bells. See 'Han-shan's autobiography, *A Journey in Dreamland*, included in *Practical Buddhism* by Charles Luk (Rider & Co., London, 1971).

MY 31ST YEAR
(1870/71)

I arrived at a mountain in Wenzhou and stayed in a grotto there. A Chan monk came along, paid obeisance and said, 'I have long heard of your lofty virtue and come to implore your instruction.'[1]

I felt very ashamed at this and replied, 'My knowledge is shallow, for as yet I have had no chance to call on learned Masters; would you be compassionate enough to give me some indication as to the Dharma?'

'How long have you adopted this austere way of life?' he asked.

I related my practice to him and he said, 'I also have had no chance to learn much and am thus unable to give you instruction; but you could go to Long-quan Temple on the Hua-ding peak of

Mount Tian-tai and call on Dharma-Master Yang-jing who is a man of pre-eminent virtue in the Tian-tai School.[2] He will be able to enlighten you.'

Thereupon, I climbed the Hua-ding peak and reached a thatched temple where I met a monk outside, asking him if the old Dharma-Master were there. He replied, 'He is the one wearing a patched robe over there,' gesturing in the old Master's direction. I approached the Master, prostrating before him. Since he paid no attention, I said, 'I have come to implore your instruction and hope you will have pity on me.'

He looked at me for a long while and then said, 'Are you a monk, a Daoist or a layman?'

'A monk,' I replied.

'Have you been ordained?' he asked.

'I have received the full ordination,' I replied.

'How long have you been in this condition?' he asked. As I related my story, he asked, 'Who instructed you to practise this way?'

I replied, 'I did it because the ancients attained enlightenment by means of such austerities.'

He asked, 'You know that the ancients disciplined their bodies, but do you know that they also disciplined their minds?' He further added 'As I see your current practice, you are like a heretic and entirely on the wrong path, having wasted ten years' training. If, by staying in a grotto and drinking water from mountain streams, you managed to succeed in living ten thousand years, you would only be one of the ten classes of *Rishis* (immortals) listed [in the 'fifty false states'] in the *Surangama Sutra*[3] and still be far away from the Dao. Even if you managed to advance a further step, thus realising the 'first fruit',[4] you would only be a 'self-enlightened fellow' *(Pratyeka Buddha)*. But as for a *Bodhisattva*, his quest is for Buddhahood from 'above' for the conversion and liberation of living beings here 'below', his way being to pursue self-liberation for the liberation of others, leaping to the supramundane plane without fleeing from the mundane.

If your method merely consists of abstaining from cereals and in not even wearing trousers, it is only a quest for the extraordinary. How can you expect such a practice to result in perfect achievement? So the Master 'pierced' my weak spot right to the core and I again prostrated myself, imploring his instruction.

Said he: 'I will teach you; if you follow my instruction properly you can stay here but if you do not, you must go away.'

I said, 'As I came here for your instruction, how could I dare to disobey it?'

Thereupon, the Master gave me garments and footwear and ordered me to shave my head and take a bath. He gave me work to do and taught me to look into the *gong-an* 'Who is dragging this corpse about?'[5] Thenceforth, I again took rice and gruel and practised the meditation of the Tian-tai School. As I worked hard, the Master praised me.

Notes

1. A very polite way of addressing strangers in China, particularly monks.
2. Originally founded by master Hui-wen in the Bei-qi Dynasty (550–78), but finally consolidated by master Zhi-yi on Mount Tian-tai, Taizhou Prefecture, Zhejiang Province, whence the school acquired its name. It bases its practices on the *Lotus, Mahiparinirvana* and *Mahaprajnaparamita Sutras,* its aim being to unlock the secrets of all phenomena by means of its 'combined triple insight' through the *zhi-guan* method. Cf. Zhi-yi's *Samatha-Vipasyana For Beginners,* in *Secrets of Chinese Meditation,* Charles Luk (Rider & Co., London, 1964, p. 111).
3. See *The Surangama Sutra,* trans. Charles Luk (Rider & Co., London, 1962), pp. 199–236.
4. *Sroto-Apanna,* i.e. one who has 'entered the stream' of holy living in meditation, but for self-enlightenment alone.
5. The *gong-an* (Jap. *koan*) 'Who is dragging this corpse about?' refers to the mind or self-natured wisdom and its superiority to the body of four elements. When the mind identifies with the body, we fall into the 'guest' position in *samsara;* when we realise that our illusory bodies are transformations which arise within the immutable mind, we take up the 'host' position and reunite with the immutable. In Chan monasteries, those attached to their bodily selves are called 'corpse-guarding demons'.

MY 32ND YEAR
(1871/72)

During my stay at the Long-quan Temple, I served the Master and he advised me from time to time how to open up my mind's innate wisdom. Though over 80 years old, he strictly observed the rules of *(Vinaya)* discipline and was well-versed in both the teaching [of the sutras] and Chan. Many a time, he ordered me to take the commentator's seat to enlighten visitors to the monastery.

MY 33RD YEAR
(1872/73)

As ordered by the old Master Yang-jing, I went to the Guo-qing Monastery to study the Chan rules and Fang-guang Monastery to study the Fa-hua (Lotus) teaching.

MY 34TH AND 35TH YEARS
(1873/75)

I stayed at the Guo-qing Monastery to study the *sutra*-teaching and from time to time, I returned to the [Long-quan] Temple to keep company with the old Master Yang-jing.

MY 36TH YEAR
(1875/76)

I went to Gao-ming Monastery in order to hear Dharma-Master Ming-xi expounding the *Lotus Sutra*. I was to bid farewell to the old Master Yang-jing at this time, so it was not without sadness to part company with him. Thus, I spent a few evenings chatting with him prior to my departure, and we wished each other well, whereafter I descended the mountain. I passed through Xue-tou and arrived at the Yue-lin Monastery, where I listened to the *Amitabha Sutra* being expounded. Thereafter, I crossed the sea to Mount Pu-tuo, where I passed the New Year in Hou-si Temple.

MY 37TH YEAR
(1876/77)

From Pu-tuo, I returned to Ningbo, where I visited the monastery of King Ashoka and made arrangements to be fed for three dollars a month. There, I revered a relic *(sarira)* of Shakyamuni Buddha and the two *Pitakas* (the Hinayana and Mahayana Canons) to reap benefits so as to repay the debt of gratitude which I owed my parents. Thence, I went to Tian-tong Monastery,[1] where I listened to a commentary on the *Surangama Sutra*.

Notes
1. Situated on the Tian-tong mountain in Zhejiang. It was built by Yi-xing of the Western Jin Dynasty in 300. It became a famous Chan centre of mixed Lin-ji and Cao-dong lineages. It was here that the eminent Japanese Master Dogen-zenji (1200–53) met his Chinese teacher, Ru-jing (1163–1228) in the Song Dynasty.

MY 38TH YEAR
(1877/78)

From Ningbo I went to Hangzhou on a pilgrimage taking me to San-tian Chu and other holy places. Half-way from the peak of Mount San-tian Chu, I called on Abbot Tian-lang and the monastery's guest-master Zhang-song, paying my respects to them. I passed the winter at Xi-tian.

The weather was very hot when on my way from Ningbo to Hangzhou, and the boat was too small for the number of passengers lying on deck, among them being young women. At night, when all were asleep, I felt someone touching my body. I woke up and saw a girl beside me taking her clothes off – offering her naked body to me. I dared not speak and promptly got up, sitting cross-legged, repeating a mantra. She dared not move after that. Had I been foolish at the time, I would inevitably have lost ground. On account of this, I have urged all devotees to be very careful under similar circumstances.

MY 39TH YEAR
(1878/79)

That year I went to the Tian-ning Monastery, where I paid my respects to Abbot Qing-guang, passing the winter there.

MY 40TH YEAR
(1879/80)

I climbed Mount Jiao to pay my respects to Abbot Da-shui. Superintendent Peng Yu-lin was staying there, and several times requested that I discuss the Buddhadharma and its methods of practice with him. I was the object of his trust and respect.

MY 41ST YEAR
(1880/81)

That year, I went to the Jin-shan Monastery in Zhenjiang calling on Masters Guan-xin, Xin-lin and Da-ding; there, I sat in meditation while passing the winter.

MY 42ND YEAR
(1881/82)

That year, I went to the Gao-min Monastery at Yangzhou and paid obeisance to Abbot Yue-lang. I passed the winter there and made good progress in my Chan practice.

Master Xu-yun at the Yong-quan Monastery on Gu-shan.
This was the temple where Xu-yun first took refuge in his youth.
The monk with him in this picture is unidentified.
It could be his old teacher, Miao-lian. No date.

CHAPTER TWO

Pilgrimage to Mount Wu-tai

MY 43RD YEAR
(1882/83)

Over twenty years had passed since I cut off my family ties in order
to leave lay life. As my spiritual attainments were as yet incom-
plete, and as I was still drifting about, I felt very ashamed. In order
to pay back my debt of gratitude to my parents, I decided to go on
pilgrimage to Pu-tuo in the east and thence to Mount Wu-tai (Five-
Peaked Mountain) in the north. I stayed a few months at Pu-tuo,
where I made excellent progress with my spiritual training in the
mountain stillness. On the first day of the seventh lunar month, I
set out from the thatched temple of Fa-hua carrying burning
incense on the way to Wu-tai. I vowed to prostrate myself at every
third step on this long journey until my destination had been
reached. On the first leg of the journey I had with me the four Chan
monks, Bian-zhen, Qiu-ning, Shan-xia and Jue-cheng. After crossing the sea by ferry, we were not many days on the road before
stopping off at Huzhou. My four travelling companions went their
ways at Suzhou and Changzhou and I carried on alone. When I
arrived at Nanjing,[1] I paid reverence to the *stupa* [round building
erected as shrine] of Master Fa-rong on Mount Niu-tou (Oxhead
Mountain and then crossed the river proceeding to Shi-zi Shan
(Lion Mountain) and Pu-kou, where I stopped to pass the New
Year in the temple.

Notes
1. Modern-day Nanjing is on the site of what used to be the ancient city of Jin-ling. Master Fa-rong (594–657) was a disciple of Dao-xin, the Fourth Chan Patriarch, and had a temple in Mount Niu-tou, south Nanjing.

MY 44TH YEAR
(1883/84)

That year, I walked holding incense-offerings from Mount Shi-zi to the north of the Jiangsu Province and entered Henan Province, subsequently passing through Feng-yang, Hao-zhou, Hao-ling and Mount Song, site of the Shao-lin temple. Passing on, I eventually reached the Bai-ma (White Horse) Monastery at Luo-yang. I walked by day and rested night, no matter whether it blew or rained, in either fair or foul weather. Thus, prostrating myself at every third step, I recited the name of Manjusri Bodhisattva with singleness of mind, oblivious of either hunger or the warmth of my fill.

On the first day of the twelfth month, I reached the Tie-xie ferry on the Huang-he (Yellow River), passed the tombs of Guang-wu and stopped at a nearby inn. The next day, I crossed the river and when I reached the other bank it was already dark, so I dared not walk on. As the place was deserted I stopped there, entering an empty thatched hut by the roadside where I sat. That night the cold was intense and there was also a heavy snowfall. When I opened my eyes the following morning, I saw the whole countryside was white with over a foot of snow. All roads were blocked and the place was devoid of travellers. As I could not resume my journey, I sat reciting the Buddha's name. I suffered greatly from hunger and cold since the hut had no enclosure, I huddled myself up in a corner. As heavier snow fell, the cold became more intense and my hunger greater. It seemed as if only my breath remained, but fortunately my 'right thought' [right mindfulness, even under duress] was intact. After three days, with the same snowfall, the same cold and hunger, I gradually sank into a state of confusion. In the afternoon of the sixth day I dimly saw a faint image of the sun but I was by then gravely ill. On the seventh day a beggar came and, seeing that I was sleeping in the snow, asked me some questions but I could not speak. He realised that I was ill from the cold, swept away the snow, took some straw from the hut, kindled

14

a fire and cooked a gruel of yellow rice, which he gave me. I was thus warmed and brought back to life.

He asked me, 'Where did you come from?'

'From Pu-tuo,' I replied.

'Where are you going?' he asked.

'On pilgrimage to Wu-tai,' I replied.

'What is your name?' I inquired.

'Wen-ji,'[1] he said.

'Where are you going?' I asked.

'I came from Wu-tai and am returning to Xi'an,' he replied.

I asked, 'Since you came from Wu-tai, do you know people in the monasteries there?'

'Everybody knows me there,' he said.

I asked, 'What places do I have to pass through from here to Wu-tai?'

He replied, 'Meng-xian, Huai-qing, Huang Shanling, Xinzhou, Tai-gu, Taiyuan, Taizhou and E-gou, thence straight into the mountains. As you first reach the Bi-mo Grotto, there is a monk there called Qing-yi who hails from the south and his self-cultivation has been excellent.'

I asked, 'How far is it from here to the mountains?'

'A little over two thousand *li* [about 620 miles],' he replied.

At sunrise, the beggar cooked up a gruel of yellow rice using ice-water to boil it with. Pointing to the contents of the pot, he asked, 'Do you have "this" in Pu-tuo?'[2]

'No,' I replied.

'What do you drink there?' the beggar asked.

'Water,' I replied.

As the snow in the pot had fully melted, he pointed his finger at the water and asked, 'What is it?'[3]

As I did not reply, he asked, 'What are you seeking for in your pilgrimage to the famous mountain of Wu-tai?'[4]

I replied, 'I did not see my mother when I was born; my purpose is to repay my debt of gratitude I owe her.'

He said, 'What with a bag on your back, the distance involved, plus the cold, would you be able to reach Wu-tai? I advise you to cancel your pilgrimage.'

I replied, 'I have taken my vow and will fulfil it regardless of the distance and time required.'

He said, 'Your vow is a difficult one to undertake. Today, the

15

weather has improved but all the roads are still blocked with snow. You can resume your journey by following my tracks. Some twenty *li* further on there is a temple in which you can stay.'

We then parted company. As the snow was deep I could not prostrate myself as I had before, but only looked at the footprints to pay my respects. When I reached the Monastery at 'Little Jin-shan' (Xiao Jin-shan) I passed the night there. Next morning, carrying incense, I continued my pilgrimage and passed through Meng-xian. On my way from there to Huai-qing, an old Abbot by the name of De-lin saw me prostrating on the road, came up, took over my stool and incense sticks and said, 'The Venerable Sir is invited to my monastery.' Then he called his disciples to take my baggage to the temple, where I was treated with great courtesy.

After food and tea had been served in the temple, my host asked about the starting-point from which I had begun my walk and prostrations. I spoke of my vow to repay the debt of gratitude I owed my parents which I had begun to fulfil when leaving Pu-tuo two years before. During our conversation, the Abbot came to know of the fact that I had been ordained at Mount Gu. With tears rolling down his cheeks, he said, 'I had two Chan companions, one from Heng-yang and the other from Fuzhou. We three went on pilgrimage together to Mount Wu-tai. After staying together at this monastery for thirty years, they left and I have not heard news of them since. Now that I hear your Hunanese accent, and since you are also a disciple from Mount Gu, I feel that I have met my old companions again, which moves me deeply. I am now 85. Our monastery's source of revenue was originally regular but has been somewhat reduced owing to the bad crops in recent years. This heavy snowfall augurs a good crop next year, so you can stay here, Venerable Sir.' Earnestly and sincerely, he urged me to stay over the winter.

Notes

1. According to tradition, Manjusri vowed to accompany every pilgrim to his holy site (Bodhimandala) at Wu-tai. He is said to appear as a beggar and in other guises in order to help pilgrims. The Chinese Buddhists believe that 'Wen-ji' who figures in the text here was actually Manjusri (Chin. *Wen-shu*) and that he wished to help Master Xu-yun.

2. Here, Wen-ji (Manjusri) probed the Master by his question, which means, 'My mind is pointing at the ice and asks you this question,' and

also 'Were you taught to realise your mind at Pu-tuo?' The Bodhisattva continued probing the Master with subsequent questions which the latter did not understand, for he was as yet unenlightened.
3. Water symbolises the self-nature and the question is loaded with meaning.
4. Again, a meaningful question, because in the practice of Chan a student is taught to avoid seeking after anything in order to realise the absolute state which is beyond gain and loss.

MY 45TH YEAR
(1884/85)

On the second of the first lunar months, I went from Hong-fu Monastery to Huai-qing carrying incense offerings *en route*, returning to the monastery again for another short stay, intending to leave soon. On the third day, I bade farewell to the old Abbot De-lin, who was tearful and did not like losing my company. With parting good wishes I left and in the same day reached Huai-qing again. Inside its walls was 'Little Nan-hai', also known as 'Little Pu-tuo'. There, guest monks could not even hang up their things or stay for the night. Thus, I had to leave the town and pass the night by the roadside. That evening, I felt severe griping pains in my belly. On the fourth, I resumed my journey at daybreak but that night I shivered with malaria. On the fifth, I contracted dysentery but forced myself to continue my walk and prostrations and the same for successive days. By the thirteenth, I arrived at Huang Shaling on the peak of which there was a ruined temple without much shelter. As I could no longer walk, I stopped there without taking food. Day and night, I stooled a dozen or more times. I was completely exhausted and had not even the strength to get up and walk about. Since the temple was on top of a mountain where there were no residents, I closed my eyes and waited for my end without a single thought of regret.

On the fifteenth, late at night, I saw someone making a fire under the west wall. I thought it was a thief but when I looked at him carefully, I saw that it was the beggar Wen-ji. I was overjoyed and called out, 'Wen-ji!' He brought me a fire-brand to lighten the place and said, 'How is it that you are still here, Venerable Sir?' I told him what had happened and he sat at my side to comfort me, handing me a cup of water to drink. After seeing Wen-ji that night, I felt purified in body and mind.

On the sixteenth, Wen-ji washed my dirty garments and gave me a cup of medicine. The next day, I recovered from my illness and after taking two bowls of yellow rice-gruel, I perspired profusely and felt great cheer and well-being within and without.

On the eighteenth, with my health recovered in full, I thanked Wen-ji, saying, 'Twice I was in danger – and twice you saved me; words fail to express my gratitude.'

Wen-ji said, 'It was nothing really.' When asked where he had been, he said, 'Xi'an.' When asked where he would be going, he said, 'I am returning to Wu-tai.'

I said, 'As I have been unwell, and what with my prostrations to do *en route*, I cannot follow you.'

He said, 'You have not covered much distance this year – when will you reach your destination? As you are still weak, it will be difficult for you to continue. Prostrations are not absolutely necessary, nor is your pilgrimage.'

I replied, 'I am most touched by your kind words, but when I was born I did not see my mother, who died at childbirth. I was my father's only son but I fled from him and because of that, he resigned his post and this shortened his life. As my parents' love for me was as boundless as heaven is vast, I have been unhappy about this business for several decades. Thus, I vowed to go on pilgrimage to Mount Wu-tai to pray for Manjusri Bodhisattva to protect them and deliver them from suffering so that they can secure birth in the Pure Land as soon as possible. However many difficulties there are to face, I must reach the holy site for it would be better to die than to fail in fulfilling my vow.'

Wen-ji said,'The genuineness of your piety is indeed rarely found. I am now returning to the mountain and since I am in no hurry, I will carry your things and accompany you. Thus, you will be able to make your prostrations, be relieved of your burden and achieve singleness of mind.'

I said, 'If so, your merits will be measurable. If I succeed in continuing my prostrations until we reach Wu-tai, I shall divide my merits into two portions, one for my parents so that they can attain enlightenment *(bodhi)* as soon as possible, and the other portion for you, Sir, to repay you for saving my life. Do you agree?'

He said, 'I am not worthy of this. You are motivated by a serious thought of filial piety, whereas my involvement is just a happy coincidence – so please, do not thank me for it.'

Wen-ji then took care of me for four days while I continued to convalesce. Since Wen-ji had offered to carry my baggage and cook for me, I resumed my journey and prostrations on the nineteenth although I was still weak. All delusory thoughts came to a sudden halt and I was no longer tied up by externals, free from erroneous thoughts within. My health was gradually restored and my body gained strength daily. From dawn till dusk I continued my walk and prostrations for a distance of forty-five *li* [about fifteen miles] yet I did not feel tired.

At the end of the third lunar month, I reached Li-xiang Monastery at Da-gu, where I was told that the Abbot was currently instructing his monks – or so the director of guests said. He scrutinised Wen-ji and asked me, 'Who is this man?' When I told him my story, he said harshly, 'You are a wandering monk and ignorant of what is going on here. In recent years there has been a great famine in these northern parts yet you are still going on pilgrimage to Wu-tai! How important you look, what with a man to serve you! If you only want to enjoy yourself, why wander about? Besides, at which monastery have you seen laymen being lodged?'

I dared not answer his reprimand so I excused myself and set about leaving. The director of guests said, 'There are no rules to allow this sort of thing. You came as you pleased, but who invited you here?'

Seeing that he was unreasonable, I said, 'This gentleman will stay at an inn; perhaps I could trouble you for a night's lodging?'

The director of guests said, 'This can be arranged.' Wen-ji said, 'Wu-tai is not too far away. I will return there first, you can come at your leisure. As for your things, there will soon be someone to take them on to the mountain for you.'

Though I did my best to keep him around, Wen-ji would not stay. I took out some small change to give him but he refused it and went his way.

After that, the director of guests changed his mien, which became pleasing and he then kindly took me to the dormitory. He boiled water to prepare tea and cooked some vermicelli, which he shared with me. Surprised at this new attitude, I looked around and nobody else was in sight, so I asked, 'How many monks are there staying here?'

He replied, 'I spent many years in places beyond the river Jiang but returned here to take charge of this monastery. Over the last few years there has been a great famine, so I am now alone here and this vermicelli is all the food I have. I was only joking with what I said outside, please do not take it seriously.'

Upon hearing this, I was struck dumb with sadness and struggled to swallow half a bowl of vermicelli. I then bade farewell to the monk and while he did his best to detain me for company, I had no mind to stay.

I left the monastery and wandered about the town visiting inns in search of Wen-ji – but without success. It was the eighteenth of the fourth month and there was a bright moon. Deciding to catch up with Wen-ji, I walked at night in the direction of Taiyuan, prostrating at every third step. I was very impatient so that next day, because of my hot mood, my nose bled incessantly. On the twentieth, I reached Bai-yun (White Cloud) Monastery at Huang Du-gou. The director of guests there noticed that my mouth was smeared with blood because of the nose-bleed and refused to let me stay for long, but reluctantly allowed me to pass the night. Early on the twenty-first, I arrived at Ji-luo Monastery in Taiyuan where I was not allowed to stay and given much abuse and rebuked.

On the twenty-second, I left town early and met beyond its northern gate a young monk called Wen-xian. He approached, took over my stool and baggage and invited me to his temple with the same respect and affection as if we were relatives. He led me to the Abbot's room and we had tea and food together. During our chat, I asked, 'Venerable Sir, you are only a little over twenty years old and not a native of this place; who made you Abbot?'

He replied, 'My father was an official here for a long time but when he was transferred to Bing-yang Prefecture, he was murdered by a treacherous minister. My mother succumbed to anger and sorrow while I held back my tears and joined the Sangha. The gentry and officials who knew me asked me to take over this temple, which I have long wished to leave. Now that I have seen how much respect you inspire, it gladdens me to have invited you here to stay so that I can receive your instruction.' As I told the Abbot of my vow to perform my prostrations and incense offerings on pilgrimage, he held me in great respect and insisted on keeping me for ten days before letting me go. He offered me garments and travelling expenses, which I declined. When I departed he carried my stool and accompanied me for over ten *li*, shed tears and bade me farewell.

On the first day of the fifth month, I headed in the direction of Xinzhou. One day, as I was prostrating myself in the road, a horse and carriage approached from behind me but slowed down in order not to overtake. Seeing it, I went to the roadside to let it pass. An official stepped down from the carriage and asked, 'What purpose lies behind the Venerable Sir's prostrations in the road?' I explained my purpose, and as the official was also a native of Hunan, we had a pleasant chat. Said he, 'If this be your purpose, I am currently staying at the Bai-yun Monastery at E-kou, which you must pass before reaching Mount Wu-tai. I can take your baggage and have it sent on to the monastery for you. I thanked him and he got back on board his carriage and left with my belongings. I continued my journey with the usual prostrations and offerings without further difficulty. In the middle of the fifth month, I reached the Bai-yun Monastery, where the official who had taken my baggage was an army officer. He welcomed me to his headquarters where I was given every courtesy and stayed three days. When I left his company, he offered me some money for my travelling expenses with other presents which I politely refused. However, he sent an escort to take my baggage and some money to Xian-tong Monastery.[1]

Holding incense sticks, I walked to Bi-mo Grotto on Mount Gui-feng, Shi-zi Wu (Lion Den Cave) and Lung-dong (Dragon Grotto) – all places with scenery beautiful beyond description. But being busy with my prostrations and incense offerings, I could not take it in properly. At the end of the fifth month, I arrived at Xian-tong Monastery to locate my baggage, which had been brought to the mountain by the soldiers. At first I went to neighbouring temples to offer incense and inquire about Wen-ji's whereabouts. Nobody knew him, but later I mentioned the beggar to an elderly monk who brought his palms together in praise and said, 'He was a transformation body of Manjusri Bodhisattva.' I then prostrated myself to offer thanks to the Bodhisattva.[2]

On the twenty-second, I began to offer incense with the usual walking-prostrations and two days later, I reached Dong-tai. That night the moon was bright and the stars were brilliant. I entered a stone temple where I offered incense, saying prayers and reciting sutras. After sitting in meditation there for seven days, I descended the peak to pay reverence at the Narayana Cave and while there, my provisions were exhausted. On the first day of the sixth month, I returned to Xian-tong Monastery. On the second day I set out to climb the Huayan (Avatamsaka) Peak, offering incense *en route* and slept the night there. On the third day, I paid reverence on the Northern Peak and subsequently passed the night on the central Peak. On the fourth day, I performed offerings on the Western Peak and again passed the night in the mountains. On the fifth, I returned to Xian-tong Monastery. On the seventh I paid reverence on the Southern Peak where I sat in Chan meditation for seven days. On the fifteenth, I descended the Southern Peak, returning to Xian-tong Monastery to attend the Great Prayer Meeting of the six month. Thus, my vow taken three years previously to pray for the liberation of my parents was completely fulfilled.

During those years, with the exception of illness, gales and snowfalls which hindered my incense-offerings and prostrations, I had realised singleness of mind and 'right thought'. While meeting with difficulties on my journey, my heart was full of joy. Each time I had the chance of checking my mind in adverse circumstances, and the more trouble I had, the more my mind became at ease. Thus, I realised what an ancient had meant by saying, 'The elimination of a portion of old habits is the gain of a portion of brightness; if all troubles can be endured successfully, some little measure of enlightenment will be realised.'

The beautiful scenery which I saw on my journey from Pu-tuo to Jiangsu, Zhejiang, Henan, the Huang-he (Yellow River) and the Tai-hang Mountain range, was plentiful and cannot be described in full. Such places have been given detailed descriptions in both ancient and modern guidebooks but they cannot really be appreciated unless one finds oneself in their midst, such as the holy site of Qing-liang on Mount Wu-tai where Manjusri sends forth bright rays and where one finds bottomless cold precipices permanently snow-covered, with stone bridges spanning over them and chambers overlooking space, none of which could be found elsewhere. As I was busy offering incense and performing my prostrations, I had practically no time to savour these views. When I had fulfilled my vow, I just happened to be there for that purpose and did not want to give the mountain gods a pretext to laugh at my stupid curiosity. At the end of the Great Prayer Meeting, I climbed the Da-luo Peak, where I paid reverence to the 'wisdom lamps' said to appear there. I saw nothing the first night but on the second, I saw a great ball of light flying from the Northern to the Central Peak, where it came down, splitting a short while later into over ten balls of different sizes. The same night, I saw on the Central Peak three balls of light flying up and down in the air and on the Northern Peak, four balls of light which varied in size.

On the tenth day of the seventh month I paid reverence and offered thanks to Manjusri Bodhisattva and then descended the Mountain. From Huayan Peak I walked northwards and arrived at Da-ying, south of Hun-yuan, where I visited the Northern Peak of Mount Heng which I climbed by way of Hu-feng Pass. There, I saw a stone arch with the inscription, 'The First Mountain of the Northern Regions'. When I arrived at the temple, I saw a flight of steps which was so high that it seemed to lead to heaven, and a forest of stone tablets and arches. I made an offering of incense and descended the mountain.

Thereafter, I reached Bing-yang Prefecture (Lin-fen) where I visited the 'Southern and Northern Caves of the Immortals'. To the south of the town I found the Temple of Emperor Yao (reigned 2357–2255 BC), which was really grand and imposing. Going south I reached Lu-cun village of Puzhou Prefecture (south-west Shansi Province), where I visited the nearby Temple of Prince Guan of the Han Dynasty. I crossed the Huang-he (Yellow River) and nego-tiated the Tong-guan Pass entering Shensi Province where, from Hua-yin, I climbed Mount Dai-hua and paid reverence at the temple of the Western Peak of Hua-shan. Ascending past very high railings with flying pennants, and through long defiles such as Lao-jun Li-kou, I saw the most beautiful scenery. I stayed there about eight days in all and as I had always admired the deeds of the two ancient sages, Bai-yi and Shi-qi, I visited Mount Shou-yang with which they are associated. I shortly reached the south-western part of Shensi Province, where I visited the Guan-yin temple on Mount Xiang (Fragrant Mountain) and the Tomb of Prince Chuan-wang. From there, I entered Gansu Province, where I reached Mount Kong-tong, via Jing-quan and Ping-liang. As the end of the year drew nigh, I returned to the Guan-yin Temple, where I passed the New Year.

Notes

1. The Xian-tong Monastery was built in 58–75 c.e. It is the second-oldest Buddhist monastery in China. It has 400 halls, set in the equivalent of 20 acres of grounds.

2. This was in fulfilment of Wen-ji's prediction that someone would carry Xu-yun's baggage to the mountain.

Master Xu-yun at Gu-shan Monastery, 1930/31.
The picture commemorates the rare flowering of the two ancient palm
trees during a precepts transmission in the spring of that year.

CHAPTER THREE

THE JOURNEY WEST

MY 46TH YEAR
(1885/86)

That spring, I left the Guan-yin Monastery on Mount Xiang, walking from the west through the Da-qing Pass and further on into Shensi Province. Passing through Yaozhou and San-yuan, I eventually reached Xian-yang, where I saw the historic sweet-pear tree under which an ancient, Zhao-bai, had lived. When I reached Xi'an (anciently known as Chang-an) with its imposing wall, I found many historic ruins. Outside the town to the north-east was the Ci-en Monastery,[1] inside of which was Wild Goose Pagoda, Its seven-storied stupa ornamented with famous calligraphic inscriptions in stone, some dating from the Tang Dynasty onwards, as well as Nestorian tablets. In front of the Prefecture's Confucian College, there was a forest of over seven hundred stone tablets. At its eastern gate, there was a viaduct with seventy-two spans and a covered pavilion where passers-by could meet and congregate before going about their business. After negotiating the triple-gateway of Yang-guan Pass, I went on to the Hua-yan Monastery where I paid reverence to the stupa of Master Du-shun[2] and State Master Qing-liang.[3] I then proceeded to Niu-tou Temple and Xing-guo Monastery, at the latter paying my respects to the stupa of Dharma-Master Xuan-zang [600–64].

I went on, reaching Eastern Wu-tai, Zhongnan Shan, thence Xiang Gu-po, the Bao-zang Monastery and Bai-shui Lang Retreat, a place formerly used by two holy monks where they lived in seclusion. I visited the former abode of Zong-mi in the Yin-dong Cave on Jia Wu-tai Peak, this Master being the Fifth Patriarch of the Hua-yan (Avatamsaka) School in China.

Next, I walked to Southern Wu-tai, where I called on Masters Jue-lang, Ye-kai, Fa-ren, Ti-an and Fa-xing, who had built thatched huts there and invited me to stay with them. Fa-ren was staying at the 'Tiger Retreat'. Ye-kai lodged under the 'Benevolent Dragon Cedar' and Fa-xing dwelt in the 'Xian-zi Cave' along with Jue-lang and Ti-an, whereas I stayed in a large, thatched hut. Early in the morning on the first day of the third month, I caught sight of a shooting-star in the heavens beyond a nearby hall, its impression remaining for some time before fading away; I did not know what it portended.

Notes
1. The 'Ci-en' or Monastery of Compassionate Grace had been built by the Crown Prince of Dai-zong in 648. The pagoda was built to be fireproof on the instructions of Xuan-zang in 652, its purpose being to house the massive collections of sutras brought back from India. He translated over thirteen hundred fascicles upon his return.
2. Du-shun (558–640). First Patriarch of the Hua-yan School in China. Famous for his essay 'Meditation on the Dharmadhatu'.
3. Alias Cheng-guan (738–840). Prolific commentator and Imperial Master to six successive Tang emperors.

MY 47TH AND 48TH YEARS
(1886/87)

During these years, I initially stayed in a hut on the Southern Peak of Wu-tai for Chan practice with my above-mentioned friends, Masters from whom I derived very great benefit.

In the second month, I descended the mountain and proceeded to Mount Cui-wei, where I paid reverence at the Huang-you Monastery, Thence at Qing-hua and Hou-an Mountains, the latter being where I visited Jing-ye Monastery to pay homage at the stupa of Dao-xuan, the Chinese Patriarch of the Lu (*Vinaya* discipline) School. I shortly arrived at the Cao-tang Monastery, where I paid reverence to the holy site of Kumarajiva.[1] Next, I visited Mount Taibai, which was 108 *li* (540 km.) high and on which snow did not thaw even in summer's heat. Thence I arrived at the Er-ban and Dai-ban Monasteries and eventually reached the Da Long-zhi (Great Dragon Pool) Peak where its waters divide into four mountain streams. Passing on through the market town of Zi-wu, I reached Han-zhong Prefecture, where I visited many historic places such as the terrace where the Han Dynasty Emperor Gao-zu paid tribute to his generals; the Temple of Zhu-gu (which commemorates a Chancellor of the second century) at Bao-cheng, and the Wan-nian Memorial in honour of Zhang-fei. Going on beyond Long-dong (Dragon Cave) and through the Tian-xiong Pass, I reached 'Little Emei', The Jian-men (Sword-gate) Pass, Bo-you Monastery, the Bai-ma (White Horse) Pass and the Tomb of Pang-tong, eventually arriving at the Wen-chang Temple in Sichuan Province. While negotiating this terrain, I had to climb Mount Qi-qu [lit. 'Seven-bends Mountain'] and cross the Jiu-qu Current [lit. 'Nine-bends Current'], besides crossing the Jian-men Pass. It indeed looked just like a sword-blade spanning two precipitous cliffs and confirmed the ancient saying that a single warrior defending the place could repulse an attack launched by an army of ten thousand soldiers.

Upon the mountain was the town of Jiang-wei, where Bai-yue had formerly commanded a garrison. It was as difficult to negotiate the bridging-planks laid across the precipice as it would be to 'stride up into the sky', as the ancients rightly put it. Moving on, I reached Nan-xin Prefecture, south of Guang-han, where I stayed at the Bao-guang Monastery to pass the New Year period. Since entering Sichuan that year, I had walked alone with only a bowl and the proper garments of a monk, thus being entirely free from all hindrances. As I wound my way across mountains and rivers, the scenery helped to clarify my mind.

Notes

1. An eminent Master of Kuchan origin who came to China in the fourth century. Noted for the number of sutra translations which he produced with the help of his able Chinese assistant, Seng-zhao. Seized as a prize of war, Kumarajiva was taken to Chang-an (modern-day Xi'an) where a translation bureau had been set up. He died there in 412.

MY 49TH YEAR
(1888/89)

In the first month, I left the Bao-guang Monastery and journeyed to the Provincial capital of Chengdu. There, I paid reverence at the Hall of Wen-shu (Manjusri) in Zhao-jue Monastery, Cao-dang Monastery and Qing-yang Temple. Thence, passing through Huayang and Shuang-liu I headed south and came to Meishan and Hungya Prefectures, walking on until I reached the foot of Mount Emei. From the Jiu-lao Cave at Fu-hu Temple (where Zhao Gong-ming formerly stayed to practise Daoism), I climbed the Jin-ding Peak of Mount Emei, where I offered incense.

At night, I saw overhead like a constellation of stars in the sky, countless 'Buddha-lights' the beauty of which was indescribable. I called on Abbot Ying-zhen at the Bao-guang Monastery, where I stayed for ten days. From the Wan-nian Temple where I paid reverence in the Vairocana Hall, I descended the mountain and carried on until reaching Yazhou Prefecture. After passing through Chong-qing Prefecture, I reached Luding nearer the western border of Sichuan Province and in the fifth month, I crossed the Lu River. In the town of Yan-an, the Da-fu River was spanned by the Luding suspension bridge, which was made of long chains over 300 feet long. It rolled and swung when in use so that travellers were usually scared and required great caution. Walking westwards, I passed through Da-jian Lu, Litang (also called Li-hua), Batang and thence going north, I reached Qamdo. As I continued my westward journey, I arrived at Shidu, A-lan-to[1] and Lhari, where the vast expanse of terrain had only a scattered population consisting of a few Han Chinese, Tibetans, Mongolians and wild tribes whose languages differed, very few of them speaking Chinese. At Litang, there was the sacred mountain of Gonga (7556 m.), a holy site for adherents of Tibetan Buddhism. At Batang, there were very high mountains and Qamdo was a town where the rivers converged. Most people in this region were adherents of Lamaism.

From Lhari I walked southwards reaching Jiang-da [probably Gyamda], beyond which was the Tibetan border. Continuing my journey across the border into Tibet, I crossed the Wusu-Jiang[2] River and later the Lhasa (Kyichu) river, soon arriving in Lhasa, the capital and joint administrative religious centre for the whole of Tibet.

To the north-west of the city was Mount Potala on which stood the thirteen-storied Potala-palace; its buildings of glittering gold against the blue sky were of an imposing majesty. It was here that the 'Living Buddha', the Dalai Lama, sat on his throne surrounded by a community of 20,000 monks. As I did not understand Tibetan, I only went to the monasteries to offer incense and pay reverence to the 'Living Buddha'.

From Lhasa, I headed west and after passing through Gonggar and Gyangze, I reached Shigatse, to the west of which stood Tashilunpo Monastery. It was a large and beautiful structure occupying an area of a few square *li* and it is the administrative and religious centre of Western Tibet where the other 'Living Buddha', the Panchen Lama, sat on his throne surrounded by a community of four to five thousand monks. During my trek from Sichuan Province to Tibet which took a year, I walked by day and rested at night. Often, I did not meet a single person for days when climbing mountains or crossing streams. The birds and beasts differed from those in China and the customs also differed from ours. The Sangha did not observe the Monastic code and most of the monks ate beef and mutton. They were divided into sects distinguishable by their red and yellow hats. I thought of the days of the Jetavana Assembly and could not refrain from tears.[3] As the year was nearing its end, I returned from Shigatse to Lhasa to pass the New Year period.

Notes

1. Shidu and A-lan-to are Chinese transcriptions of local place-names. Happily, Lhari can be identified and gives an idea of the vicinity.
2. 'Wusu-Jiang' is probably a tributary of the Brahmaputra (Yarlong Zangpo) River.
3. Xu-yun's observations about the status of Tibetan Buddhism seem less than salutary at this point, though his account is otherwise generous towards the Tibetan tradition. Special circumstances need to be taken into account here. The Buddhist Sangha generally prohibits meat-eating and Xu-yun introduced rigorous reforms in the Chinese monasteries when and where he found meat-eating going on. Consequently, he was shocked to discover that it is fairly common for Tibetan Buddhists to eat meat as a matter of course. The Tibetan climate and terrain does not readily yield up vegetable crops and cereals are often scarce. Thus out of sheer necessity, the Tibetan monks often live on meat. Barley and millet are sometimes available, but rarely in quantities sufficient to meet all needs. Having said that, Xu-yun was a strict vegetarian throughout his stay in Tibet and obviously found sufficient food to sustain himself. Strangely enough, the Vinaya code does not explicitly rule out meat-eating, largely because monks are supposed to beg or eat what their patrons offer. In China, the Vinaya code is linked with the *Brahmajala-sutra,* which does rule out meat eating, like the *Lankavatara Sutra.* Thus in China, the precepts do explicitly prohibit meat-eating.

As regards Xu-yun's criticism of the Tibetan schools and their differences, the problem was more apparent than real. Tibetan Buddhism has developed its own schools as did the Chinese Buddhist tradition. Presumably, the Master thought that these different lineages represented sectarian views. As we know from Xu-yun's remarks elsewhere, he regarded all aspects of the Dharma as complementary and taught his disciples not to discriminate in favour of one method. Had the Master spoken or read Tibetan, he would have recognised that the Tibetans find it expedient to express the Dharma through different methods, just as the Chinese schools do.

MY 50TH YEAR
(1889/90)

I did not wish to stay in Tibet, so with the coming of spring, I headed southwards passing through La-ko and Ya-dong (alias Mao-dong), which was the gateway to India from Tibet. I entered Bhutan crossing the mountain ranges, the names of which were unknown to me, though I had sometimes heard them referred to as the 'Onion Range' or the Snowy Range' (the Himalaya Range). I availed myself of this opportunity to compose a poem which contained the following lines:

> What crosses the horizon
> Looking like clear emptiness?
> Such a bright and silvery world
> Differs not from brilliant jade.

Once in India, I reached the town of Yang-pu,[1] where I pilgrimaged to various holy places. Later, I reached the great Bengalese city of Calcutta from which I sailed to Ceylon. Whilst there I made further pilgrimages to holy sites, after which I crossed the sea again, this time reaching Burma. There, I visited the great Golden Pagoda of Shwedagon (in Rangoon) and paid reverence inside the temple. When I reached Chi-ti-li near Moulmein, I saw an unusual boulder said to have been placed on its rocky prominence by Maudgalyayana in ancient times.[3] Many devotees went there to pay reverence.

In the seventh month I returned to China. Proceeding from Lashio, I passed through the Han-long Gate and entered Yunnan Province. After passing through Nian-ning, Long-ling, Jing-dong, Meng-hua, Chaozhou and Xiaguan, I reached Da-li Prefecture. There, I visited the great Er-hai Lake, where the din of its silvery cascades could be heard for several *li* around; it was a most remarkable scene.

Upon my return to China, my first vow was to visit the Cock's Foot Mountain, where I wished to pay reverence to Mahakasyapa – to whom the mountain is sacred – and where he is said to be wrapped in *samadhi* inside a cave, awaiting the Future Buddha, Maitreya. From Er-hai Lake, I headed in a north-easterly direction and after passing through Wa-se, Bai-dan, Bing-sha, Shan-jiao and the Temple of Da-wang at An-bang, I reached the Arch of Ling-shan (Vulture Peak) assembly at the base of Cock's Foot Mountain. Halfway from its peak was the Ming-ge Terrace where, in former times, it is said that eight princes followed Mahakasyapa to the mountain. Unable to bear the thought of leaving him, they are said to have stayed on the mountain to continue their self-cultivation, all becoming Dharma-protectors (on account of which they are now revered in the near-by Temple of Da-wang).

I climbed the mountain, reaching the Cave-Shrine of Mahakasyapa where his image is kept inside. It is said that when Ananda went there to pay reverence, the stone door at the front of the cave opened by itself. It was a high mountain cave, blocked off by a stone wall resembling a door. The door is called the 'Hua-shou Men' ('Flower Blossom Gate')[3] and Mahakasyapa is supposed to be sitting in *samadhi* within. The door closing off the cave opening had the appearance of a huge city-gate, measuring a few hundred feet in height and over a hundred feet in width. The two portions of the door were closed, but the line of juncture between them was clearly visible.

That day, there were many visitors with local guides. While I was offering incense and making prostrations, the sound of a large bell unexpectedly rang out thrice. The locals present were over-joyed and paid reverence, saying, 'Whenever an enlightened person comes here, the sound of a bell, drum or musical instrument is heard. We have all heard that of a drum or musical instrument once or twice to date, but so far, we have never heard the sound of a large bell. Seeing that you came to pay reverence today – and that the sound of a large bell was heard, that surely means you have attained the Dao?' I immediately denied that I was qualified for the welcoming bell. It was the last day of the seventh month.

Next, I ascended the Tian-zhu Peak (Pillar of Heaven); it was the highest point of the whole mountain and the distance between it and the ground was about thirty *li* [approx. 15 km.] Upon it were a bronze shrine and the Surangama Stupa. According to the annals of Cock's Foot Mountain, there were once 360 hermitages and 72 great temples on it, but now less than ten temples remained. Monks and laymen were no longer distinguishable and the owner-ship of temples passed from generation to generation on a heredi-tary basis, each community appropriating its own temple and refusing to allow monks from other places to come and stay, even for a short period. I thought of the past prosperity of the Dharma assemblies and compared it with the present decadence – I could not help sighing. In spite of my ardent desire to restore the former grandeur of these places, I did not know whether the chance to do so would come.

I descended the mountain, crossing through the Liang-wang and Jiu-feng peaks before reaching a district of Yunnan. From there, I passed through the Shui-mu, Ling-qiu and Zi-qi Mountains reach-ing Chuxiong Prefecture. There, I stayed at the Gao-ding Monas-tery beyond its western gate. Shortly after my arrival, the monastery was filled with the fragrance of orchids. The Managing-monk at the temple congratulated me on this rare occurrence. Then the Abbot came and said, 'This divine fragrance has only been smelt a few times before. According to the Annals of the Prefecture, there are divine but invisible orchids on the mountain which only exude their fragrance when an enlightened person comes here. As the whole moutain is filled with such a fragrance today, this must be due to your pure virtue.' He accorded me every courtesy and insisted that I stayed for a long time. As I was in a hurry to return to my native Province of Hunan, I politely declined his request. After one night's stay, I left the monastery and after passing through Kunming and Qu-jing Prefectures, I reached Bing-yi on the border of Guizhou Province. I went on in an easterly direction, passing through Kue-yang and Zhen-yuan, before long reaching Ma-yang District and Zhi-jiang in western Hunan. I continued my trek, passing through Bao-qing and arrived at Heng-yang. There, I visited and paid obeisance to Master Heng-zhi on Mount Qi. After staying there ten days, I carried on northwards.

Upon my arrival at Wuchang in Hubei Province, I went to the Bao-tong Monastery, where I paid my respects to Abbot Zhi-mo. After studying the rules for repentance and reform of the Kuan-yin rite, I proceeded to Jiu-jiang, where I climbed Mount Luo to pay reverence to Abbot Zhi-shan at the Hai-hui Monastery. Whilst there, I attended a meeting held for the recitation of the Buddha's name. Next, after passing into Anhui Province and following a visit to Mount Huang, I climbed Mount Jiu-hua[4] and paid my respects at the Stupa of Ksitigarbha Bodhisattva and the Bai-sui Temple. I also paid obeisance to Abbot Bao-wu, who was a strict disciplinarian and whose imperturbable mind was of the first order. Thence, I crossed the river and arrived at Mount Bao-hua to pay my respects to Abbot Sheng-xing who retained me there for the passing of New Year.

During the two years gone by, although I travelled ten thousand *li*, I always walked on foot, the only exception being when crossing the sea by boat. I forded streams and climbed mountains braving rains, gales, frost and snow. The scenery changed every day but my mind was pure like a bright and solitary moon hanging in the sky. My health grew more robust and my steps became rapid. I felt no hardship on this march but on the contrary, I realised the harmfulness of my former self-indulgence. An ancient rightly said that 'after reading ten thousand books, one should travel ten thousand miles.'

Notes

1. Probably Benares. It is sometimes impossible to locate foreign place-names given in Chinese transliteration, often a 'rough and ready' business. For instance, in the account of Xu-yun's Tibetan sojourn, two identical phonetics are used for entirely different places, though happily to say, they were readily identifiable by plotting his course.
2. 'Chi-ti-li' is Kyai Khtiyo, near Moulmein. Devout Burmese Buddhists plaster this rock with gold-leaf, often saving for years in order to do so.
3. The door to Mahajasyapa's Cave-Shrine was called 'Hua-shou Men' or 'Flower Blossom Gate' to commemorate the Buddha's 'Flower-sermon' in which he had held a flower aloft, thus directly pointing to the Mind. Mahakasyapa was the only disciple to understand the profound meaning of the gesture, responding with a smile. The Chan tradition regards this episode as the point at which the 'Transmission of the Mind' began, Mahakasyapa being the First Indian Patriarch in the Chan lineage.
4. Mount Jiu-hua (1841 m.). One of the four sacred Buddhist mountains. Bodhimandala of Di-zang (Ksitigarbha) or 'Earth-store' Bodhisattva. It is in Anhui Province.

Xu-yun at the Temple of Six Banyans, Canton 1946/47.
The picture commemorates the unseasonal flowering of peach blossoms
in the courtyard during the course of Buddhist rites held in November.

CHAPTER FOUR

ENLIGHTENMENT AND ATONEMENT

MY 51ST YEAR
(1890/91)

I arrived at Yi-xing (in Jiangsu Province) where I paid obeisance to Abbot Ren-zhi. Although Xian-qin Monastery (where Zong-mi, the Fifth Huayan Patriarch joined the Buddhist Sangha) was being repaired, I passed the summer there. I then went on to Gu-rong, where I paid obeisance to Abbot Fa-ren; I assisted him in repairing the Chi-shan Monastery and passed the winter there.

MY 52ND YEAR
(1891/92)

At Nanjing, I stayed with Abbot Song-yan and assisted him in repairing the Jin-cheng Monastery. Upasaka Yang Ren-shan often called on me and we had interesting discussions on the *Hetuvidya Shastra*[1] and the treatise called 'The Lamp of Prajna-Wisdom'.[2] I stayed in Jin-cheng Monastery for the winter period.

Notes
1. *Hetuvidya Shastra*. One of the five *pancavidya shastras* explaining causality or the science of causation *(hetu)* in logical reasoning. The founder of the school was Aksapada.
2. A commentary by Bhavaviveka on the verses of the *Madhyamika-karikas* of Nagarjuna.

MY 53RD YEAR
(1892/93)

With Masters Pu-zhao, Yue-xia, and Yin-lian, I climbed Mount Jiu-hua, where we repaired the huts on Cui-feng Peak for our sojourn there. Master Pu-zhao expounded the five divisions of the Huayan School. As the Xian-shou teaching had been buried in oblivion long ago, people who now heard of it being taught again came in great numbers to listen. Since then, the Xian-shou teaching was revived in the region south of the river Jiang (Yangtze).[1]

Notes
1. Xian-shou (643-712) was the Third Patriarch of the Huayan School and a prolific commentator, As there were Five Patriarchs of the Huayan School in China who each made commentaries, the books of this school are divided into five portions. Xian-shou means 'wise head' and this name was given to him as a tribute to his understanding, He is also know aŝ Fa-zang.

MY 54TH AND 55TH YEARS
(1893/95)

I stayed on Cui-feng Peak studying the sutras. Dharma-master Di-xian came to pass the summer with me in the mountain. He left for Jin-shan to pass the winter there. The following year, I remained on Cui-feng to study the sutras.

MY 56TH YEAR
(1895/96)

Abbot Yue-lang of the Gaomin Monastery at Yangzhou came to Jiu-hua and informed us that one of his patrons by the name of Zhu had promised to give financial support for twelve weeks of meditation, including the current four weeks. He also informed us that the old Master Fa-ren of Chi-shan had returned to his monastery and that he hoped all of us would go there to assist him in supervising the meditation weeks. When the opening date drew near, I was asked to leave the mountain first. When I reached Di-gang Harbour at Da-tong, I walked following the river bank. The river was rising and I wanted to cross it but the boatman asked me for six coins; as I was penniless, the boat left without me. Walking on, I suddenly slipped and fell into the water and thus bobbed on the current for one day and night until I drifted to Cai-shi Jetty, where a fisherman caught me in his nets by chance. As I wore a monk's robe, he called a monk from Bao-ji Temple who recognised me as we had previously stayed together at the Jin-shan Monastery. He was frightened for my life and exclaimed, 'This is Master De-qing!' (i.e. Xu-yun, ordained as De-qing). I was subsequently carried to the temple where I was revived. As a result of the battering which I had received in the swift current, I bled from the mouth, nose, anus and genital organ. After a few days' stay at Bao-ji Temple, I went on to the Gao-min Monastery. When I saw the director of duties (karmadana) there, he saw that I looked pale and thin, and asked if I was well, I replied that I was not. I then called on Abbot Yue-lang who, after inquiring about Mount Jiu-hua where I had been, immediately asked me to take up a temporary post at the forthcoming meditation-weeks. I politely declined his request, saying nothing about my fall into the water, asking only that I be allowed to attend the meditation meeting. According to Gao-min Monastery's rules of discipline, to reject a post given by the Abbot was regarded as an affront to the whole monastic community. Thus, I was found to be an offender and punished by being beaten with a wooden ruler. While I willingly accepted this punishment,[1] it did aggravate my illness. I bled continuously and also passed drops of seminal fluid in my urine. Waiting for my end, I sat firmly in the meditation hall day and night with increasing zeal.[2] In the pure single-mindedness of my meditation, I forgot all about my body[3] and twenty days later, my illness vanished completely.[4] When the Abbot of Cai-shi Jetty came with an offering of garments for the assembly, he was reassured and delighted to see that my appearance was radiant. He then spoke of my fall into the water and all the monks held me in great esteem. I was thus spared the trouble of working in the hall and could continue my meditation.

Henceforth, with all my thoughts brought to an abrupt halt, my practice took effect throughout day and night.[5] My steps were as swift as if I were flying in the air. One evening after the set meditation period, I opened my eyes and suddenly perceived a great brightness similar to broad daylight wherein everything inside and outside the monastery was discernible to me.[6] Through the wall, I saw the monk in charge of lamps and incense urinating outside, the guest-monk in the latrine, and far away, boats plying on the river with the trees on both its banks – all were clearly seen; it was just the third watch of the night when this happened. The next morning, I asked the incense-monk and guest-monk about this and both confirmed what I had seen the previous night. Knowing that this experience was only a temporary state I had attained, I did not pay undue regard to its strangeness. In the twelfth month during the third night of the eighth week set for training, an attendant came to fill our cups with tea after the meditation session ended. The boiling liquid accidentally splashed over my hand and I dropped the cup which fell to the ground and shattered with a loud report; instantaneously, I cut off my last doubt about the Mind-root and rejoiced at the realisation of my cherished aim.[7] I then thought of the time when I left home, and of the time during which I had lived a wanderer's life, my illness in the hut on the banks of the Yellow River, and the difficult questions put to me by the layman (Wen-ji, who saved me).

What would Wen-ji have said if I had kicked over his boiler and stove at the time?[8] If I had not fallen into the water and been gravely ill, and if I had not remained indifferent to both favourable and adverse situations, I would have passed another life aimlessly and this experience would not have happened today. I then chanted the following *gatha:*

> A cup fell to the ground
> With a sound clearly heard.
> As space was pulverised
> The mad mind came to a stop.[9]

I also chanted a further *gatha:*

> When the hand released its hold, the cup fell and was shattered.[10]
> 'This hard to talk when the family breaks up or someone dies;
> Spring comes with fragrant flowers blossoming everywhere,
> Mountains, rivers and the great earth are but the Tathagata.[11]

Notes

1. This was the Master's practice of *ksanti-paramita* or spiritual patience under all conditions.
2. This was his practice of *virya-paramita* or zealous effort.

3. Thus he relinquished his attachment to the ego.

4. This was how he cured his illness.

5. This is the prerequisite for a major awakening *(Wu)*.

6. His mind was now stripped of all attachments, which expanded and became all-embracing; hence, he saw his near and distant surroundings.

7. Mind is the root-source of a myriad things. When the mind returns to its inherently still condition, one perceives that all things in *samsara* (birth and death) rise and fall within the immutable Mind. This was how the Master succeeded in leaping over the worldly stream. 'Doubt' here means doubt about the underlying nature of 'birth and death'.

8. If at the time I had just kicked over Wen-ji's boiler and stove to eliminate all traces of externals to expose the self-nature, what would he have said?

9. When the mind ceases to discriminate about externals, the self-nature resumes its normal (non-dual) function of direct perception, exposing the self-nature. The Master's mind had returned to its inherently still condition because of his long meditation; thus, when the cup dropped to the ground with a loud report, the Master directly perceived the self-nature from which all phenomenal things spring, instead of mere sense-data. He thus realised the inherent voidness or emptiness of all conditioned things, wiping out the illusion of space and eliminating his last doubt about the birthless and deathless Mind. The *Surangama Sutra* says, 'When the mad mind halts, it is Bodhi.'

10. The word 'hold' here stands for the mind clinging to externals and when it has become disengaged from them, it is as hard to express as the state when a family has broken up – symbolic of the elimination of surrounding phenomena. Equally, it is hard to speak when someone dies, symbolic of the 'death of the ego' or conditioned selfhood. This according to the Vajracchedika, is the last, subtle attachment to 'ego and Dharmas' which has to be relinquished before one can attain enlightenment.

11. 'Spring' symbolises enlightenment after which 'fragrance' or bliss prevails everywhere. Mountains, rivers and the great earth are illusory forms which spring from the Tathagata or 'Thusness' of the Buddha-body. The *Surangama Sutra* speaks of 'fragrant form' or 'wonderful form', referring to the marvellous appearance of sense-data after it has been transmuted by wisdom.

MY 57TH YEAR
(1896/97)

In the summer of that year, I arrived at Jin-shan Monastery in Zhen-jiang, where I stayed to observe the period set for studying the rules of discipline. The old Abbot Da-ding allowed me to stay there to pass the winter period.

MY 58TH YEAR
(1897/98)

Upon my return to Jin-shan Monastery after pilgrimaging to Mount Lang to pay reverence to Mahasthama Bodhisattva, Abbot Dao-ming invited me to Yangzhou to help him at the Zhong-ning Monastery. In the fourth month, Dharma-Master Tong-zhi expounded the *Surangama Sutra* on Mount Jiao, the audience there numbering about one thousand people. He invited me to assist him in expounding the sutra and after doing so, I left the assembly and descended the mountain. When I was born, I lost my mother whom I never saw. I only saw her picture at home and each time I thought of her, my heart broke. Previously, I had taken a vow to go to the Ashoka (A Yu Wang) Monastery in order to revere the Buddha's relics and to burn off a finger there as an offering to the Buddha for the liberation of my affectionate mother. As I now wished to fulfil this vow, I went to Ningbo (where the Ashoka Monastery is situated). At the time, Dharma-Master Huan-ren and Chan-Master Ji-chan (alias 'Ba-zhi Tou-tuo' or 'The Eight-fingered ascetic') were in charge of the Tian-tong Monastery (near Ningbo) and Master Hai-an was compiling the Annals of Ashoka Mountain. They all invited me to help them but since I had come to fulfil my vow, I politely declined. At the Ashoka Monastery, I paid reverence to the Buddha's relics and every day, from the third watch of the night until the evening meditation, except when I was in the main hall, I used only my own cloth mat instead of the Monastery's hassocks when making three thousand prostrations. One night, while sitting in Chan meditation – as if in a dream – I suddenly saw a dazzling bright golden dragon which was many feet in length. It descended through the air, flying to the pool before the reliquary hall. Thereupon, I climbed on its back and flew into the sky until it reached a place where the mountains, streams, trees and flowers were most beautiful to behold, with palaces and chambers of an exquisite grandeur. I saw my mother in a room and called out, 'Mother, please ride this dragon to the Western Paradise [of Amitabha Buddha].' As the dragon came down again, I was shaken and woke up. My body and mind were cheerful and the vision had been entirely intelligible to me. This was the only time in my life that I saw my mother.

Henceforth, everyday when visitors came to have a look at the relic in the hall, I always accompanied them. The visitors' opinions about the relic varied greatly. I had seen it many times; at first it looked to me as if the size of a green bean and of a dark purple colour. In the middle of the tenth month, after I had paid reverence to the Hinayana and Mahayana *Tripitakas*,[1] I went again to look at it and it was the same size as before but like a brilliant red pearl this time. As I was impatient to see how it would transform itself, I again performed prostrations and felt pains throughout my body; the relic now appeared bigger than a yellow bean, half yellow and half white. I then realised that its size and colour varied according to the visitor's sense organ and its field. Being in a hurry to see its further transformations, I increased the number of my prostrations but at the beginning of the eleventh month, I fell badly ill. I could not continue and as my illness grew more severe, I was moved to the recuperating hut where all medicines given to me were of no avail. I could not even sit but had to lie down all the time. The chief monk Xian-qin, superintendent Zong-liang and Miss Lu spared no money and effort to try and save me but all failed at the time. Everyone thought I was nearing the end of my causal transmigration. Although I was prepared to let the sickness take its course, I was very concerned about my failure to burn off a finger (in fulfilment of my vow). On the sixteenth, eight visitors came to see me in the hut. They thought that I was not seriously ill and especially came to assist me in burning my finger. I remembered that the following day had been fixed for the ceremony and insisted that they came to participate as arranged. The chief monk and the others present did not approve because of the risk involved. I burst into a flood of tears and said, 'Who can escape from death? I wanted to repay my debt of gratitude to my mother and took a vow to burn off a finger. Why should I live if I have to cancel my decision at this point? I am ready to die . . .'

Superintendent Zong-liang, who was only 21 years old, heard my plea and with tears in his eyes, he said, 'Do not worry, I will pay for tomorrow's vegetarian food and arrange everything for you.' I brought my palms together to thank him. On the seventeenth in the early morning, Zong-liang came with his Dharma brother Zung-xin to assist me in burning off my finger. Several people helped me to the main hall where together with the assembly, I paid reverence to the Buddha, performed the ritual and recited the rules of repentance and reform. With singleness of mind, I recited the Buddha's name and prayed that he would liberate my affectionate mother.

At the beginning of the ceremony, I still felt pain but as my mind gradually became pure and clean, my awakening wisdom clearly manifested itself. When I came to the sentence, 'The whole Dharmadhatu is contained in the body of Amitabha Buddha,' every hair in the 84,000 pores of my body stood on end. As my finger finished burning, I arose to prostrate before the Buddha. I did not require others to support me (as I had done previously) and entirely forgot about my illness. After walking unaided to present my thanks to the assembly, I returned to the hut. All the next day I bathed my hand in salt water and had no more bleeding. Within a few days, I had recovered from my illness and gradually resumed my prostrations. I stayed at the Ashoka Monastery to pass the New Year.

Note by Cen Xue-lu, Xu-yun's Editor

The monastery had originally been called A-Yu Wang (King Ayu or King Ashoka) Monastery but was later named Guang-li Monastery. It was built on Mount Mou forty *li* to the south of Nanxiang village in the Yin district of Ningbo Prefecture. Formerly – a few hundred years after the Buddha's Nirvana – Central India was ruled by King Ashoka (reigned approx. 274–37 BC. He is said to have placed 84,000 relics of the Buddha in precious stupas and ordered the gods to bury them in the ground at various places. In the east, these stupas appeared one after another in nineteen locations in China, among them being Mount Wu-tai and the Ashoka Monastery. On Mount Wu-tai, the relic was placed inside a stupa and could not be seen. As for that of the Ashoka Monastery, in the third year of the Tai-kang reign (282–3 CE) of Emperor Wu-ti of the Jin Dynasty, after Hui-ta had prayed for it to appear, it emerged from the ground; a monastery was then erected and the relic was placed in a stone stupa, the door of which was locked. When visitors wished to look at the relic, the guardian of the stupa was notified. Once inside the hall, visitors first paid reverence to the Buddha and then went outside to kneel on stone steps forming a queue, each waiting in turn to go and see the relic. The guardian took out the stupa, which was one foot, four inches in height and over one foot in width. It was hollow and enclosed a solid bell having a needle, the point of which held the relic. When observed, the relic appeared as either big or small, as one or many, and as still or moving, according to each visitor's vision. Some people saw but one, while others saw three or four relics. The colour also varied – it might be blue, yellow, red or white. Thos seeing in it a lotus flower or image of the Buddha were regarded as being endowed with an excellent karmic link with the Dharma.

In the Wan-li reign of the Ming Dynasty (1573–1619), Lu Guang-zu, head of the civil office board, came with his friends to pay reverence to the stupa and its relic. First, he saw the relic as small as a tiny bean, then it gradually changed to the size of a big bean, a date, a melon and finally – it appeared the size of a large, glittering wheel – which refreshed his mind's-eye. Lu repaired the dilapidated hall which has since remained in its imposing condition to this day. The Tathagata was compassionate and left behind this Dharma-body of his so that living beings in the following generations could develop the right believing mind.

Notes
1. The *Tripitaka* or 'Three Baskets' of the Buddhist Canon, comprising the *Vinaya* or disciplinary rules, *Sutras* or discourses of the Buddha, and *Shastras* or commentaries.

MY 59TH YEAR
(1898/99)

That year in the early spring, as a large bell was being cast for the Qi-ta (Seven Pagodas) Monastery at Ningbo, the old Abbot Ben-lai invited Dharma-Master Mo-an to expound the *Lotus Sutra* there and came to the King Ashoka (Guang-li) Monastery to ask if I would help in expounding it. Thus, I went to Qi-ta Monastery and after expounding the sutra, I proceeded to Mount Dong-guan where I built a thatched hut in which to pass the New Year period.

MY 60TH YEAR
(1899/1900)

Master Jie-sen and Bao-lin invited me to Dan-yang to help repair the Xian-tai Temple, where I passed the summer. In the seventh month, I went to Zhu-yang in Jiangsu Province where Master Fa-ren of Mount Chi let me have his hut for the winter.

Xu-yun with Ananda Jennings, 1948/49.
Ananda Jennings was the American Buddhist who called on the Master
when in his 109th year. She had been a Theosophist, worked for the
League of Nations, and eventually turned to Buddhism in the cause of
world peace. The picture was probably taken during her ordination at
the Nan-hua Monastery, Guangdong.

CHAPTER FIVE

INTERRUPTED SECLUSION

MY 61ST YEAR
(1900/01)

I had stayed for some ten years in Jiangsu and Zhejiang Provinces and now wished to make a distant journey to Mount Wu-tai, after which my intention was to cultivate my practice in the seclusion of Mount Zhong-nan. I subsequently left Mount Chi and proceeded to Zhenjiang and Yangzhou and thence pilgrimaged to Mount Yun-tai (Cloud Terrace Mountain). Moving on, I entered Shandong Province to visit Mount Tai (1,524 m.), the eastern sacred peak. Heading easterly again, I went on to Mount Lao, where I visited the Narayana-cave in the vicinity where the Ming Master Han-shan[1] had rebuilt the Hai-yin (Ocean-seal) Monastery. I then proceeded to Qu Prefecture to pay reverence at the Tomb and Temple of Confucius.[2]

I then headed in a westerly direction and one night, I stayed at a ruined temple wherein there was only a rotten coffin with its lid turned upside down. Knowing it was not in use I slept on it, but about midnight, I felt something moving inside the coffin and unexpectedly heard a voice saying, 'I want to get out.'

I asked, 'Are you a man or ghost?'

'A man,' the voice replied.

'Who are you?' I asked.

'A beggar,' the voice replied.

I smiled, got up and let him out of the coffin. He was as ugly as a ghost and asked me, 'Who are you?'

'A monk,' I replied.

The man was angry, saying I had squashed his head. As he wanted to strike me, I said to him, 'I sat on the lid of the coffin but you could not even be bothered to move; how can you think of hitting me now?'

Thus cowed into submission, he went out to pass water and

46

returned to sleep in the coffin again. I left the place just before sunrise.

At this time, there were already signs of the Boxer Movement[3] rising in rebellion in many districts of Shandong Province. One day, I met a foreign soldier on the road who pointed his gun at me and asked, 'Are you afraid of dying?' I replied, 'If my fate is to die by your hand, then go ahead and shoot!' Seeing that I was not in the least perturbed, the soldier said, 'Right, you may go.' I then hurred on my way to Mount Wu-tai and after offering incense, I intended to proceed on to Mount Zhong-nan. However, since the Boxer Rebellion had broken out, I returned to Beijing, where I visited the Xi-yu Monastery and paid reverence at the Cave of the Stone Sutras. I called on Yi-xing, a monk on Mount Tan-zhe who was renowned for his remarkable conduct. Next, I reached the Jia-tai Monastery where I paid my respects at the stupa of Chan-Master Fei-bo. Thence, I climbed Mount Hong-luo to participate in a meeting held for the recitation of the Buddha's name and visited the Monastery of the Big Bell. There, I saw the bronze bell which had been cast by Yao Guang-xiao. It weighed 87,000 *catties*[4] and measured 15 feet in height; its hanger-top was 7 feet long, and it was 14 feet in diameter. The whole *Avatamsaka Sutra* was cast on the outside of the bell, with the *Lotus Sutra* inscribed inside; the *Diamond Sutra* was inscribed on the edge of its case, and the *Surangama Mantra* on its hanger-top. The bell had been offered by Emperor Cheng-zu of the Yung-luo reign (1403–24) in the Ming Dynasty for the liberation of his deceased mother.

Thereafter, I headed back to the Long-quan (Dragon Spring) Monastery just south of the capital and stayed there a while. In the fifth month the Boxer Rebellion came to a climax. Its rallying cry was, 'Support the Manchu Dynasty, Exterminate foreigners!' The secretary of the Japanese Legation and the German minister were assassinated at the secret instigation of the Empress-dowager. On the seventeenth of the month, an imperial mandate was issued declaring war on the foreign powers. The capital was thrown into disorder. In the sixth month, Tianjin was captured by the allied armies which occupied the capital, Beijing, in the following month. The princes and ministers who knew of me from their stay at the Long-quan Monastery urged that I should leave with them and follow the Imperial retinue then fleeing westwards. In the utter confusion during the departure, there was a complete absence of the proud pomp usually shown by the spoiled son of heaven. By day and night, everybody made forced marches and endured great hardship. On the arrival at Fubing, the Emperor and Empress-dowager were delighted to see Viceroy Chen Chun-xuan of Gansu Province with his soldiers coming to welcome and protect their majesties and accompany them beyond the Great Wall. When the Emperor arrived at Yun-men Pass, he met an old monk in the Yun-men Monastery who was 124 years old. He gave him some thin, yellow cloth for his robe and ordered that a dedicatory arch be erected at the site. We continued our westward march and arrived at Bingyang Prefecture where a severe famine prevailed. The inhabitants offered their food of *taro* [a tuber] and sweet-potato tops to their majesties who were very hungry and found it delicious. When we reached Xian, their majesties stayed at the Viceroy's headquarters. At the time, as the hungry masses were even eating corpses in the streets, the authorities took steps to stop this by erecting eight booths from which free meals were given to the starving people. Free meals were also distributed in the countryside.

Viceroy Chen Chun-xuan invited me to the Wo-long (Reclining Dragon) Monastery to pray for snow and rain to end the long drought. After prayers were said, the old Abbot Dong-xia invited me to stay at the monastery, but seeing that the Imperial court was held at Xian with its clamour and bustle, I left the place in secret. In the tenth month, I climbed Mount Zhong-nan's range in order to build a thatched hut. Behind Jia Wu-tai's peak I found the 'Lion Cave', which was a secluded place for spiritual retirement. I then changed my name to Xu-yun (Empty Cloud) to avoid unwanted visitors. As there was no water on the mountain, I had to drink melted snow and eat coarse herbs which I cultivated. Living in the mountain at the time were Masters Ben-zhang on Po-shi Peak, Miao-lian at the Temple of Guan-di, Dao-ming in Wu-hua Grotto, Miao-yuan in an old thatched hut, plus Masters Xiu-yuan and Qing-shan on Mount Hou. Master Qing-shan was a native of Hunan Province and was very much respected by the monks on the mountain. He lived comparatively close to me and we frequently exchanged visits.

In the eighth month of the following year, Masters Fa-cheng, Yue-xia and Liao-chen came to my hut and when they saw me they were surprised and said, 'We have had no news of you for years;

who would have expected that you were sleeping here?' I said, 'Let's put "here" aside, how is it "there?"[5] We then exchanged greetings and after serving them with *taro*, I accompanied them to Po-shi Peak. Yue-xia said, 'The old Abbot Fa-ren of Mount Chi is currently expounding the *Lotus Sutra* in the Gui-yuan Monastery at Hanyang. He does not like its noisy surroundings and wants to come north; he asked me to come here so that I could find a place for him.' Yue-xia asked me to help him find an appropriate site for the old Abbot but since I was practising meditation, I politely declined. After I had completed my week of Chan meditation, Masters Hua-cheng, Yin-yue and Fu-jia came from Mount Cui-wei, where they had found a site for the old Abbot. Master Yue-xia said that the place was suitable but I thought otherwise since it faced the 'White Tiger' influence to the north without a supporting hill for the evening star [geomantic terms for subterranean and cosmic currents in the Feng Shui science for selecting auspicious sites].[6] They did not listen to my advice and so they were responsible for what happened [by way of misfortune the following year].

That winter on the solstice day, the old Master Qing-shan asked me to go to Xian Prefecture to do some shopping for him. On my return, I was caught in a heavy snowfall. After climbing the mountain, just as I reached the newly thatched hut, I slipped and fell into a bank of snow at the foot of the precipice. I shouted for help and Master Yi-quan who was in a nearby hut came to my rescue. All my garments were thoroughly soaked with water; it was already dark and thinking that the snow would block all the tracks the following day, I negotiated the snowy path and went to see Master Qing-shan. Seeing my disorderly appearance, he laughed at me, jokingly saying that I was of no real use. I smiled and nodded assent and then returned to my hut where I passed the New Year period.

Notes
1. Han-shan (1546–1623). The Narayana-cave is between Deng-zhou and Lai-zhou in Jing-zhou district. It is traditionally held to be the seat of certain bodhisattvas. The nearby monastery was a ruin when Han-shan found it. He rebuilt it and called it 'Hai-yin' or Ocean-seal.
2. Confucius (Kong Fu-zi) 551–497 BC. Famous for his *Analects* and other writings. The Kong family still live in Qu Prefecture, Shandong Province.
3. The Boxer Movement or Yi-he-quan: a secret society with quasi-Daoist origins.

4. An ancient grain measure equalling one pint.

5. Master Xu-yun asked his companions to forget about what could be found 'here' in the phenomenal realm, hinting instead about that which could be found 'there' in the uncreated self-nature which is beyond all locations. These terms carry a Chan meaning and were not used in their conventional sense.

6. 'Feng-shui (lit. 'wind and water') is an ancient Chinese science used to determine the most auspicious place and time to site homes, farms, wells, temples, graves, etc. It is based on the idea of harmonising the negative and positive (yin and yang) energies of a given location. Some places are regarded as having an innate balance of favourable energies, others are regarded as malific because of an innate imbalance, which must either be corrected or else avoided altogether. Experts in this science use a divining board and compass marked off with complex calibrations involving the 'five directions', the 'eight trigrams' *(ba-qua)*, the 'nine directions', the 'five activities' *(wu xing)* and hourly divisions based on Chinese sexagenary cycles, etc. Even the most modern Chinese take this science very seriously and very few banks, hotels or other modern buildings are built without consulting a 'Feng-shui' expert. Like most traditionally minded Chinese, Master Xu-yun attached great importance to the principles of 'Feng-shui'. For a more detailed study of Feng-shui, see S. Skinner, *The Living Earth Manual of Feng-Shui* (Routledge, 1982).

MY 62ND YEAR
(1901/02)

I stayed at my hut during the spring and summer. The old Master Fa-ren of Mount Chi arrived in Shensi Province and erected a hut on Mount Cui-wei. With him came sixty people, about one half of whom stayed at the Huang-yu Monastery [the former summer retreat of the Emperor Tai-zong (627–49) of the Tang Dynasty], while others were at the new hut and Xing-shan Monastery. At the time in this northern region, Commander Su who was in charge of clearing land for tillage – donated one hundred *qings* of land (about 1,515 acres) on Ya-bai Mud-bank as a source of local provisions for the monks on Mount Cui-wei. The local people argued that they had lived there for generations and insisted that building land should be given to them in exchange for the rice-fields appropriated. The monks did not agree and the case was brought before a court which ruled in favour of the natives of the region. The old Master Fa-ren was disappointed and returned to the south the following year. Before leaving, he returned all his possessions to

Masters Ti-an and Yue-xia and disbanded his following. When I thought of this untoward situation, I realised that mere reliance upon men of influential power could only result in harm and misfortune. This incident greatly affected those southern monks coming to the north; thus I could not dismiss as nonsensical the effects of geomantic influences upon a site. The year was nearing its end; all the surrounding mountains were covered with snow and the intense cold penetrated to the bone. I was alone in my hut but my body and mind felt pure and clean. One day I cooked *taro* in a cauldron and sat cross-legged while waiting for my meal to cook and involuntarily entered the state of *samadhi*.

MY 63RD YEAR
(1902/03)

Master Fu-cheng and others who stayed in nearby huts were surprised that I had not called on them for a long time and came to my hut to present their New Year greetings. Outside my hut, they saw tigers' tracks everywhere with no traces of man. They entered my hut and seeing that I was in *samadhi*, they awoke me with a *qing* [a musical instrument made of stone, the sound of which is subtle but penetrating]. When I returned to self-consciousness, they asked me, 'Have you taken your meal?' I replied, 'Not yet, the *taro* in the cauldron should be well cooked by now.' When its cover was lifted, the cauldron was covered with an inch of mould. Fu-cheng was startled and said, 'you must have been in *samadhi* for half a month.' We then melted ice, cooked *taro* and ate our fill. They joked with me and left.

A few days after Fu-cheng had left me, monks and laymen in nearby and distant places came to see me. In order to avoid the trouble of meeting people, I left at night with my baggage on my back for the wilderness where there is not an inch of grass.[1] I reached Mount Taibai (3,767 m.), where I lived in a grotto. But after a few days, Master Jia-chen followed my footsteps and came to my locale. We then agreed to make the long journey to Mount Emei together. We made our exit through the Bao-ya Defile, arrived at Mount Zibai, passed through Miao Tai-zi Terrace, visited the temple of Zhang-liang and passed through Zhao-hua District where we saw the Zhang-fei Cedar. Walking on, we

51

reached Chengdu, where we rested in a temple for a short while. We then walked again and via Jiading Prefecture, we eventually arrived at Emei Shan, which we ascended to the Jinding Peak. The 'Buddha-lights' we saw there were exactly the same as those seen on Cock's Foot Mountain. Late in the night, we saw countless heavenly lamps whose brilliance was akin to the 'wisdom lamps' previously seen on Mount Wu-tai. I went on to the Xi-wa Hall, where I paid reverence to the old Abbot Zhen-ying who was over 70 and leader of all the monks on the mountain, being an enlightened master of the Chan School. He gladly kept me with him for a few days' stay.

Afterwards, I descended the mountain, followed my way round the Xixiang Pool, I passed by the Da-er Monastery, reaching Zhang-lao Plain, The Vairocana Temple and the Emei and Jiajing Districts, intending to cross the Liusha River at Yin-cun Village. It happened that the river current was rising and from morning until midday I waited for the boat. When it arrived, after all the other passengers had gone aboard, I asked Jia-zhen to board ahead of me and passed him our baggage. Just as I was about to climb aboard, the mooring rope broke but I managed to catch hold of the half attached to the boat. As the current was swift and since there were many passengers on board, the slightest inclination of the boat would have caused it to capsize so I did not move and was thus dragged through the water by the boat. At sunset, it made towards land and I was lifted ashore. My garments and both my feet were cut by stones. It was cold and raining. When we arrived at Shai-jing Customs Post, the nearby inns refused to admit monks. There was a temple in the street but the only monk there also refused to let us stay despite repeated demands; he only permitted us to pass the night under a theatrical platform outside. As our garments were soaked and the ground wet, we gave money to the monk to sell us some dry straw. Instead, he brought us two bundles of wet straw which would not burn. We patiently endured these annoyances and sat until sunrise. Then we bought a few coarse fruits to fill our stomachs and continued our march. We passed over Mount Huo-ran, arrive at Jian-zhang and Ning-yuan Prefecture, eventually reaching Hui-li Zhou. We crossed the border of Yunnan Province, passed through Yung-bei District, visited the holy site of Avalokitesvara, crossed the Jinsha River and made a pilgrimage to Cock's Foot Mountain, where we passed the night under a tree; once again, the sound of the bell was heard from within the stone door.

The following day, we climbed the mountain until reaching the Jinding Peak, where we made incense offerings. I again thought of this sacred site of the Buddha and Patriarch which was now in such a dilapidated condition, and of the degeneration of the whole Sangha order in the Province of Yunnan. I vowed to build a hut on the mountain to receive visiting pilgrims but was prevented from doing so by the monastic hereditary system prevailing in the locality. I was sad and could not refrain from tears.[2]

We then descended the mountain, arriving at Kunming. There, Upasaka Chen Kuan-ci who was a Dharma-protector, invited me to stay at the Fu-xing Temple, where, with the help of Master Jia-chen, I isolated myself for meditation, passing the New Year period in seclusion.

Notes

1. This means that the Master preferred not to be disturbed by phenomenal hindrances.
2. The 'hereditary ownership' of temples had become fairly common by Xu-yun's time. It meant that the control and management of monasteries was decided by arbitrary rules, the temples virtually being regarded as private property and nepotism rather than spiritual merit dictated what could be done by whom. This prevented visiting monks from making free use of many facilities or even staying for the night when on long pilgrimages. In principle, no Buddhist monastery should be regarded as property in the possession of its occupants, but as belonging to the whole Sangha order under the standing rules.

MY 64TH YEAR
(1903/04)

While I was in retreat, a monk came from Ying-xiang Temple to tell me that someone there had set free a cock weighing a few *catties* and that the bird was aggressive and wounded the other fowl. I went to the temple and expounded the refuge formula and precepts to the bird, also teaching it to recite the Buddha's name. Soon, the cock ceased to fight and stood alone on the branch of a tree; it no longer killed insects and ate only when given cereals. After a while, whenever it heard the bell and *qing* rung, it followed the monks to the main hall and after each prayer meeting it would return to the same branch in the tree. It was again taught to recite the Buddha's name and eventually crowed, 'Fo, Fo, Fo,' [Chinese for 'Buddha']. Two years had elasped when, one day after a prayer-meeting, the cock stood up in the hall, stretched out its neck, fanned its spread wings thrice as if to recite the Buddha's name and died while standing. Its appearance did not change for several days; it was eventually placed in a box and buried. On the occasion I composed the following poem:

> This cock of fighting nature
> Wounded fowl and shed their blood.
> When its mind came to a stop, by precepts sacred
> It fed on grain and stood alone, to insects harmless.
> Gazing at the golden yellow statues
> How easily it crowed the Buddha's name!
> After turning thrice, suddenly it passed away,
> Where did this being differ from the Buddha?

MY 65TH YEAR
(1904/05)

That spring the Dharma-protectors and Abbot Qi-ming of Gui-hua Temple invited me to end my seclusion and visit his place in order to expound the *Sutra of Complete Enlightenment* and the *Sutra of Forty-Two Sections.* At the time, over three thousand people became my disciples. In the autumn, Abbot Meng-fu invited me to expound the *Surangama Sutra* at the Qiong-ju Monastery. I supervised the carving of wooden blocks for printing the *Surangama Sutra* and the poems of Han-shan.[1] These blocks were kept at the monastery. I was also asked to expound the precepts and at the end of the meeting Commander-in-Chief Zhang Song-lin and General Lu Fu-xing came with other officials and gentry to invite me to Dali Prefecture and to stay at the Chong-sheng Monastery in San-ta. There, I asked to expound the *Lotus Sutra* and those who became my disciples on the occasion numbered a few thousand. Li Fu-xing asked me to stay at the monastery but I said, 'I do not wish to live in towns. Previously, I took a vow to stay on Cock's Foot Mountain but the monks there would not admit me. As you are now protectors of the Dharma, my vow could be fulfilled if you gave me a site on which to build a hut on the mountain to receive pilgrims, thus saving the Sangha from disaster and restoring the holy site of Mahakasyapa.'

They all approved and ordered the sub-prefect of Binchuan to lend his aid (so that my vow could be fulfilled). A ruined temple called Bo-yu was found on the mountain for me. I went there to stay and although it had no living rooms and while I had no food with me, I received courteous visits from monks, nuns, male and female lay-devotees who came from all quarters. The Temple of Bo-yu had been abandoned since after the Jia-qing reign (1796–1820) of the Qing Dynasty, because to its right a big rock had been found from which emanated the malefic 'White Tiger' influence, thus causing the site to be uninhabitable. I wanted to break up the rock and dig a pool in which fish and other river creatures could be set free. Labourers were hired for the purpose but to no avail, for when the earth around it was removed, its base could not be found. It emerged 9 feet 4 inches above ground and it was $7\frac{1}{2}$ feet in width; One could sit on it with crossed legs for meditation. A foreman was called to remove it to a distance 280 feet to the left, and over a hundred men came but they failed to shift it despite their combined effort for three successive days. After they had left, I offered prayers to the guardian spirits of the temple and recited mantras. I took ten monks and together we succeeded in moving the rock to the left. Those who gathered to watch us were in uproar and wondered at the divine aid. Someone wrote three characters on the rocks, 'Yun Yi Shi' ('A rock moved by a cloud'[2]). Officials and scholars who heard of the story came to write inscriptions on the rock. On the occasion, I also wrote the following poem:

> This strange rock stands out boldly,
> Wrapped in moss since times of old;
> It was left to me when the vault of heaven cracked.[3]
> Seeing the Chan School's decline, I determined to restore it[4]
> And mocked at Yu-gong's silliness in moving mountains.[5]
> Looking for truth, a hearer of Dharma
> Seemed to find it on a hill where tigers roamed.[6]
> Henceforth, unmoved by the eight worldly winds,[7]
> He lived among the clouds with a few firs.[8]
> The Bo-yu Peak penetrates to Brahma's palace;

A seeker of the Dao will walk ten thousand *Li*
To visit the golden-hued ascetic's home.[9]
I have overcome a thousand obstacles to
Enter this mountain and reach this old, moss-covered rock,[10]
In bright moonshine, while fish with the fir shadows play.[11]
He who from above looks beyond the illusory world
Will hear the sound of bells borne on the heavenly breeze.[12]

I began repairing the temple for the reception of pilgrims from all quarters and was in a hurry to raise the required funds. Therefore, I left Master Jia-chen to look after the temple and went alone to Tengyue for the purpose (of raising subscriptions). From Xaiguan I went on to Yungchang and eventually reached the Hemu Tree. The road there was long – several hundred *li* – and appeared very rough and difficult to negotiate as it had not been repaired for many years. However, the locals said that a monk from another province had decided to brave great hardship to repair it. He had not asked for contributions, accepting only voluntary gifts of food for his merest subsistence from passers-by. He had worked on the road unflinchingly for several decades. Thanks to his efforts, about ninety per cent was now in good condition again. To mark their gratitude for his work, the people at Pupiao intended to renovate the Temple of the Peacock King[13] for him to stay there.

However, he declined their offer and concentrated only on repairing the road. I wondered at the story and went out to find the monk. About sunset I met him on the road; he was carrying a hoe and basket and was about to leave. I approached, joining my palms in salute, but he only stared at me wide-eyed without saying a word. I took no notice of this and followed him to the temple where he put down his tools and sat cross-legged on a hassock. I went to pay my obeisance to him but he ignored me, remaining speechless. So I also sat face to face with him. The next morning, he rose to cook rice and I poked the fire; when the rice had cooked, he did not call me but I filled my bowl and ate. After the meal, he carried the hoe while I took the basket and together, we went to move stones, dig the ground and spread sand. Thus, we worked and rested together for over ten days without exchanging a single word. One evening, in the bright moonlight which was as bright as broad daylight, I went outside the temple and sat cross-legged on a large rock. It was late but I did not return to the temple. The old monk approached me stealthily from behind and shouted, 'What are you doing here?'

I opened my eyes slowly and replied, 'I am here to see the moon.'

He asked, 'Where is the moon?'

'A glowing rosy light,' I replied.

He said:

> 'In the midst of falsehood the real can hardly be seen;[14]
> Mistake not then the rainbow for the radiant light.'

I replied:

> 'The light which embraces form is neither past nor present;
> Unhindered, it is neither positive nor negative.'[15]

Thereupon he grasped my hand, laughed loudly and said, 'It is very late, please return to rest [at the temple].' The following day, he was joyful and began to talk, saying that he was a native of Xiangtan (in Hunan Province). His name was Chan-xiu (Cultivator of Chan). He had retired from the world when young and at 24 he entered the Chan-hall of Jin-shan Monastery where he succeeded in putting a stop to his wandering mind. Later, he went on pilgrimage to the sacred mountains (in China) and proceeded to Tibet, returning to China through Burma. As the road was rough, he took pity on the people and horses negotiating it. He was impressed by the former deeds of Dharanimdhara Bodhisattva and undertook to repair the road alone. Thus, he had been there several decades and was now 83 years old. He had not met a bosom-friend before and was gladdened to have a favourable karmic link which enabled him to pour out his story, kept untold for so long. I also related the circumstances leading to my retirement from home life.

The following day, after breakfast, I bade farewell and we parted company, laughing loudly. I then walked to Tengchong (also called Tengyue) which faces Bhamo across the border in Burma, thus to raise funds for renovating my temple. On arrival, I stayed at Hunan Guildhall. Before I had laid down my baggage, a few men in mourning came and bowed down before me, saying, 'Venerable Sir, our request is that you recite sutras for us.'

I replied, 'I am not here to recite sutras.'

One of them in filial mourning said, 'We know that venerable monks, like yourself, recite sutras.'

I said, 'I have heard nothing about there being monks in this region.'

Thereat the head of the guildhall interjected and said by way of explanation, 'Venerable Sir, you should go to their place to recite sutras for them; this is a rare coincidence. They are the grandsons of academician Wu, known as the "Virtuous One". He was over 80 years when he died and his children and offspring number several dozen, among whom there are a few well-known scholars and academicians. The grand old man passed away a few days ago and before his death, he said that he had been a monk in his previous life and ordered that his body should be dressed in monastic garments, that those in the house should not weep, that no killing of fowl or cattle should be allowed, and that no Daoist priests should be called in to recite their scriptures for him. He also predicted that an eminent monk would come to liberate him. He then sat cross-legged and passed away. The following day, his complexion remained fresh. Venerable Sir, as you came here today, was it not an occasion caused by the good karma of the deceased?'

Hearing this, I then accepted the invitation and went to the house to recite sutras and to perform the ceremony for the bestowal of food to hungry ghosts over a seven-day period. The whole district with its officials and literati invited me to stay at Tengyue but I said to them, 'I came here to appeal for funds to rebuild a temple on the Cock's Foot Mountain and regret that I am unable to stay here.' Upon hearing this, they were delighted and enthusiastically donated substantial funds. After my return to the mountain, I bought provisions for the community, erected buildings with extra rooms, set up monastic rules and regulations, introduced meditation and expounding of the sutras, enforced discipline and transmitted the Buddhist precepts. That year, the number of monks, nuns, male and female lay devotees who received the commandments was over 700 persons. Gradually, all the monasteries on the mountain followed our example and took steps to improve themselves; their monks again wore the proper monastic garments and ate vegetarian food. They also came to stay at my temple to receive instruction.

Notes

1. Han-shan or 'Cold Mountain' was a remarkable adept who lived in the Jin-guan reign (627–64) of the Tang Dynasty. He is regarded as a transformation body of Manjusri. He lived in a grotto and wrote inspirational poems to teach Chan. Many of these were inscribed on dead trees, disused buildings and similar places.

2. 'Cloud' stands for the Master, whose name (Xu-yun) means 'Empty Cloud'.

3. According to Chinese mythology, when two gods waged war with each other, the four cardinal pillars of heaven crumbled and the sky was badly damaged. Nu-wa, one of the two gods, used a magical five-coloured stone to mend it. Master Xu-yan was a great poet and many Chinese poets allude to ancient myths to make a point. The Master really meant that his duty was to 'mend' the Dharma which was being under-mined on the Cock's Foot Mountain.

4. Lit. 'The Cloud saw the change and wanted to follow the dragon.' 'Cloud' stands for Xu-yun, and to 'follow the dragon' means to follow good examples set by the ancients who always spread the Dharma and revived the Chan School when it showed signs of decline. This sentence is metaphorical and has been rendered into plain English above.

5. Yu-gong appears in an ancient fable known to most Chinese. Even as an old man of 90, he wanted to move two mountains which faced the door of his house. People laughed at his foolishness in wanting to move mountains, but he said, 'Though I will die, there will still be my sons. When they die, there will be my grandsons to carry on. As our family line increases, the mountain-stones will decrease.' According to the tradi-tional story, the old man's attempts to shift the mountains so moved the 'heavenly ruler' that he sent down two angels to cart the mountains away. Here, Master Xu-yun utilises this story to lay stress on the Mind which alone could move mountains and all obstructions to instantaneous enlightenment.

6. This shows the difficulty of hearing the correct Dharma.

7. The 'eight worldly winds' which disturb the mind are: gain and loss, eulogy and defamation, praise and ridicule, joy and sorrow.

8. The practitioner retires to a mountain peak which is cloud-hidden, with but two or three fir-trees as companions for meditation.

9. The Cock's Foot Mountain, said to be the place where Mahakasyapa – otherwise 'the golden-hued ascetic' – is in the state of *samadhi*, awaiting there the coming of Maitreya to this earth. Mahakasyapa is said to have swallowed light, hence his 'golden hue' and his name of 'Light Drinker'. These two lines show the difficulty which a seeker of the Dao should overcome when visiting the holy site of the First Chan Patriarch, symbolic of the path leading to enlightenment.

10. The rock symbolises the resistance from degenerate monks on the mountain.

11. The bright moonshine stands for the inherently enlightened self-nature and fish for the deluded living beings who play with the illusory shadows of the fir-trees, symbolic of the 'non-existent' phenomena.

12. The last three lines of the poem mean that in the midst of illusions, he who can look into that which is beyond the phenomenal will attain enlightenment and be praised by Mahakasyapa who rings the invisible bell, the sounds of which are conveyed by a heavenly breeze, symbol of the bliss enjoyed by successful devotees.

13. A Bodhisattva with four arms who rides on a peacock.

14. When a meditator's mind has become completely still, it is usually the case that beautiful colours are seen which may be mistaken for the light of wisdom.

15. The light of wisdom can contain all illusory forms but it is eternal, that is beyond spatial and temporal limitations. It is all-embracing and meets no obstruction for it is free from all dualism, this being the cause of the sense of separation between subject (the 'knower') and object (the 'known'). Thus, it is like the 'pure light' which enables a rainbow to appear, the colours of the spectrum having no reality of their own. In the same way, all phenomenal forms arise within the clear light of wisdom but none of them have their own subsistent reality.

The body of Master Han-shan at the Monastery of the Sixth Patriarch.
Master Han-shan (1546-1623) was an eminent Chan monk of the Ming
Dynasty. He restored the Sixth Patriarch's Monastery at Cao-xi,
Guangdong Province some three hundred years before Xu-yun
appeared, doing the same thing himself.

CHAPTER SIX

TAKING THE *TRIPITAKA* TO JI ZU SHAN

MY 66TH YEAR
(1905/06)

That spring, Abbot Bao-lin of Shi-zhong (Stone Bell) Monastery invited me there to transmit the precepts and those who came to receive them numbered over eight hundred persons. After the transmission of the precepts, while Jia-chen isolated himself in seclusion for meditation at the Bo-yu Temple, I went to various lands in the South Seas to appeal for funds. Initially, I arrived at Nantian (in Yunnan Province), where I expounded the *Amitabha Sutra* at the Tai-bing Monastery and while there, several hundred persons became my disciples. Thence, by following high cliffs and making my way through tribal regions I entered Burma, passing through the Shan States I arrived at Xinjie and then Mandalay. While passing through the miasmal Shan States, I caught a disease which developed and became serious. Ill as I was, I managed to reach the Temple of Avalokitesvara at Liudong where there was a Chinese monk called Ding-ru. I paid obeisance to him but he ignored me. I then went to the hall where I sat cross-legged. That evening when he sounded the *qing*, I assisted him in ringing the small bell and beating the drum. After reciting the rules for repentance and reform, he chanted, 'Kill, kill, kill!' and made three prostrations. The next morning, after reciting the same text in the hall, he again chanted his violent remarks as on the previous night and prostrated himself thrice. I wondered at his manners and purposely stayed there to observe. His morning, midday and evening meals consisted of foods with onion, garlic and milk. I did not eat but remained silent about the strange diet, only taking water. He knew why I did not take his food and ordered that I be served with gruel and rice without the onion and garlic. I was then able to eat.[1]

On the seventh day, he invited me to tea and I asked why he chanted 'Kill, kill, kill!' in the hall. He replied, 'Kill foreigners! . . . I was a native of Bao-qing in Hunan Province. My father was a military officer and after his death I retired from the world and learned about the Dharma on Pu-tuo Island. I followed Master Zhu-chan who taught me painting. Ten years previously, I had gone from Hong Kong to Singapore by ship on which I was ill-treated by foreigners. Their treatment was unbearable and I will hate them for the rest of my life. I am now selling pictures which are treasured by the people here and for this reason I have had no worries about my upkeep these last ten years. The monks who have passed through here before usually put on airs and graces and were very temperamental; it is rare to meet someone like you who is unobstructed and in harmony with all.[2] This is why I tell you the truth about myself.'

I urged him to treat friend and foe alike, but failed to lessen his hatred of foreigners. After I had gradually recovered from my illness I took leave of him, but he insisted on keeping me. When I told him that I was raising funds for my temple, he gave me provisions and travelling expenses, bought me a railway ticket and telegraphed Upasaka Gao Wan-bang at Rangoon to receive me. He gave me every courtesy and wished me good luck. When I reached Rangoon, Upasaka Gao with all his family, Superintendent Xing-yuan and the monks of Long-hua Monastery were at the railway station to meet me. I stayed at Upasaka Gao's house, where I was treated with great honour. He said, 'The Venerable Master Miao-lian has always thought of your austere life over the decades but never received news from you. He was most delighted to hear that you were going to visit here and wrote to me, telling me that he was returning to China to repair the Gui-shan (Tortoise Mountain) Monastery at Ning-de (in Fujian Province). He came here recently and I accompanied him when visiting the Great Golden Pagoda (Shwedagon) and other holy sites for a few days, after which he returned to his monastery to await you lest you return to China quickly.'

Upasaka Gao accompanied me to the boat and telegraphed Ji-luo Monastery to send some monks to receive me. When the ship arrived, there was a passenger on board who had died from an epidemic so a yellow flag was hoisted and all travellers were quarantined on a distant hill where over a thousand people were left without shelter, exposed to sunshine by day and to rain at night. Each person was given a food ration consisting of only a small bowl of rice and two carrots to be cooked by themselves. A doctor came twice daily to examine them. One-half of the passengers left within seven days and the rest on the tenth, so I was left alone on the hill and was thus very impatient.

I was seriously ill and felt miserable. Eventually, I could no longer eat. On the eighteenth day, the doctor came and ordered me to move to a vacant house. I was glad to be there. I asked the old watchman there some questions and he said that he was a native of Zhuanzhou. He then sighed, saying, 'This room is for those who are about to die; you were ordered to move here as a post-mortem will be necessary.' When I told him that I had come to visit the Ji-luo Monastery, the old man was moved and said, 'I will give you some medicine.' He then prepared a bowl of *shen-qu* [a medicine] which he gave me to drink, and after taking it twice, I felt slightly better by the following day. He said, 'When the doctor comes again, as soon as you hear me coughing, get up and try to be in high spirits as best as you can; if he gives you medicine, do not take it.'

As warned by the old man, the doctor actually came just as he had said and after mixing some medicine in water, he forced me to swallow it. As I could not refuse, I reluctantly drank it. After the doctor had left, the old man was alarmed and said, 'You will not live much longer now; tomorrow, he will come back to dissect your body. I gave you medicine, hoping that the Buddha would protect you.' The following morning, when the old man came, I was sitting on the ground but could not see anything although my eyes were wide open. He helped me to stand up and saw that the ground was covered with blood. He again brought me medicine which I drank, then changed my garments, cleaned the ground and sighed, saying, 'Another man taking the medicine you were given yesterday would have been dissected even before breathing his last; you are not fated to die and this must be because of the Buddha's protection. When the doctor comes again at nine o'clock, I will cough as a signal and you must feign high spirits. 'When the doctor came and saw me alive, he pointed his finger at me, smiled and left. When asked why the doctor smiled, the old man replied, 'Because you are not fated to die.' I told him that Upasaka Gao had given me some money and asked him to give some of it to the doctor to set me free. I promptly took out forty dollars which I handed over to him [as my ransom-money] and another twenty dollars as a present for what he had done for me. He replied, 'I must not take your money. Today, the doctor will be a European and this cannot be arranged; tomorrow, the doctor will be a Karen and it can be arranged.' That evening, he called again and said, 'I have arranged things for you with the Karen doctor and have given him the twenty-four dollars; you will be released tomorrow.' I was thus reassured and thanked the old man.

The next morning the doctor came and after his visit a boat was called to take me across the bay. I was helped on board by the old man and on reaching the opposite shore, a vehicle was hired to take me to the Guang-fu Hall where the monk in charge of guests left me unattended and waiting for two full hours because of my disorderly appearance. I could not help having mixed feelings, both sad and glad at once; glad because I had just escaped from death and sad because of the irresponsible attitude of the director of guests. Finally, an old monk whom I later knew to be the head monk called Jue-kong came and I said to him, 'I am disciple so-and-so,' he bowed, touching my head to the floor. As I was too weak to get up, he helped me up and sat me on a chair and said, "Upasaka Gao sent us a telegram as notice of your impending arival, but we have heard no news from you. The Venerable Abbot and the whole community have been worred about you; how did you come to be in this condition?' Without further ado, young and old monks crowded into the hall, instantly transforming the atmosphere to something like a warm home in springtime. Shortly after, the old Abbot Miao-lian came and said, 'Day after day I have been waiting for news of you and I have been apprehensive that you might be in some danger. I had wanted to return to Fujian to repair the Gui-shan Monastery, but having heard that you were coming I have awaited you here.' After a long chat I said, 'This is my fault,' and then related my own experience. The old Abbot and monks were impressed and pleaded to hear my story in full. They then brought their palms together in salute and we all returned to the Ji-luo Monastery. The old Abbot urged me to take some medicine but I said, 'As I have returned home, all my false thoughts have stopped; I will be all right after a few days rest.'[3] Later, when he noticed that I sat for several consecutive days each time I meditated, he warned me, 'The weather in the South Seas is hot and differs from that in China. I am apprehensive that a long sitting will be harmful to your health.' However, I did not feel that anything was wrong in my meditation. The old Master said, 'You should now expound the *Lotus Sutra* to form a propitious cause here. I am returning to China; after you have expounded the sutra do not return to Yunnan Province but go to Mount Gu as I still have something to tell you there.'

After accompanying the old Abbot to the ship, I returned to the monastery and began expounding the sutra. A few hundred persons became my disciples and the Dharma-protectors at Malacca invited me to expound the *Sutra of the Medicine Buddha (Jnanabhaisajya)* in Qing-yun Temple. I then went on to Kuala Lumpur where Upasakas Ye Fu-yu and Huang Yun-fan asked me to expound the *Lankavatara Sutra* in Ling-shan Temple. In all the Malaysian cities where I expounded the sutras, over ten thousand persons became my disciples.

That winter I received a telegram from representatives of the whole Sangha order in Yunnan Province, informing me of the Government's intention to impose a levy on monastic property. At the same time, Master Ji-chuan and others at Ningbo wired me a telegram requesting that I return to China as soon as possible to discuss these matters. As the year was drawing to its close, I stayed Kuala Lumpur to pass the New Year period.

Notes

1. Buddhist monks are prohibited from eating the 'five hots' or five pungent roots which are garlic, shallots, chives, onion and leeks, because they are known to heat the blood and cause anger and lust.
2. A Buddhist idiom meaning perfect harmony among all differences, as in delusion and enlightenment, *samsara* and *nirvana*, life and death, etc., all phenomenal differentiation being like waves which arise within the *Bodhi*-ocean, in itself still and free from concern.
3. Meaning, 'I have recovered my own Self after the ordeal and since my true nature has never been ill, I will be all right and do not require treatment.'

MY 67TH YEAR
(1906/07)

I returned to China in the spring. When the ship called in Taiwan

en route, I visited the Long-quan Monastery and when she arrived
in Japan I visited monasteries in various places. As China and
Japan were not on friendly terms at the time, Chinese monks were
closely watched and Japanese monks were not allowed to visit
China. Because of this, my wish to set up a confederation of
Chinese and Japanese Buddhists failed to materialise.

In the third month I reached Shanghai, where, together with
Master Ji-chan and representatives of the Buddhist Association, I
proceeded to Beijing in order to present our petition to the Central
Government. After arrival there, we stayed at Xian-liang Monastery where Masters Fa-an, Director of Buddhist Affairs, Dao-xing
of the Long-quan Monastery and Jue-guang of the Kuan-yin
Monastery personally welcomed us. There, Prince Su Shan-qi
invited me to expound the Buddhist precepts to his wife. Princes,
Dukes and high officials who were old acquaintances of mine
(from the days of the Boxer Rebellion when they followed the
imperial retinue fleeing westwards) all came to see me with advice
as to how our petition should be presented. Since the Dharma-
protectors were willing to give me assistance, I did not encounter
any difficulty. In response to our petition, the following imperial
edict was decreed:

The Thirty-Second Year of the Guang-xu Reign: Imperial Edict
In the matter of the collection of the contributions, it has been repeatedly
decreed that no high-sounding pretext will be permitted to oppress the
poor. It has come to our knowledge that the establishment of schools and
factories has been done harshly, disturbing the provinces where even the
Buddhist Sangha has not been spared. Such a state of affairs cannot be
tolerated and it is hereby decreed that all viceroys should immediately
order provincial authorities to give protection to all monasteries, whether
large or small, and to all the monastic properties within their jurisdiction.
Henceforth, no gentry or public servants shall be permitted to disturb
them under any pretext whatsoever and no regional authorities are
allowed to extort contributions from monastic property. To act thus is to
be in conformity with our form of government.

After the promulgation of this imperial edict, all provincial
levies imposed on monastic properties were abolished. I stayed in
the capital to confer with the Dharma-protectors there about the
fact that no Emperor had presented a copy of the *Tripitaka* to

Yunnan Province since the beginning of the Qing Dynasty, and drew attention to the advisability of presenting a petition so that this distant border region could receive the benefit of the Dharma. Prince Su gladly agreed to sponsor the petition which the Minister of the Interior presented to the Emperor. It read:

The Director of Buddhist Affairs and Seal-Keeper Fa-an has petitioned the Ministry that according to Abbot Xu-yun of the Ying-xiang Monastery of Boyu Peak on Cock's Foot Mountain, Bin-chuan in Da-li Prefecture, Yunnan Province, the said Monastery is an ancient holy site but currently lacks a copy of the *Tripitaka*. He now requests the bestowal of an Imperial Edition so that it can be revered there in perpetuity. The above site is known as the holy seat of Patriarch Mahakasyapa and the present temple is all that remains of the ancient monastery complex. The object of this petition is to ask for the gracious bestowal of a set of the Imperial Edition of the *Tripitaka* for the purpose of extolling the Buddha Dharma. It has been presented by Prince Su, the Minister of Civil Administration, Abbot Cheng-hai of Bai-lin Monastery and Abbot Dao-xing of Long-xing Monastery. In case of Your Majesty's approval, my humble request is that the Buddhist office should be ordered to donate the copy of the *Tripitaka*.

On the sixth day of the sixth month, the petition was given imperial sanction and the following imperial order was decreed on the twentieth of the seventh month in the thirty-second year of the Guang-zu Reign (1907):

His Imperial Majesty has been pleased to bestow upon the Ying-xiang Monastery of Boyu Peak of the Cock's Foot Mountain, Yunnan Province, the additional title: 'Chan Monastery of Zhu-sheng' ('Invocation of the Holy One') for the national welfare, plus a royal chariot with the Imperial 'Dragon Edition' of the *Tripitaka*, and upon its Abbot, a purple robe, a bowl, a jade seal, staff and sceptre. Abbot Xu-yun is hereby given the title, 'Great Master Fo-ci Hung-fa' (Vast Dharma of the Buddha's Compassion). He is commanded to return to the mountain, there to transmit Buddhist precepts for the welfare of the nation and its people. The Minister of the Interior is hereby commanded to inform Master Xu-yun of this Imperial edict so that he can collect the gifts offered and return to the mountain, act as its guardian and spread the Buddha's teaching.

All officials and inhabitants of the locality are required to obey and execute this Imperial edict and give protection to the monastery; all irreverent acts on their behalf are strictly forbidden.

My request for the *Tripitaka* had thus been granted and everything was now in order. On the twentieth I received a letter from Miao-lian who had written from Gu-shan, saying, 'When conveying the *Tripitaka*, you will first have to call at Amoy (Xiamen); please leave the sutras there temporarily and come immediately to see me at Mount Gu.'

Assistance was given to me by Dharma-protectors in the capital for obtaining the *Tripitaka*. Abbots Chuan-dao of Yang-zhen Hall and Wen-zhi of Mount Fu-ding especially gave me tremendous help for conveying the huge collection of texts from the capital to Shanghai, thence to Amoy. As the year was nearing its end, I stayed in Beijing to pass the New Year period.

MY 68TH YEAR
(1907/08)

That spring in the first month, I went to Shanghai and Amoy thanks to the help of Masters Wen-ji and Chuan-dao. Upon my arrival I received a telegram from Mount Gu informing me that the old Abbot Miao-lian had passed away on Mount Gu. At the time, monks from all the monasteries in Amoy had gone to Mount Gu to attend the ritual cremation of the Abbot's body, whose stupa had been moved to a minor hall of the monastery awaiting decision as to its final resting place. I immediately headed for Mount Gu to supervise the erection of the pagoda and help perform the ceremony for the transmission of Buddhist precepts to the dead. I was kept very busy and on the tenth of the fourth month, as soon as the building of the pagoda was completed, it rained very heavily for fifteen successive days, giving a great deal of anxiety to the whole community.

On the eighth of the following month, after the ceremony for the transmission of the Bodhisattva precepts, it stopped raining. On the ninth, the weather was fair and the literati and people came to the mountain in great numbers. On the tenth, when the stupa (containing ashes) was placed in the pagoda, a hundred tables with vegetarian food were offered on an open platform where the assembly gathered to recite sutras. After offering prayers, when the food-transmuting mantra was being chanted, a whirlwind suddenly raised all the offerings into the air and a bright ray of red light emanated from the stupa and went upwards towards the top of the pagoda. All those present praised the rare occurrence. After the ceremonies and upon our return to the monastery, torrential rains fell. Half of the relics were placed in the stupa and half were taken to the Ji-luo Monastery at Penang for worship there.

When I arrived at Penang with the *Tripitaka* and the relics of the late Abbot Miao-lian, monks of the Avalokitesvara Hall and others who came to receive me numbered several thousand persons. After the recitation of sutras, while the food – transmuting mantra was being chanted, a whirlwind suddenly scattered thousands of floral offerings there. The box of relics emitted a brilliant ray of light which reached the top of the pagoda, two *li* away. The above two remarkable occurrences took place during my performance of the rituals and were clearly witnessed by me, personally. For this reason, the Buddha said, 'The response from esoteric rites is mysterious.' Of the Abbot's lifetime of self-cultivation, I knew nothing. He did not insist on either Chan or Pure Land methods but his chief aim was to repair dilapidated monasteries and to form auspicious karma by receiving and converting all who came to him. The events after his passing were indeed very remarkable. After he had shaved my head as a novice years ago, I received no news about him. I was really guilty of ingratitude to my master and my last connection with him was the care of his stupa and the distribution of his brilliant relics. I remembered his last words from which it could be inferred that he knew of his death in advance. As it is impossible to make accurate guesses in this respect, I only relate the facts for others who will come after me, thus to draw their own conclusions.

I next went by boat to Dan-na and the Avalokitesvara Hall invited me to expound the *Hrdaya (Heart) Sutra* there. Thence, I took another boat to Siam (Thailand) but since there was no vegetarian food on board, I sat cross-legged for most of the time. An Englishman came to my deck and after glancing at me a few times, he asked:

'Where does the Venerable Master happen to be going?'

Seeing that he spoke Chinese, I replied, 'I am going to Yunnan.' Thereupon he invited me to his cabin and offered me cakes and milk, which I politely declined.

'Where do you stay in Yunnan?' he asked.

'At Ying-xiang Monastery on the Cock's Foot Mountain,' I replied.

He said, 'The monastic rules are observed with excellence there.'

I asked him, 'What were you doing there, Sir?'

He replied, 'I was the British consul at Tengyue and Kunming and I visited the monasteries in the region. "The British Consul then asked the purpose of my visit to foreign lands. I said that I was conveying the *Tripitaka* to Yunnan and that as I was short of travelling expenses, I had first gone to Kuala Lumpur to ask for donations. He asked, 'Have you any official documents?' I then showed him official proofs and the book of subscriptions. The consul entered in the book a subscription of 300 dollars.[1] This was an extraordinary karmic event. He then invited me to a meal consisting of fried rice with vegetables. When the boat arrived in Siam, I went ashore and parted company with him.

Next, I stayed at the Long-quan Monastery, where I expounded the *Sutra of Ksitigarbha* (or 'Earth-Store Bodhisattva'). One day, the British Consul came to see me and gave me 3,000 dollars. In order to build a hall for housing the *Tripitaka* upon my return to Yunnan, I required a large sum amounting to several tens of thousands of dollars, but until the Consul's offering, I had only collected a small sum. A few days after I had finished expounding the *Sutra of Ksitigarbha*, I continued to expound the *Universal Door*[2] to an audience of several hundred people.

One day as I sat cross-legged, I involuntarily entered the state of *samadhi* and thus forgot all about expounding the sutras. After I had been so sitting for nine successive days, the news spread in the capital (Bangkok). The King, high ministers, male and female disciples came to pay their reverence. I came out of *samadhi* and after I had finished expounding the sutras, the King of Thailand invited me to his palace to recite them once more. He presented me with many offerings and respectfully requested me to accept him as a disciple. The literati and people who became my disciples numbered several thousand persons. After this experience of *samadhi*, both of my legs became numb and I could only walk with difficulty. Soon my whole body became paralysed and as I could not hold my chopsticks, others had to feed me. The Dharma-protectors called in Chinese and Western doctors to treat me but medicines, acupuncture and cauterisation were of no avail. When I could no longer speak or see, all the physicians had no further resources. I was, however, indifferent to this and did not feel any suffering for I had laid down everything. But there was one thing I could not afford to lay down, and this was a bank draft sewn inside my collar. Nobody knew of this and since I could not reveal it in speech or writing, in the event of my death and cremation with the draft, the *Tripitaka* would fail to be conveyed to Cock's Foot Mountain and the hall for keeping it would not be built. How then, could I bear the heavy karmic burden for this? As I thought of it, I shed tears and silently prayed for Mahakasyapa to protect me.

At the time, Master Miao-yuan, who had previously stayed with me on Mount Zhong-nan happened to be present. He saw my tears and noticed my lips moving, leaning close to listen. I asked him to give me some tea to perk me up so that I could continue my prayers to Mahakasyapa. After drinking the tea, my mind became clear and I fell asleep. While dreaming, I saw an old man who looked like Mahakasyapa sitting at my bedside, he said, 'Bhiksu, you should never stray from the commandments that go with the bowl and robe. Do not worry about your bodily condition; use your folded robe and your bowl as a pillow and everything will be all right.' Upon hearing this, I immediately used my folded robe and my bowl as a pillow and when I had finished readying them for use, I turned my head but could not see the Honoured One. My whole body perspired profusely and I felt indescribably happy. I could now murmur a few words and asked Miao-yuan to pray for a prescription at the shrine of Wei-tuo. The prescription given consisted solely of *mu-jieh* and bat's excrement. After taking this I was able to see and speak again. Miao-yuan prayed for a second prescription which consisted of just small red lentils to be mixed with rice *congee* [a thin soup], and instruction to abstain from all other foods. After taking this for two days, I could move my head a little. Another prescription was prayed for, this time consisting of only small red lentils. Since then, I just took the *congee* of red lentils which thus enabled me to ease nature, my excrement being as black as lacquer. Gradually, my senses recovered and I was now able to get up and walk. My illness had lasted over twenty days and I thanked everybody present for their good care of me. I was greatly moved by the kind attention of Master Miao-yuan who had looked after me day and night. I then went to thank Wei-tuo and vowed to build a shrine dedicated to him whenever erecting or repairing a monastery in the future. In the shrine of Wei-tuo, a few lots drawn by me predicted good fortune.

After my recovery, I continued expounding the *Awakening of Faith Shastra* and by the time I had about finished it, Ji-lou Monastery in Penang sent Masters Shan-qin and Bao-yue to welcome me back there. The King of Thailand along with his court and high officials as well as Dharma-protecting Upasakas and Upasikas came to present donations and see me off. The sum received was very great.

In reward for my recitation of sutras at the royal palace, the King gave me 300 *qings* (about 4,550 acres) of land at Tong-li, which I in turn donated to Ji-luo Monastery, requesting that its Abbot Shan-jin should set up a rubber factory there as a source of income for his monastic community. With Masters Shan-jin and Bao-yue, I passed the New Year period at the factory site.

Notes
1. This was a considerably large amount at the time and might have represented one half of the Consul's yearly income.
2. 'The Universal Door' refers to a chapter of the *Lotus Sutra* in which Avalokitesvara Bodhisattva's universal compassion is related. Avalokitesvara vowed to take on whatever form is required to save living beings from suffering, the only precondition being that devotees should cultivate a single-minded faith in the Bodhisattva's saving powers. In its broadest sense, the 'universal door' represents the spirit of the Mahayana, which teaches salvation for all.

MY 69TH YEAR
(1908/09)

That spring, together with Master Shan-jin, I went to the Temple of Avalokitesvara which he had built at Selangor. Thence, I went to Ipoh and Perak where I visited several holy sites and then proceeded on to Ji-luo Monastery, where I expounded *The Awakening of Faith Shastra* and the Samantabhadra's *Conduct and Vows*, the epilogue of the *Avatamsaka Sutra*. When I passed through towns and cities, the number of people who asked to become disciples was very great, and I passed all my time receiving those people who came to see me. After I had expounded the sutras at Ji-lou Monastery, I isolated myself for a temporary period of retreat, stopping for a while my explanation of sutras and the reception of visitors. I passed the New Year period in the monastery.

MY 70TH YEAR
(1909/10)

My conveyance of the *Tripitaka* started in Penang and when I arrived at Rangoon, I was received by Upasaka Gao Wan-bang who retained me for over a month's stay at his house, after which he personally accompanied me to Mandalay. At Rangoon, Upasaka Gao bought a reclining Buddha statue of jade which he wished to send to Zhu-sheng Monastery for worship there. When the boat arrived at Xin-jie, I stayed at the Temple of Avalokitesvara and hired pack-horses to carry the *Tripitaka* and the Jade Buddha to the Cock's Foot Mountain. Over three hundred pack-horses were needed for the sutras but the statue was too heavy to be carried on horseback. As no labourers could be found for the purpose, the statue was left at the Temple of Avalokitesvara for the time being so that it could be carried to the mountain in a few years time. Upasaka Gao stayed there for over forty days to supervise preparations for the convoy, sparing neither toil nor money for the purpose; it would have been hard indeed to find another man like him. The convoy, consisting of about a thousand men with three hundred horses, passed through Tengyue and Xiaguan and was welcomed by people in the towns and trading centres. Although it had taken several days to arrive there, the men and animals were in good shape. From Xiaguan to Dali Prefecture no rain fell but thunder suddenly crashed and rolled with lightning furrowing rapidly through the clouds; waves rose on Lake Er Hai and a mist developed, all of which presented a remarkable spectacle. Upon arrival at the outer gate of the monastery, a ceremony was held to welcome the *Tripitaka* and after the cases of sutras had been secured just before the last leg of the journey, rain fell in torrents after which the weather cleared. [At the time] people said that the old dragon in Er Hai Lake had come to welcome the Imperial Edition of the *Tripitaka*.

Viceroy Li Jing-xi of Yunnan and Guizhou Provinces – who had received an imperial command to send his men to Dali Prefecture to welcome the *Tripitaka* – came with provincial officials and notables and personally witnessed this marvel; all of them praised the boundlessness of the Buddha Dharma. We rested in Dali Prefecture for ten days. Carrying on through Xiaguan and Zhao-zhou the convoy arrived at Binchuan Prefecture, thence straight to the Zhu-sheng Monastery. The whole journey was without an ill event, not a drop of rain wetting the cases of the sutras. The texts were placed in the monastery and on the last day of the month an incense offering was held. The whole community was joyful at the auspicious arrival of the scriptures without a single hitch in the long journey. The petition for the *Tripitaka* had now come to a satisfactory conclusion.

There was another event worth recording. After my arrival at the Wan-shou (Long Life) Monastery in Tengyue, while talking with Zhang Sun-lin in the hall, a dun cow which had escaped from its owner came in and knelt down, shedding tears, shortly followed by its owner Yang Sheng-chang and others. I learned that Yang was a butcher and said to the cow, 'If you want to flee for your life, you should take refuge in the Triple Gem.' The cow nodded and I immediately taught the animal the Triple Refuge formula. After this I helped the cow up and it was most placid like a human being. I took out some money which I gave to its owner who, however, refused it. He was deeply moved by what he saw, swore that he would change his occupation and asked for his conversion to the Dharma. As he also became a vegetarian, Commander Zhang, who was deeply impressed by the man's transformation, recommended him for work in a shop.

75

The body of Master Hui-neng (638-713) at Nan-hua Monastery.
The Nan-hua Monastery (formerly Bao-lin) became famous under
Hui-neng's influence, whereafter all the great Chan Schools flourished,
descendants of his two main disciples, Huai-rang and Xing-si.
Xu-yun also restored this famous temple.

CHAPTER SEVEN

FAMILY NEWS

MY 71ST YEAR
(1910/11)

As a result of the imperial decree forbidding any levies on monastic property and what with the arrival of the *Tripitaka* at the monastery, the whole Sanga order of Yunnan Province was able to live in peace. Viceroy Li of Yunnan Province sent a representative to the monastery to enquire after me and also ordered members of his family to become disciples. They brought me gifts from the Viceroy and I wrote to thank him. I asked Master Jia-chen to come out of retreat and to call on monasteries, urging them to observe with us the rules of discipline, to begin educating the younger monks and to abolish all evil customs and habits. Since then, the Dharma flourished again on the Cock's Foot Mountain. I also conferred with the magistrate of Binchuan over the release of all the monks still held in gaol and the setting free of all other prisoners who had committed lesser offences.

In the summer I received a letter from my family which had been forwarded to me from Gu-shan Monastery. I thought of the fifty years that had passed since I left home and composed three poems which contained the following lines:

> A pure karma in this life
> Otherwise an empty mind
> . . .
> Since all worldly things have been long forsaken, beware
> Of taking habits that remain to the land of clouds.

When Upasaka Chen Yung-chang, the chief secretary for the central government, saw my poems, he added them to the following account of Bhiksuni Miao-jin's *gathas,* which he had inscribed on a stone tablet:

77

Bhiksuni Miao-jin's Gathas

Bhiksuni Miao-jin's lay surname was Wang. She was the stepmother of Master Xu-yun, whose other Dharma names were Gu-yan and De-qing. He was a native of Xiangxiang and his surname was Xiao, his family being descendants of Emperor Liang Wu-di. His father Xiao Yu-tang was an officer of Quanzhou Prefecture in Fujian. His mother's family name was Yan. When she was over 40 years old, she prayed to Avalokitesvara Bodhisattva for the birth of a son and became pregnant. One night both she and her husband saw in a dream a man with a long beard wearing a blue robe, carrying the Bodhisattva's statue on his head. He came riding upon a tiger which jumped upon their bed. His mother was scared and awoke, finding that their room was filled with unusual fragrance.

When the Master was born, only a fleshy bag was visible and his mother was bitterly disappointed to see it, succumbed to her desperation and died. The following day an old man selling medicinal herbs came to the house, cut open the fleshy bag, taking out the male child who was to be Master Xu-yun and subsequently raised by his stepmother.

Master Xu-yun did not like eating meat as a child. As he grew up he received his schooling but disliked the Confucian classics, his penchant being the Buddhist Sutras. His father was disappointed and severely reprimanded him. When he was 17, as he was also heir to his uncle, his father chose two wives for him from the Tian and Tan families. The Master did not want to be married and fled to Mount Gu in Fujian, where he followed Abbot Miao-lian as a disciple. In the year Jia-zi (1864/65), after the death of his father, his stepmother – together with his two nominal wives – entered a Buddhist convent where they joined the Sangha order as *Bhiksunis*. Miss Tian, who had previously suffered from tuberculosis, had a relapse four years later and passed away. As for Miss Tan, she is still living and is staying on Mount Quan-yin in Xiangxiang, where she is known as Bhiksuni Qing-jie. In her letter to the Master, she informed him of the death of his stepmother in the year Ji-yu (1909/10), who sat with crossed-legs, chanted the following *gathas* and passed away:

First Gatha

What use was there in rearing
A son who fled once he was strong?
His pregnant mother's life hung by a thread,
So thanks were only offered after he was born.
Diligently was he suckled; despite ordure and urine
He was treasured like a ball by the unicorn.[1]

When he grew up and left his stepmother
To whom could she look in her older years?
As you had no brothers when your father died,
On whom could your stepmother and two wives depend?
You did not know how troublesome it was to rear
A child: the more I think of this the sadder I become.
Though willing to be a ghost mother searching for her son,[2]
How can I be when parted by mountains wreathed in cloud?
Thinking so hard on birth and death, you did not
Recall that Pang-yun stayed at home.[3]
Worldly feelings and love of Dharma, are they not the same?
Even mountain birds know they must roost with the setting sun.
Though our calling's the same to fulfil our vows,
Each day we wash the cold mountain of its blue-green.[4]
Being a son of the void's king, you should know
That the Bhagavat freed His mother's sister.[5]
I hate this troubled world and set my mind
At rest for my return to the Land of Bliss.

Second Gatha

If one stays in the world for love of it, delusion
And desire will cause one to forget the real self.
For more than eighty years my life has been a delusion and a dream.
Nought will remain when the myriad things return to the void.
Free now from my past life's entanglements, I will put
On a pure and wonderous body in the Lotus Realm.
Those who can recite the Buddha's name to return to the West
Should not permit themselves to sink in the bitter-ocean.

Bhisuni Qing-jie's Letter

Salutations from afar, Revered One. I have not ceased thinking of you
since you left us but due to the cloud-wreathed mountains that separate
us, I have been unable to obtain news of you. I trust that you have
established good health in the Dharma-substance and that you have
harmonised the states of stillness and activity. Over fifty years have
passed since you left home, but since you are as elusive as a rustic
immortal, I regret that I have been unable to come and serve you. In the
first month of this year, I heard indirectly that you were living a free and
easy life of retreat somewhere in Fujian Province. I was half sad and half
happy when the news came, but I was most puzzled as to just where you

79

were living. The more I think of your inability to pay back your debt of gratitude to your parents, and of your casting aside all feelings towards your wives, the more I am at a loss trying to understand how you have been able to bear all this.

Moreover, as you had no brothers and since your parents were old when they had you, we are unfortunate in that we have not been able to continue the family-line. At home, there was no one to support the family which was thus left without a successor. Whenever I think of all this, I cannot refrain from tears. The Confucian teaching stresses the importance of the five human relationships and filial conduct.[6] Formerly, even the immortal Han-xiang still thought of saving his uncle, Han-yu, and the latter's wife. As to our Lord Buddha, he treated both friend and foe alike. He first liberated Devadatta [his cousin and opponent] and his own wife, Yasodhara. Is it really true that there is no karmic affinity between us? If you cannot be moved by the thought that we are fellow natives of the same district, you should at least remember the debt of gratitude you owe your parents. I feel obliged to give you some news of the family affairs.

After you left home, your father sent out messengers to search for you – but in vain. He was very sad and because of his declining health, he resigned his post and returned home to seek for a cure. Over a year later, he passed away on the fourth of the twelfth month in the year Jia-zi (1864/65). After his funeral, your stepmother, Miss Tian and I entered a convent and joined the Sangha under the respective Dharma names of Miao-jing (Profound Purity), Zhen-jie (True Cleanness) and Qing-jie (Clear Chastity). The affairs of our family were entrusted to the charge of your uncle and aunt who gave away most of our possessions as alms.

After four Dharma-years, Miss Tian vomited blood and passed away. In the year Yi-hai (1875/76), your uncle died at Wenzhou. My elder brother is now Prefect at Xining. Your cousin, Yong-guo, went to Japan with Miss Tian's third brother. Your cousin, Hun-guo, has been made your successor and as to your cousin Fu-guo, no news has been received from him since he left with you.

An ancient said, 'Those of great virtue have no descendants.' In your past life, you must have been a monk who has now reincarnated, but you have been responsible for the discontinuity of two family lines. Although you are a Bodhisattva seeking the liberation of all living beings, you cannot prevent the ignorant from slandering you because of your failure to fulfil your filial piety. I have also failed in my filial duty but I admire the genuine roots of your spirituality and your unshaken determination which is like a lotus flower that cannot be soiled by the mud from which it grows. But why should you leave your native province and thus forget all about your origins? That is why I am writing you this letter.

Last winter, on the eighth of the twelfth month (18 January 1910), your stepmother, Bhiksuni Miao-jin, departed for the Western Land [of Bliss]; she sat cross-legged and chanted her *gathas* before passing away. She departed immediately after chanting the *gathas* and the convent was filled with a rare fragrance which lasted for a few days during which her body, erect in the sitting position, looked exactly as if she were alive. Alas! Although this world is like a dream and an illusion, even a wooden man could not refrain from tears under the circumstances. This letter is to keep you informed of your family affairs and I do hope that upon receipt of it, you will return immediately along with your cousin Fu-guo. Morover, the holy teaching is in decline and you should know that it is your duty to restore it. Could you not follow Mahakasyapa's example and send forth the golden light so that I can be your Dharma companion? I am full of tears and will cherish this hope for the rest of my life. Talk is cheap and even a thousand words could not convey all my feelings, the meaning of which must be inferred.

> You are like a goose that has left its abode
> Preferring to soar in the sky, flying south alone.
> Pity its companion deserted in the nest whose grief
> Is deepened by the distance separating them.
> My gaze pierces the moon on the horizon
> And my eyes are filled with tears that never cease.
> On the banks of the River Xiang I have stayed long
> And the bamboos are marked with many joints.
> You will surely realise the great Dao
> And your wisdom-sun will brightly shine.
> Once we were companions in the burning house,[7]
> Now we are relatives in Dharma-city.

(Respectfully written by Bhiksuni Qing-jie, choked with sorrow on Guan-yin Mountain, this nineteenth day, the second month of the year Geng-shu (29 March 1910).)

Note by Cen Xue-lu, Xu-yun's Editor

When the Master received the above letter, he had mixed feelings; he was sad because he had not repaid the debt of gratitude he owed his parents, but also joyful because after over forty Dharma years, Bhiksuni Miao-jin's mind was not disturbed at her death, as shown in her two *gathas* which foretold her rebirth in the Western Paradise.

Notes

1. The fabulous unicorn is represented in China as always embracing or chasing after a ball which it treasures.

2. i.e. – I could wait until I die to become a ghost to search for you, but in the meantime we are separated. This recalls a Chinese sentiment that 'a life parting is more painful than death'.

3. Upasaka Pang-yun attained enlightenment but did not join the Sangha. This line means 'Why did you not follow his example and stay at home to take care of your old parents and wives?'

4. The 'Cold mountain' here symbolises the self-nature which is passionless and turns its cold shoulder on the worldly. The 'blue-green' symbolises worldly habits. This line means that the Bhiksunis were only 'scrubbing' their self-nature clean of all worldly feelings and passions, although they were not performing Bodhisattva-works as did the Master.

5. The 'Void's King' is the Buddha. The old woman reprimanded her stepson for failing to think of liberating his parents and two wives.

6. Relationship between (1) prince and minister; (2) father and son; (3) husband and wife; (4) brothers; and (5) friends.

7. The *Lotus Sutra* compares this world to a burning house in which there is only suffering. Qing-jie's *gatha* alludes to this parable.

The Bell Tower of Yun-xi Monastery, Yunnan. No date.
Note the lotus pond. The Yun-xi Monastery was situated on Bi Ji
Mountain, West of Lake Kunming in Yunnan Province. It was one of
the monasteries restored by Xu-yun. This picture, along with that of the
Master at Gu-shan 1930/31 (facing p.00), has obviously been folded up
and carried around by a monk. While this did little to preserve the
technical quality of these shots, they are unusual and worth recording.

CHAPTER EIGHT

THE PEACEMAKER

MY 72ND YEAR
(1911/12)

In the spring, the transmission of the Precepts was followed by seven weeks of Chan meditation, the aim being to introduce longer sitting periods, each measured by the time it took for several incense sticks to burn. The summer retreat was instituted with its rules and regulations. In the ninth month, the news that a revolution had broken out at Wuchang reached Yunnan Province, where it created a great disturbance. The walled town of Binchuan was beseiged and hostilities were imminent. I played the role of peacemaker. Due to a misunderstanding, Commander Li Gen-yuan sent his troops to surround the Cock's Foot Mountain, but he was satisfied with my interpretation of events, embraced the doctrine of the Triple Gem and led his men away.

Note by Cen Xue-lu, Xu-yun's Editor

The Master dictated only the above few lines, but I have read the full account in the Provincial records of Yunnan, from which I quote the following: The Master's modest silence revealed the extent of his virtue:

While the Master was spreading the Dharma and working for the salvation of living beings in Yunnan, the following calamities were averted thanks to his timely intervention . . .
1. At the end of the Manchu Dynasty [1911–12], the Prefect of Binchuan was called Zhang. He hailed from Changsha and was a fierce and meddlesome man. The district was infested with bandits and although he had arrested and shot many of them, they increased and banded together in secret societies. For their own safety, the gentry joined with them and they were severely punished by Zhang, who also arrested several unscrupulous monks on the Cock's Foot Mountain, but otherwise held the Master [Xu-yun] in great reverence. When the revolution broke out, the people of Binchuan joined it and laid siege to the prefecture which was,

however, firmly held by Zhang. As he could not count on reinforcements, his case was hopeless. When the Master descended the mountain and went to the prefecture, the besieging ranks said, 'Master, please entice Zhang out so that we can kill him to allay public anger.' The Master replied evasively, but when their leader made the same request, he said, 'It would not be difficult to kill Zhang. This border region is full of rumours and the situation is still very confused. If you lay siege to the town with the hope of killing its officials, you will be punished when reinforcements arrive.'

The leader asked, 'What do you advise?'

The Master replied, 'Dali Prefecture is only two days' march away and the Provincial Governor of Sichuan is on an inspection tour there. If you go there to present your case against Zhang, the latter will be condemned to death and you would then avoid having to take the law into your own hands.'

The leader followed the Master's advice and stationed his troops outside the town. When the Master entered the headquarters of the prefecture, he saw Zhang, who was armed, ready to meet the insurgents. Zhang shook hands with the Master and said, 'I am doing my duty and shall be grateful if you would reserve a grave for me on the Cock's Foot Mountain in case I die.'

The Master replied, 'That will not be necessary; everybody here respects Prefect Zhang Jing-xian. Please send for him.'

When Zhang Jing-xian arrived, he arranged a truce and the revolutionaries withdrew. Prefect Zhang then went to Dali Prefecture to ask for reinforcements and when they arrived, they lifted the siege on the town. When Prefect Zhang left, Yunnan had already proclaimed its independence [from the Manchu Emperor]. General Cai-o was appointed Governor and his old schoolmate, who was Zhang's son, became Secretary for Foreign Affairs. To thank the Master, Zhang wrote to him, saying, 'You have not only saved my life but you have also been a benefactor of Binchuan Prefecture. Without your intervention, I might have been killed and my son would now be seeking to avenge me.

2. After the proclamation of the Republic, the living Buddhas and high lamas of Tibet took advantage of the breakdown of communications to ignore the new regime's order to hoist the Republican flag.[1] The central government ordered Yunnan to send Yin Shu-huan with two divisions of troops to punish them and the vanguard had already reached Binchuan. The Master thought that if hostilities were started, endless troubles would be caused in the border region. He followed the vanguard to Dali Prefecture, where he said to the commander, 'The Tibetans are Buddhists and if you send someone who is well-versed in the Dharma to discuss the matter with them, there will be no need to dispatch an army to punish them.'

Yin listened to the Master's advice and asked him to go to Tibet on a mission of peace. The Master said, 'I am a Han Chinese and I am afraid that I shall fail, but at Lichuan there is a Lama called Dong-bao who is advanced in Dharma years and whose great virtues are well known and respected. The Tibetans revere him as he is called the "Dharma King of the Four Gems".[2] If you send him, the mission will be successful.'

Yin therefore wrote a letter for the Master to deliver to the Lama and he also sent some officials to accompany the Master to Lichuan. Dong-bao at first declined to get involved on the grounds of old age, but the Master said, 'The Tibetans still tremble at the thought of the previous expedition sent to Tibet by Zhao Er-feng. Do you really want to spare your "three inches of tongue" and so disregard the lives and properties of thousands of people?" The Lama then rose from his seat and said, "All right, I will go, I will go . . . He was assisted by an elderly monk called Fa-wu; both entered Tibet, obtained a signed truce document and returned. The signature of this new agreement brought about peace for the next thirty years.

3. The Master's conveyance of the *Tripitaka* to Yunnan and his teaching of the Dharma there to convert many people made him well known and much revered in the locality where everybody called him 'The Grand Old Monk Xu-yun'. The revolution and the Emperor's abdication were followed by the expulsion of Buddhist monks and the destruction of their temples. Li Gen-yuan who commanded the provincial troops hated monks who did not observe the monastic rules. When he was about to lead his soldiers into the mountains of Yunnan to drive out the monks and destroy their monasteries, he asked himself how the Master, who was only a poor monk, could win the hearts of the local populace? This intrigued him so much that he issued a warrant for the arrest of Master Xu-yun.

Seeing that trouble was imminent, nearly all the monks fled from their monasteries. Over a hundred were staying with the Master and were seized with panic. Someone advised the Master to hide but he said, 'If you want to leave, do as you please, but what is the use of fleeing if one has already earned karmic retribution? I am prepared to die as a martyr for my faith in the Buddha.'

The community then decided to stay with him. A few days later, Li Gen-yuan led his troops to the mountains and stationed them at Xitan Monastery; they pulled down the Bronze statue of Maharaja (the protector of the monastery) on the peak of Cock's Foot Mountain and destroyed the Buddha-hall and *deva*-shrine. Seeing that the matter was now a pressing one, the Master descended the mountain and called on the commander, presenting his card of identity to the guard at the gate. Those there who recognised him warned that he was in imminent danger of being apprehended and refused to take the card to their superior.

Paying no attention to them, the Master entered the gate. Commander Li was in the main hall chatting with Zhao-fan, the former Governor of Sichuan Province. The Master came forward and saluted the commander, who took no notice of him. Zhao-fan, who knew the Master, asked where he had come from so the Master gave his reason for calling.

Flushing with rage, the Commander shouted, 'What is Buddhism good for?'

The Master replied, 'The holy teaching is for the benefit of this generation and for the salvation of those in distress; it extols good and eschews evil. From olden times the practice of government and religion has been going on side by side, the former to secure peace and order and the latter to turn the people into good citizens. The Buddha's teaching stresses control of mind, which is the root of the myriad phenomena; if the root is correct, everything else will be in order.'

Li was not angry now but asked, 'What are clay and wooden statues good for? Are they not a waste of money?'

The Master replied, 'The Buddha spoke of the Dharma and its formal expression; the latter reveals the doctrine which, without symbols, cannot be known and will never arouse feelings of awe and reverence. A man devoid of these feelings is apt to commit evil and so cause trouble and misfortune. The use of clay and wooden statues in China and of bronze ones in foreign countries, serves to arouse feelings of admiration and respect and their effect on the masses is incalculable. However, the ultimate pattern taught by the Dharma is, "If all phenomenal forms are not regarded to be real as such, the Tathagata will be perceived." '

Li was rather pleased with this explanation and called for tea and cakes. He then asked, 'Why is it that, instead of doing good, the monks act strangely and so become useless to the country?'

The Master replied, 'The title "Monk" is just a name, for there are holy monks and worldly monks. It is not fair to blame the whole Sangha because there are one or two bad monks. Can we blame Confucius because there are bad Confucian scholars? You command the provincial troops but despite military discipline, do you expect all your soldiers to be as intelligent and honest as you are? We regard an ocean as large because it does not have to reject a single fish or shrimp, and the Self-nature is like the ocean of the Buddhadharma because it can contain all things. The duty of the Sangha is to preserve the Buddha's teaching, guard the Triple Gem and to convert and guide others in hidden ways but its influence is tremendous; it is not altogether useless.'

Commander Li was very pleased with his explanation; he smiled and bowed his head in reverence. He then retained the Master for a vegetarian dinner. Candles were lit and the conversation turned upon the law of causation in worldly entanglements and the fruits of karma with the continuity of the world and living beings. In the course of the conversation, deeper principles were also dealt with. Li now became both sympathetic and respectful towards the Master. Finally, he sighed and said, 'The Buddhadharma is indeed great and boundless, but I have killed monks and destroyed monasteries. Mine is, therefore, an evil karma and what shall I do about it?'

The Master said, 'This is due to the prevailing modernism and is not entirely your fault. I hope that you will endeavour to protect the Dharma in future and there is no merit greater than that.' Li was very glad and moved to the Zhu-sheng Monastery, where he mixed with the monks and shared their vegetarian food for a few days. One day, a ray of golden light suddenly appeared linking the peak with the foot of the mountain on which all the vegetation turned yellow like gold. It is said that there are three kinds of light on the mountain: The Buddha-light, silver light and golden light. The Buddha-light has been seen every year, but after the monasteries were built, silver and golden lights have been seen only a few times. Li Gen-yuan was very impressed and asked to be the Master's disciple. He also asked him to be the head abbot of the whole Cock's Foot Mountain and then led his troops away. If the Master's sublime virtues had not been in accord with the Dao, how could he have changed the commander's mind in so short a time?'

(Conclusion of the notes from the Provincial Annals of Yunnan.)

That winter, because of a dispute between the Chinese Buddhist Association and the Universal Buddhist Society at Shanghai, I received a telegram from the former asking me to visit them immediately in Nanjing. On arrival, I called on Master Pu-chang, Tai-xu, Re-shan and Di-xian to discuss the matter with them. We agreed to establish the headquarters of the Buddhist Association at Jing-an Temple. Then with Master Ji-chan, I went to Beijing, where we stayed at the Fa-yuan Monastery. One day, Master Ji-chan suddenly felt unwell and passed away sitting in meditation. I saw to his funeral and took his coffin to Shanghai. At Jing-an Temple, the headquarters of the Buddhist Association was officially inaugurated and a memorial service was held for Master Ji-chan. I received official documents authorising the formation of branches of the Association in Yunnan and Guizhou Provinces and the Yunnan-Tibet area. When I was about to return to Yunnan, Upasaka Li Gen-yuan (also called Li Yin-juan), gave me letters of introduction to Governor Cai-o and other provincial officials asking them to protect the Dharma.

Notes

1. This extract from the Provincial Records of Yunnan raises the old issue of China's suzerainty over Tibet. The official responsible for setting them down took such suzerainty for granted. Centuries ago, both Burma and Tibet were nominally under the political control of China. Readers are strongly urged not to identify the political ideas in this extract with the personal views of Xu-yun. Master Xu-yun's role was simply that of a peacemaker who obviously spared some thought for the fate of the Tibetan people and all others. The question of Tibet's autonomy cannot be discussed here, but a passage has been deleted here from the provincial records because of its insensitivity on this point.

2. The 'Four Gems' of Tibetan Buddhism are: Lama (Guru), Buddha, Dharma and Sangha.

Yun-men Monastery: The Complete Prospect.
Yun-men Monastery after Xu-yun's restoration, circa 1951/52.
Note the vegetable plots.

CHAPTER NINE

THE JADE BUDDHA

MY 73RD YEAR
(1912/13)

After my return to Yunnán, I immediately began organising branches of the Buddhist Association and convened a general meeting at Wen-Chang Temple, where I asked Master Lao-chen to set up a branch in Guizhou Province. Tibetan *Hutuktus*[1] and Lamas came in great numbers from distant places. We decided to form groups to spread the Dharma and to open Buddhist schools, hospitals and other charitable institutions. That year, there was an unusual event worth recording. A villager brought to the Buddhist Association of the Yunnan-Tibet area a raven to be set free there. The bird was a good mimic. At first it was fed on meat but after it had been taught the refuge formula and the mantra for reciting the Buddha's name, it refused to take meat. It was tame and enjoyed freedom of movement. All day long it never stopped calling Amitabha and Avalokitesvara Bodhisattva. One day it was caught by an eagle and while being carried away in the air it continued calling the Buddha. Though it was a bird, it did not cease to think of the Buddha in time of danger. How then can we human beings allow ourselves to be inferior to a bird?

MY 74TH YEAR
(1913/14)

After its opening, the Buddhist Association began to register monastic property and plan new projects which required frequent contact with the civil authorities. We had great trouble with a man called Lo Yung-xian who was head of civil administration in the province and who put obstacles in our way. Constant intervention in our favour by the military governor Cai-o proved of little avail.

The Tibetan *Hutuktus* and the Buddhist Association asked me to visit Beijing to take up the matter with the central government. The Prime Minister, Xiong Xi-ling, who was a fervent Buddhist, gave us his valuable help and support and transferred Lo Yung-xian to the capital; Ren Ke-qing was then appointed Civil Governor in his place. After my return to Yunnan I found that Ren was sympathetic to the Dharma which he gave full support.

Notes
1. *Hutuktu* is a Sino-Mongolian term which is more or less equivalent to the Tibetan 'Tulku', meaning a Lama of high rank, usually regarded as the reincarnation of an adept with unusual powers. In Mongolian Lamaism, a *Hutuktu* is generally in charge of many temples over a whole region.

MY 75TH YEAR
(1914/15)

General Cai-o went to Beiking and Tang Ji-yao was appointed Military Governor of Yunnan in his place. As I intended to return to the Cock's Foot Mountain to rest, I handed over management of the Buddhist Association to its committee. After my return to the mountain, I immediately began repairing the Xing-yuan Monastery there and the Lo-quan Temple at Xiayang. As soon as I had completed my plans for these repairs, the abbots of the monasteries on Mount He-qing and the neighbourhood invited me to Mount Long-hua to expound the sutras.

Following that, Abbot Zhen-xiu asked me to the Jin-shan Monastery at Lijiang to teach the sutras and so I was able to make pilgrimage to Taizi Grotto on Mount Xue. I visited Weixi, Zhongtian and A-tun-zi, eventually reaching the border of Tibet, where I called at thirteen great monasteries. I then returned to the Cock's Foot Mountain where I passed the New Year period. There was one other thing of note.

That year, while staying at the Long-hua Mountain to expound the sutras, all four districts of Dali Prefecture were suddenly hit by an earthquake. Virtually all the buildings collapsed, including the city walls, about the only exception being the Yu-bao Pagoda at the monastery, which remained erect. During the earthquake, many fissures opened in the earth, spewing forth a blazing fire which spread everywhere. The people of the city struggled to flee for their lives, but at almost every step the earth cracked open underfoot so that they often fell into crevices. Just when many tried to get out, the earth closed back around them, dismembering their bodies, the heads of some just barely visible above ground. This grave scene resembled the fiery hells mentioned in Buddhist texts and it was unbearably sad to behold. There were about a thousand homes in the city, many of which were in dire trouble.

At the time, there was a Gilding shop in the city run by the Zhao and Yang families. Zhao's Buddhist name was Wan Chang and Yang's was Zhan Ran. The raging fire mysteriously abated itself before reaching their dwelling, nor was it hit by the earthquake. There were over ten members in each family and they had remained perfectly tranquil and made no fuss during this terrifying incident. Someone who knew the two families said that they had revered the Dharma for many generations and that they firmly upheld the Pure Land practice of reciting the Buddha's name. I was much gladdened to hear of their example amid this tragic scene.

MY 76TH YEAR
(1915/16)

In the spring, after the transmission of the precepts, a strange event took place. An academician of the former Manchu Dynasty, by the name of Ding, lived in Dengchuan Prefecture. He had an unmarried daughter of 18, and one day, she suddenly fainted and her family did not know what to do. When she revived, she spoke with a male voice and, pointing to her father, she cursed him and said, 'Ding! Presuming upon your influence, you falsely accused me of being a bandit and were responsible for my death. I used to be Dong Zhan-biao of Xichuan in Dali Prefecture, do you still remember me? I have accused you before the God of the Dead[1] and now come to take my revenge for the crime you committed [against me] eight years ago. "The girl then seized an axe and chased her father with it. Ding was scared, went into hiding and dared not return home. Every day when the spirit came to take possession the girl's manner changed and she created a great disturbance in the house much to the annoyance of the neighbours.

At the time, the Cock's Foot Monastery sent two monks called Su-qin and Su-zhi to its town office at Dengchuan and as they passed by Ding's house, they saw many people around the girl in her possessed state of mind.

One of the monks said, 'I advise you not to disturb the peace.'

The girl replied, 'You are a monk and should not mind other peoples' business!'

The monk said, 'Of course, this is not really any concern of mine, but my master has always said that mutual enmity should not be persisted in but dropped. If preserved, it grows greater and never ends.'

The girl thought for a while and then asked, 'Who is your master?'

The monk replied. 'The Venerable Abbot, Xu-yun of Zhu-sheng Monastery.'

The girl said, 'I have heard of him but I have never met him. Would he agree to transmit the Precepts to me?'

The monk replied, 'He has a greatly compassionate heart and has vowed to liberate all living beings. Why should he refuse your request?'

The monk also advised her to ask Ding to spend some money on a prayer meeting for her deliverance, but the girl said, 'I do not want his money, he is a murderer.'

The monk said, 'What about if the people of this town gave you the money so that peace can be restored?'

The girl angrily said, 'If this grievance is not avenged I will never be satisfied; on the other hand, if mutual enmity is preserved, it will go on and on. I will ask the God of the Dead for advice. Please wait for me here tomorrow.'

After the demonic spirit left the girl, she stood up, noticed the people around her, blushed with embarrassment and withdrew. The following day, the possessed girl came before the monks and blamed them for breaking their promise. The monks excused themselves on the grounds that some monastic business had kept them at the town office. The girl said, 'I have consulted the God of the Dead.[1] He said that the Zhu-sheng Monastery is a holy site and that I can go there on the condition that you accompany me.'

Thus, the two monks returned to the mountain along with the girl and about ten other people, relating details of the preceding events. The following day an altar was erected for reciting the sutras and to transmit the precepts to the girl. Henceforth peace returned to Ding's house and the people of Dengchuan made frequent pilgrimages to the [Zhu-sheng] Monastery.

Notes
1. Yama was originally the God of the Dead in the Vedas with whom the spirits of the departed dwell. In Buddhist mythology, he is regarded as the King of Hades and regent over the hells. He is thus thought of as a judge of the dead and held to apportion punishment.

MY 77TH YEAR
(1916/17)

As I intended to take the Jade Buddha to China which Upasaka Gao had given me a few years earlier, I returned to the South Seas [to fetch it]. Having heard that most of the Tribesmen *en route* had faith in Buddhism, I passed through their regions. I visited Rangoon again, where I paid reverence at the Great Golden Pagoda (Shwedagon). Thence, I called on Upasaka Gao, besides expounding the sutras at the Long-hua Monastery. From there, I took the boat for Singapore. Upon arrival, a police officer declared to the passengers, 'Our friend, the President of the Republic of China, is restoring monarchy on the mainland and all revolutionaries are being arrested. All passengers who are mainland Chinese intending to stay overseas must be carefully interrogated before being allowed ashore.

A few hundred passengers were taken to the police station for questioning but were eventually released except for our group of six monks. We were suspected of being left-wingers of the Gemingdang. We were all held as detainees, tied up and beaten. We were then left out in the sun and not allowed to move; if we moved, we were beaten again. We were not allowed food or drink, nor were we allowed to relieve ourselves. This went on from six in the morning until eight at night. When a refuges-disciple of mine called Hong Zheng-xiang and a company manager called Dong heard of our detention, they went to the police station to guarantee our *bone fides*, paying 5,000 dollars bail for each of us. After fingerprints had been taken, we were released and invited to Zheng-xiang's warehouse, where we were invited to stay for the New Year period and later given assistance for transporting the Jade Buddha to Yunnan.

MY 78TH YEAR
(1917/18)

In the spring, the conveyance of the Jade Buddha began from the Guan-yin Pavilion. Eight labourers were hired and it was arranged that a lump sum would be paid to them at the Cock's Foot Mountain. The convoy had to cross mountainous terrain for several weeks by obscure tracks. One day, as we reached Mount Yeren, suspecting that the Jade Buddha might contain bank-notes, gold and gems, the labourers set it down and claimed that it was too heavy to be carried further. As they asked for an increase in pay several times the original sum fixed, I did my best to calm them but they became noisy and aggressive. I found it was useless trying to reason with them and seeing a large boulder by the roadside which weighted several hundred *catties*, I smiled and asked them: 'Which is the heavier, this boulder or the statue?'

In unison, they replied, 'The boulder is two or three times heavier than the statue,'

Then with both hands, I raised the boulder over a foot above the ground.

Gaping in astonishment, they put out their tongues and said, 'Old Master, you must be a living Buddha!' They then stopped arguing and when we reached the Cock's Foot Mountain, I gave them a substantial reward. I know that my own strength could never have raised the boulder and I attributed this to divine assistance.

Later, I went to Dangchong to expound sutras at the monasteries there.

MY 79TH YEAR
(1918/19)

Governor Tang Ji-yao ordered the magistrate of Binquan to accompany his personal representative to the mountain with a letter inviting me to Kunming. I declined their offer to send a sedan chair with military escort and walked to the provincial capital along with my disciple Xiu-yuan. At Chuxiong some bandits searched me; they found the Governor's letter and struck me.

I said to them, 'There is no need to beat me, I want to see your chief.'

They led me to Yang Tian-fu and Wu Xu-xian. On seeing me,

Wu shouted, 'Who are you?'

'I am the Abbot of the monastery on Cock's Foot Mountain,' I replied.

'What is your name?' asked Wu.

'Xu-yun,' I said.

'Why are you going to the provincial capital?' inquired Wu.

'To perform Buddhist ceremonies, I replied.

'Why?' asked Wu.

'To pray for the welfare of the people,' I said.

Wu said, 'Governor Tang Ji-yao is a bandit; why do you want to help him? He is a bad man and since you are on friendly terms with him, you are also a bad man.'

I said, 'It isn't easy to say whether a man is bad or not.'

'Why?' said Wu.

I replied, 'If you speak of a man's good nature, then everybody is good; if you speak of a man's bad nature, then everybody is bad.'

'What do you mean by hat?' asked Wu.

I replied, 'If you and Tang worked together for the welfare of the country and people, and if your soldiers did the same, wouldn't that make you all good men? But if you and Tang accuse each other of being bad and are so prejudiced that you fight each other and make the people suffer, wouldn't that make you all bad men? Innocent people would be forced to follow either you or Tang and all would become bandits; then they would all be most pitiable.'

After hearing this, both men laughed and Wu asked, 'What you have said is correct but what shall I do?'

I replied, 'In my opinion you should stop fighting and call for peace.'

Wu said, 'Do you want me to surrender?'

I said, 'No, I do not mean that. By calling for peace, I mean calling all good men like you to work for peace in the country. I only ask you to give up your prejudices and work for the welfare of the country and people; isn't that a good thing?'

Wu asked, 'How do I start?'   'With Tang,' I replied.

'With Tang?' he replied. 'No, he has killed and imprisoned many of our men. This is the time for revenge; how can we surrender?'

I said, 'Please don't misunderstand me. I mean this: since Tang is an official of the Central Government, he has the power to make peace and you too would then become an official appointed by Beijing. As to those of your men who have been killed, I am going to Kunming to hold Buddhist rites for the welfare of all those who have fallen in battle. As for the prisoners, I shall ask Tang to proclaim an amnesty which will also benefit them. If you don't listen to my advice, hostilities will continue and the outcome for you is uncertain. You and Tang each have resources but yours are limited and cannot compare with his abundant manpower, finance and reinforcements with powerful backing by the Central Government. I am not asking you to surrender. I am here because of a propitious cause that prompts me, though a powerless monk, to use my tongue to urge for the cessation of hostilities and thus help the country and people.'

Yang and Wu were deeply moved and asked me to act on their behalf. I said, 'I am not qualified but if you state your conditions, I will present them to Tang.' They then deliberated and put forward six conditions which were: (1) the release of all their men held captive; (2) no disbandment of their troops; (3) no loss of rank; (4) to retain command of their own troops; (5) no investigations into past activity; and (6) equal treatment for both armies.

I said, 'Tang may well agree and after I have discussed it all with him, an official reply will be brought by his representatives who will discuss the whole thing with you.'

Wu said, 'I am sorry to have troubled the Venerable old Master; if the matter can be satisfactorily arranged, we shall be very grateful to you indeed.'

I said, 'Don't mention it; what I am doing for you is merely a matter of convenience because I am passing through anyway.'

Yang and Wu then gave me every courtesy and we had a friendly chat in the evening. They wanted to keep me for a few days but since I had no time to spare, I bade them farewell the following morning. After breakfast they gave me travelling expenses, food and carts, ordering their men to escort me. I refused all this except for a little food. About half a *li* from their headquarters, I saw a few men who knelt and touched their heads to the ground in respect; I recognised them as the bandits who had beaten me the previous day. They implored, 'Will the Bodhisattva forgive us?' I consoled them, urging them to do good and to refrain from evil acts. They wept and withdrew.

At Kunming, I was welcomed by provincial officials sent by Governor Tang. I stayed at the Yuan-tong Temple and in the evening Tang came and said, 'I have not met the Venerable Master for several years, during which my grandmother, father, wife and brother have died one after another. I am deeply distressed and on top of all this, there are bandits all over the province who molest the people, while the spirits of the officers and men they have killed have to be comforted. Therefore I want to do three things; (1) To hold Buddhist rites praying for the Buddha's protection so that misfortunes can be averted and to pray for the welfare of the dead; (2) To turn this temple at Yuan-tong into a large monastery in order to spread the Buddhadharma and (3) To found a university to educate the young.

My people can look after the university but apart from the Venerable old Master, there is no one to help me achieve the first two tasks.'

I said, 'Your vow is great and rarely made in the land during these times; it comes from a Bodhisattva's mind. I am not competent to help you in all this. There are many virtuous monks who can assist you to build a large monastery, but Yuan-tong is a small temple which can only accommodate a community of about one hundred people; please reconsider this question. As for the Buddhist rites which do not take long to perform, I shall be glad to hold them for you.'

Tang said, 'You are right about Yuan-tong not being suitable for a large monastery; we can discuss this later. As for the Buddhist rites, how are we going to perform them?'

I said, 'Mind and Buddha are of one substance and are mutually responsive. As you have decided to hold Buddhist rites for the welfare of the country and people and to benefit both the living and the dead, I suggest that three things should be done: (1) Forbid the slaughter of animals for food during the rites; (2) Proclaim an amnesty; and (3) Relieve the distressed.'

Tang said, 'The first and last can be done but the other is within the jurisdiction of the Ministry of Justice and so beyond my power.'

I said, 'There are now so many problems to be solved all over the country that the Central Government cannot cope with them. If you arrange this with the Provincial Department of Justice, you will be able to announce an amnesty and so obtain divine blessings for the country.' Tang nodded assent and I then spoke of the two bandit chiefs, Yang and Wu, whom I had met while on my way to Kunming, and suggested a general pardon for their men still held captive so as to convert the insurgents still at large. Tang was pleased with my suggestion and immediately discussed the proclamation of an amnesty.

The year was drawing to its end. When Upasakas Ou-yang, Jing-wu and Lu Qiu-yi arrived in Kunming to raise funds for the Chinese Dharma Study Centre at Shanghai, they also stayed at Yuan-tong Temple. I invited them to expound the *Mahayana-samparigraha Shastra.*[1] I passed the New Year period at Kunming.

Notes
1. A collection of Mahayana *shastras* ascribed to Asanga, three of which were translated into Chinese by Paramartha in 563.

MY 80TH YEAR
(1919/20)

In the spring a *bodhimandala*[1] was set up at the Temple of the Fallen Patriots where Buddhist rites for the welfare of the spirits on earth and in water began, while an amnesty was announced and the slaughter of animals for food was forbidden. Governor Tang then sent provincial officials to discuss peace with Yang and Wu and the matter of their appointment as military commanders. After this these two insurgents remained loyal to the provincial authorities.

What was remarkable was that after the Buddhist rites had begun, the flames on the candles in the various shrines opened into flowery shapes like lotus blossoms, the variegated colours of which were wonderful. Devotees who came to worship there gathered to see this unusual occurrence. Before the end of the forty-ninth day and during the welfare rites, jewelled banners and canopies appeared in the clouds overhead and were seen by the crowd, who then knelt to pay reverence.

After the rites, Governor Tang invited me to his house to read sutras for the welfare of the deceased members of his family. When he agains saw auspicious signs which caused him to develop a firm faith in the Dharma, all his people were converted to Buddhism. I then stayed at Kunming for the winter.

Notes

1. *Bodhimandala.* Though this term is often used to mean a temple or sacred place in general, it has a specific context in this case. The 'Earth and Water Rites' held by Xu-yun involve the setting up of tables, rituals objects, etc., in the shape of a protective mandala, the bestowal of food and symbolic offerings being regarded as the equivalent to a Tantric rite, capable of guiding the dead to Nirvana or favourable rebirth. This rite was initiated by Emperor Liang Wu-di many centuries ago, and first held at Jin-shan in Zhenjiang, after the Emperor dreamed that a Bhiksu appeared to him, advising him to initiate such a ceremony for the welfare of the dead.

MY 81ST YEAR
(1920/21)

In the spring Governor Tang again asked me to set up another *bodhimandala* and perform Buddhist rites for the welfare of the spirits on earth and in water, after which I expounded the sutras.

The Hua-ting Monastery on the Western Hill at Kunming was an ancient holy site in very beautiful scenery but the monks, instead of keeping it in good condition, had allowed it to fall into ruin and now decided to sell it to the European residents who wished to build a club-house there for which they had obtained permission from the local authorities. I was sad about this and spoke to Governor Tang, urging him to preserve this holy site. He listened to me and secretly discussed the matter with local notables, among them being Wang Jiu-ling and Zhang Jue-xian. The latter then invited me to a vegetarian meal, during which they presented their formal invitation, written on red paper, asking me to become Abbot of the temple so that they could restore the holy site. They made this request thrice verbally and I finally accepted it.

That year, Upasaka Zhang Jue-xian took a pair of geese to Yun-xi Monastery to set them free. I was asked to teach them the refuge formula and both birds bowed their heads and kept silent as if to receive it. After that, they raised their heads and seemed to be very happy. From them on they went with the monks to the main hall and looked at those reciting the sutras. For three years they followed the monks when the latter walked in procession round the statues of Buddhas and Bodhisattvas; everyone in the temple liked them.

One day, the goose [i.e. the female] went to the door of the main hall, where she stood still, then walked round three times, raised her head to gaze at the statues and died, her feathers remaining lustrous when placed in a wooden box for burial. The gander cackled ceaselessly as if he could not bear to part with his mate. A few days later, he refused to feed and swim and then stood in front of the main hall to gaze at the statues of the Buddha, spread his wings and died; he was also placed in a small box and buried in the same place as his mate.

Note by Cen Xue-lu, Xu-yun's Editor

In the autumn of that year, Gu Bin-zhen who commanded the army in Yunnan, plotted to overthrow Governor Tang who still had twenty loyal regiments. Since Tang held Master Xu-yun in high esteem, he called on him one night seeking his advice. The Master said, 'Although you have won the hearts of the people, you have not won that of the army. If hostilities break out, neither side will win and our neighbours will take advantage of the situation to invade Yunnan. Your best course is to leave and wait for the right moment to return.' Tang heeded this advice, asked for leave and handed over the Governorship to Gu. He then left for Tongking on his way to Hong Kong. The Master told me this ten years ago.

The Bell Tower: Yun-men Monastery, Guangdong, circa 1949/50.

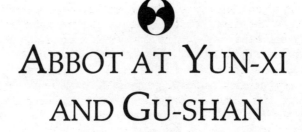

CHAPTER TEN

ABBOT AT YUN-XI
AND GU-SHAN

MY 82ND YEAR
(1921/22)

In the spring, Gu Bin-zhen became Governor of Yunnan Province. From the second to the seventh month, rains fell unceasingly so that boats could sail in the streets of the provincial capital. Every day from the tower over the city gate, big guns were used to bombard the heavy clouds to try and disperse them but this was of no avail. From the seventh month onwards a drought persisted so that by winter, dust arose from the dry river bed. This had never happened before in Yunnan. In the autumn an epidemic of diphtheria broke out and claimed serveral thousand victims. At the time I was with Master Zhu-xin at the Hua-ting Temple where all activities came to a complete standstill. One day we went to the city and on our way back in the afternoon, while resting under a tree, we found a parcel containing gold and jade bracelets, gold hairpins, earrings and a watch, along with 8,000 Yunnan dollars and over 10,000 Indo-Chinese piastres. We waited for the owner to turn up but about sunset, seeing that we were still far from our temple, I took the parcel and left the place with the thought of returning next day to the city to try and find the owner by putting an advertisement in the newspaper.

Just as we reached the foot of the mountain and were about to cross the lake, we caught glimpse of a girl jumping into the water. I went to rescue her and as she was beginning to drown, I jumped in to save her. She struggled, refusing my help, so I forced her ashore. As she seemed intent on ending her life, we compelled her to go to our temple; it was already dark when we arrived. We then gave her clothes and food but she refused to eat. We tried to comfort her and after a long silence, she eventually told us that she was a native of Changsha by the name of Zhu, born in Yunnan some eighteen years ago, being the only child of a shopkeeper who sold medicine in Fuchun Street in the city. She then told us her story: One day, a Divisional Commander called Sun had called at her home, saying that he was a bachelor, asking her parents if he could take her hand in marriage. Her parents believed what he had said but after the wedding, she found out that Sun already had a wife. Thus she had been cheated and it was too late for her to do anything about it. She was frequently beaten by the first wife, who was very cruel. Though her in-laws intervened, it was in vain; her own parents were frightened of the Commander's power. She said, 'I lost hope and so took some of my belongings, intending to run away to the Cock's Foot Mountain to follow Master Xu-yun as a nun.'

Since she did not know the way, she had already walked for two days and being afraid that she might be chased by her husband's men, she had run and lost her parcel. She then felt that the only course left was to kill herself.

I asked her about the things she had lost and found that they were what I had picked up. I consoled her and instructed my companion to explain the refuge formula to her. The following day, I called the Zhu and Sun families, comprising about thirty or more people, to the temple to discuss this matter. I also expounded the Dharma to them. At this point Commander Sun and his first wife knelt down before the Buddha-shrine, repented their previous wrong-doings and then embraced each other with tears running down their cheeks. Those who had come along were deeply moved and stayed at the temple for three days. On that occasion about thirty or more people, the men, women, young and old of the two families, were converted to the Dharma and received the Precepts before going away.

MY 83RD YEAR
(1922/23)

That year, the Temple of Hua-ting (also called 'Yun-xi' or 'Abode of Clouds') was rebuilt. West of Lake Kunming was a mountain called Bi-ji (Emerald Cock). When the second son of the Indian King Ashoka went there, he saw a flock of Emerald Phoenix and decided to stay on in order to practise self-cultivation and thereby realised the Way. He was known as the 'Spirit of the Emerald Phoenix' and the mountain was then named after him. Its screen-like peaks later became the site of the Hua-ting Temple where in the Yuan Dynasty [1280–1367] Chan Master Xuan-feng – who had practised and realised the Dharma under his eminent teacher, Zhong-feng [1263–1323] – built a temple called Yuan-jue (Complete Enlightenment), but it was later called Hua-ting (Flower-arbour) after the mountain on account of its flowery abundance. Two years ago, when this holy site was about to be sold to the foreigners in Yunnan, I had intervened so that Governor Tang bought it and then asked me to be its Abbot. In the course of reconstruction, an ancient stone tablet was dug up. It was undated but bore an inscription with the two characters 'Yun-xi' (Abode of Clouds) upon it. It was later placed on top of the Hai Hui Stupa containing the ashes of dead disciples.

[As an act of generosity] Academician Chen Xiao-fu exchanged his own flower-garden for the former site of Sheng-yin Temple, which had been the property of the school of agriculture so that we could build Yun-xi's secondary temple with its main hall and dormitories. At the foot of the mountain, we built a new temple called Zhao-di and the village there was named after it. We felled timber from the thick forest behind the mountain and one day, we found a package containing gold and silver coins worth over 200,000 dollars which I proposed to hand over to the Government for use as a relief fund. When those present suggested that the find be kept to ease the monastery's financial difficulties, I said: 'According to Buddhist regulations, a monk is forbidden to pick up money lost by others; we broke them when we picked up the package and it would be unpardonable if we kept it for ourselves. You could make contributions in your own names to cultivate the field of blessedness [i.e. to give alms, particularly to the Sangha] and the monks can appeal for funds when they are in need of provisions, but I dare not keep lost property for the temple.' My suggestion was approved and the coins were handed over to the Government for a relief fund.

The Province of Yunnan suffered greatly from a long drought which had continued from the previous year and the number of diphtheria victims could not be counted. The whole population, from army commanders to the man in the street, thought of the lofty virtue of the former Governor Tang and agreed to welcome him back as Governor of the Province. After his return, he came to the temple and asked me to pray for rain. I then set up an altar for the purpose and within three days torrential rain fell. At the time it had not rained for five months. As the diphtheria remained unchecked, Tang said, 'I have heard that a snowfall can stop an epidemic of diphtheria but spring is drawing to its end; how can we obtain snow?'

I said, 'I will set up an altar for the purpose and on your part, please pray for snow with all your heart.'

Tang then observed the rules of pure living and I prayed for snow. The next day a foot of snow fell; the epidemic suddenly ended and everybody praised the inconceivable Buddhadharma.

MY 84TH YEAR
(1923/24)

That year saw the building of the stupa for the ashes of the seven classes of disciples.[1] When the foundations were dug, a coffin was found more than ten feet below ground bearing the inscription: 'Mrs Li, a native of Fan-yang, this fourth year of the Jia-jing Reign [1525–6].' Her face was fresh as if she were still alive and when her body was cremated, the flames opened into the shape of lotus blossoms. Her ashes were then placed in the space reserved for *Upasikas*. All the tombs to the right of the temple were exhumed and after cremation, the ashes were also placed in the stupa.

One of the tombs had a stone tablet inscribed with the life of Bhiksu called Dao-ming who was born in the Dao-guang reign (1821–50) and was eventually sent by his parents to the temple in order to join the Sangha. After ordination he held confessional rites and concentrated on reciting the name of Avalokitesvara Bodhisattva. One night he dreamed that the Bodhisattva ordered him to take a bath, after which he never saw him again but felt that his legs were now very comfortable. The next morning, when he rose from his bed he found that he could walk as well as others. Since then his innate wisdom manifested itself and that is why he continued to call upon the Bodhisattva for the rest of his life. The cover of the coffin had been damaged by white ants with marks that clearly suggested the outline of a seven-storied octagonal stupa, thus testifying to the effectiveness of the monk's practice.

Notes
1. The seven classes of disciples: (1) *Bhiksu*, or fully ordained monks; (2) *Bhiksuni*, or fully ordained nuns; (3)*Siksamana*, or novices who observe six precepts; (4) *Sramanera*, or novice monks who observe the minor precepts; (5) *Sramanerika*, or novice nuns who observe the minor precepts; (6) *Upasaka*, or laymen who observe the first five precepts; and (7) *Upasika*, or laywomen who observe the first five precepts.

MY 85TH YEAR
(1924/25)

That year we repaired all sixteen stupas, including that of the 'Seven Buddhas of Antiquity' on the mountain and all statues of the Buddhas, the 'Five Hundred Lohans [Arhats]' in the monastery. At Sheng-yin Temple, three bronze statues were cast for the main hall and three clay ones for the shrine of the Western Paradise. Chan Bhiksu Zhu-xing died after receiving the rules of discipline in the spring and I recorded his life-story as follows:

The Story of Chan Bhiksu Zhu-xing
Bhiksu Ri-bian, also called Zhu-xing, was a native of Huili and was orphaned as a child. A man called Ceng took care of him and later married his daughter to him. They had two sons but were very poor. When I came to the Cock's Foot Mountain, his family of eight worked at the monastery. In the first year of Xuan-tong's reign [1909], after my return to the mountain with the convoy containing the *Tripitaka*, I transmitted the preliminary precepts to him when he was 20. The following year, when he was 21, his whole group of eight [family members] sought to join the Sangha.

He had an ugly face and was both deaf and illiterate. He worked in the vegetable gardens during the day and offered prayers to Avalokitesvara Bodhisattva in the evening. He also practised meditation and at times read the sutras but never asked others to teach him. He was diligent in his practice and in 1915 he asked for leave to call on learned Masters elsewhere in the country. In 1920 when I was at the Yun-xi Temple, he returned and resumed his duty as a gardener. He could then read the sutras in the main hall and spent his spare time making garments and bamboo-ware for the community. He gave away all the surplus vegetables to form propitious karma, keeping nothing in excess of the necessities of life and never spoke without due reason.

While I was at Sheng-yin Temple, I noticed his work in the gardens and inner cultivation which was exemplary and rarely found. That year, during the transmission of the rules of discipline elsewhere on the mountain, he came and asked me to verify his achievements and after he had been fully ordained, he asked for leave to return to the Sheng-yin Temple.

On the twenty-ninth of the third month, after midday meditation he went to the courtyard behind the main hall where he put on his robe, heaped up some bundles of straw and sat upon it cross-legged, his face turned towards the West, reciting the Buddha's name and then, with one hand ringing the bell and the other beating the wooden fish, he set fire to the straw. The numerous people in the temple at first knew nothing about what was happening, but when those outside saw the blaze they entered the temple but could not find the Bhiksu. When they went to the courtyard, they saw him sitting motionless with crossed legs on the ashes. His clothing was intact but the wooden fish and handle of the bell were reduced to ashes.

I was told of his death but since I was preparing for the ceremony for the transmission of the Bodhisattva precepts on the eighth of the following month, I could not descend the mountain. I then wrote to Wang Zhu-cun, head of the Financial Department and Zhang Jue-xin, Chief of the Conservancy Bureau, asking them to see to his funeral on my behalf. When they saw the remarkable occurrence, they reported it to Governor Tang, who came with all his family to observe it. When the bell was removed from the Bhiksu's hand, his body, which had until then remained erect, collapsed into a heap of ashes. Those present praised the occurrence and developed their faith in the Buddhadharma. Governor Tang ordered the provincial authorities to hold a memorial service for three days and those attending it numbered several thousands. He then set down the life record of the Bhiksu, which was deposited in the provincial library.

MY 86TH YEAR
(1925/26)

That year, after the transmission of the Precepts, I expounded the sutras and held a week of Chan meditation. As the monastery's property on the mountain occupied a great deal of ground which had to be cleared of trees, I called in the villagers who came to work with the community; they were happy when they were given half the quantity of logs felled. That year, the governorship of the province was abolished and replaced by an administrative committee. Thus, Governor Tang went into retirement and often came to stay on the mountain.

MY 87TH YEAR
(1926/27)

That year, troubled conditions prevailed in the Province of Yunnan, with soldiers billeted in private houses so that nobody lived in peace or dared go to the fields during the harvest. I went to the army headquarters and discussed the matter with the Commander, who then issued an order forbidding his men to interfere with the peasants when they were being escorted to the fields by the monks. As a result, a few thousand peasants came to stay at the temple, where they shared with the community first meals of rice, then rice gruel, then bran when the rice ran out – and finally, only water to stave off their hunger pangs. They were deeply moved and wept when they saw the monks endure the same hardships as themselves. It was only after things had improved that the peasants returned to their homes and since then, they always volunteered to protect the monastery with a whole heart.

Since I had become Abbot of Yun-xi Monastery, each year I transmitted the precepts, expounded the sutras and held weeks of Chan meditation. That year during transmission of the Precepts, some withered trees in the courtyard in front of the main hall suddenly blossomed with lotus-like flowers. All the green vegetables in the temple garden bore lotus-like green flowers, each one having something like a standing Buddha in the centre. Upasaka Zhang Jue-xian recorded the rare occurrence in a *gatha* which was inscribed on a stone tablet at the monastery.

MY 88TH YEAR
(1927/28)

That year I transmitted the Precepts, expounded the sutras and held weeks of Chan meditation as usual. The construction of additional shrine halls and dormitories was completed and the bell-tower was rebuilt.

MY 89TH YEAR
(1928/29)

I went with Upasaka Wang Jiu-ling to Hong Kong in order to raise funds for making new statues of the Buddhas. The Governor of Guang-dong, General Chen Zhen-ru, sent a representative to Hong Kong inviting me to Canton where I stayed at the Yi Yang-yuan Sanatorium. I then accompanied the Governor to Neng-ren Temple on Mount Bai-yun and whilst there, I had to decline his invitation to assume the role of Abbot at the Nan-hua Monastery in Cao-xi. I then proceeded to Amoy and Fuzhou, returning to Gu-shan where I expounded the sutras. Afterwards, I went to the King Ashoka Monastery at Ningbo to revere the Buddha-relics there and thence to Pu-tuo Island, where I met Master Wen-zhi. He accompanied me to Shanghai where I stayed at the Gandhama-dana Hermitage in Long-guang Temple. Towards the end of that Autumn, Abbot Da-gong of Gu-shan Monastery died and the community there sent a representative to see me in Shanghai. As the year was drawing to its end, I stayed in Shanghai to pass the New Year period.

MY 90TH YEAR
(1929/30)

In the first month I left Shanghai, returning to Mount Gu. While there, the Navy Minister, Yang Shu-zhuang, also Chairman of Fujian Province and Fang Sheng-dao, the former Chairman, came with gentry and officials inviting me to become Abbot of Gu-shan Monastery. I thought of the place where I had first had my head shaved when joining the Sangha and of the august virtues of my late Master, and could find no excuse to shrink from this duty; consequently, I accepted their request.

MY 91ST YEAR
(1930/31)

During my previous year at Mount Gu, I had improved the

organisation of the monastery. In the spring, I asked Master Wen-zhi to assist me as Director of Duties *(karmadana)* during the transmission of the Precepts and in the first month of that year, I lectured on the *Brahma-Net Sutra* to the whole assembly. In the courtyard of the Abbot's quarters, there were two feathery palm trees which are said to have been planted some ten centuries ago in the Tang Dynasty, one by the Prince of Min State [now modern-day Fujian], and the other by Abbot Sheng-jian. These trees grow slowly and last very long, sprouting only one or two leaves each year. Both were then ten feet high but had never flowered, and it is said that they take a thousand years to bear blossoms. But during the transmission of the Precepts, they were in full bloom. People came from far and near, crowding into the monastery to see them. On this occasion, Master Wen-zhi recorded this rare occurrence on a stone tablet at the monastery.

MY 92ND YEAR
(1931/32)

I continued to be Abbot of Gu-shan Monastery, where I transmitted the Precepts, expounded the sutras, founded a school of Vinaya discipline and built the temples of Bing-qu, Xi-lin and Yun-wo.

MY 93RD YEAR
(1932/33)

In the spring, during the transmission of the Precepts, an old man of unusual mien with white hair and beard came and went straight to the Abbot's room, where he knelt down and asked me to teach him the Vinaya rules [of discipline]. When asked, he said that his name was Yang and that he was a native of Nan-tai. A monk called Miao-zong who was receiving the Precepts at the time also came from Nan-tai, but told me he had never met the old man before. After the transmission of the Bodhisattva Precepts and distribution of certificates of discipleship, no trace of the old man could be found.

When Miao-zong returned to Nan-tai he found at the Temple of the Dragon King a statue which not only strongly resembled the old man, but which also held in its hand a certificate of discipleship. The news spread all over Nan-tai that the Dragon King had received the transmission of the Precepts. At this time, a 66-year-old Cantonese Upasaka called Zhang Yu-dao, who had been an academician of the former Manchu Dynasty, came to the monastery to receive full ordination. He was given the Dharma name of Guan-ben (Contemplating the Root) and entrusted with cataloguing the sutras in Gu-shan monastery's library. After the ceremony, I asked the old Master Ci-zhou to expound the four-division Vinaya in the Dharma Hall, and Dharma Masters Xin-dao and Yin-shun to teach novices at the Vinaya school.

MY 94TH YEAR
(1933/34)

That spring I asked Dharma-Master Yin-ci to expound the *Brahma Net Sutra* during the transmission of the Precepts. In the first month, the Japanese Army occupied Shanhai Pass and created a tense situation all over the country. As the Nineteenth Route Army declared a state of alert, all the temples in the province refused to receive guest-monks except Gu-shan Monastery, which still admitted those monks coming by sea. There were fifteen hundred to sixteen hundred monks gathered at the monastery but in spite of our limited provisions, we managed to let them have rice gruel at breakfast and rice at noon. In the sixth month, the park intended for the release of living creatures was completed. Among the flock of geese sent by Upasaka Zheng Qin-qiao to be set free in the park, there was an unusual gander which weighed about sixteen *catties*. When it heard the monastery's wooden fish being beaten, it spread out its wings and stretched out its neck. In the main hall, it gazed at the Buddha-rupa all day. A month later, it died while standing before the Buddha's image but did not fall to the ground. Upasaka Zheng wondered at this rare occurrence and asked for the bird to be cremated according to Buddhist rules. Seven days later when it was cremated, there was no smell. A common grave was then dug for the ashes of all birds and animals cremated at death.

Master Xu-yun at the Zhen-ru Monastery, 1957/58.

CHAPTER ELEVEN

NAN-HUA MONASTERY

MY 95TH YEAR
(1934/35)

In the spring, as a further step to improve the Vinaya School, I asked Dharma-Master Ci-zhou to be its headmaster. In the second month, during an evening meditation, I saw, in a state which seemed to be but was not really a dream, the Sixth Patriarch,[1] who came and said, 'It is time for you to go back.' The next morning I said to my disciple, Guan-ben, 'Last night I dreamed that the Sixth Patriarch called me back; is my causal life [in this world] coming to an end?' Guan-ben said a few words to comfort me. In the fourth month, I again dreamed that the Sixth Patriarch urged me thrice to go back. I was very surprised by this, but shortly after I received telegrams from the provincial authorities in Guangdong inviting me to take over and renovate the Sixth Patriarch's Temple. I thought of the holy site of the Sixth Patriatch [Hui-neng], which badly needed repairing after its last renovation by Master Han-shan [1546–1623] and set out on my journey to Lingnan [ancient name for Guangdong Province].

Previously General Li Han-yun, who commanded the army in Northern Guangdong, had noticed that the Nan-hua Monastery was in a dilapidated condition and made some minor repairs which began in November 1933 and ended in October 1934. That winter, the protectors of the Dharma asked me to transmit the Precepts. As some of the halls and buildings of Nan-hua Monastery had collapsed and the dormitories were uninhabitable, we built thatched bamboo lodgings in order to house a few hundred guests. The officials and notables of Canton and Shaoguan came with their families in great numbers to receive the Precepts and become disciples of mine. On the evening of the seventeenth of the eleventh month, during the transmission of the Bodhisattva-rules, a tiger came in as if to receive the Precepts, scaring all those present. However, I spoke the Refuge Precepts to the tiger and it was receptive, became tame and went its way.

The Master's Arrival At Cao-xi
(From the Xu-Yun He Shang Fa Hui)

In 1934 on the second day of the eighth moon, Master Xu-yun arrived from Gu-shan and, followed by the district officials, literati and people, proceeded to Cao-xi. It happened to be the day when people in the district were celebrating the anniversary of the Patriarch's birthday and about ten thousand of them were converging on the monastery to offer incense.

AT THE CAO-XI GATE

On his arrival at the gate, the Master pointed his staff at it and chanted:

A dream has now come true at Cao-xi[2]
From far away the poor man has returned.[3]
Let us no more think of what is and what is not,[4]
Even to call it a bright mirror is still wrong.[5]
Since the midnight transmission of robe and bowl at Huang Mei[6]
Imposingly the light for centuries has shone.
Who of the House descendants will carry on the line
So that the Lamps succeed each other to reveal Spiritual Majesty?[7]

AT THE GATE OF THE BAO-LIN MONASTERY[8]

The Master pointed his staff at the gate and chanted:

Here clearly is the road to Cao-xi.
Wide open is the Gate of Precious Wood
Where students of the Sect from the Ten quarters
Come and go on their long journeyings.
When this place of Transcendental Bliss is reached,
The Pure Void is free from dust.[9]
The Dharma realm has nor centre nor circumference,[10]
This One Door holds the wonder of all schools.[11]

116

IN THE MAITREYA HALL

The Master entered the Hall and chanted:

When the big belly thunders with loud roar of laughter[12]
Thousands of white lotus rain through all the worlds.[13]
With his bag of cloth vast is he as the Universe,[14]
He will succeed the Buddha, preaching in Dragon Flower Tree Park.[15]

Then the Master prostrated himself before the statue of Maitreya.

IN FRONT OF THE SHRINE OF WEI-TUO[16]

The Master chanted:

In answer to the needs of all as a youth you come
To conquer ghouls and demons with awe-inspiring majesty.
Hey! The sermon on the Vulture Peak is still ringing in all ears,
O fiery General, O Protector of the Dharma![17]

Then the Master prostrated himself before the statue of Wei-tuo.

IN THE HALL OF THE FIFTH PATRIARCH

The Master chanted:

The Transmission handed down in this Eastern Land
Produced a flower with petals five.[18]
From Xiu in the North and in the South from Neng[19]
Shot leaves and branches spreading everywhere.

Then the Master prostrated himself before the Fifth Patriarch.

IN THE HALL OF THE SIXTH PATRIARCH

Holding incense sticks the Master chanted:

Each year on this second day of the eighth and eighth day of
the second month[20]
In the sky appear the tracks of birds.[21]
Although it never hid within the Universe,[22]
It could not be perceived e'en by Li Lou,[23]
How can it ever then be known?

Burning incense sticks he continued:

Today clearly is it pointed out!

IN FRONT OF THE SHRINE OF MASTER HAN-SHAN

Holding incense sticks, the Master chanted:

> In all the land there never was a rival.[25]
> But now a rival comes by name Gu-shan.[26]
> Occasionally a recollection
> Makes one repent one's restlessness.[27]
> What restlessness?

Calling followers, the Master continued:

> Two clay oxen struggle to stride into the sea.[28]
> Each time I offer incense sticks, my heart is full of sadness.[29]

After offering incense sticks, the Master continued:

> Today this is De-qing,[30]
> It was De-qing before.[31]
> When past and present meet, there is change of form.[32]
> The Dharma prospers and declines as good and bad prevail;[33]
> Yet it has never ceased in wood and grass to dwell.[34]

Then the Master prostrated himself before Han-shan.

IN THE MAIN HALL

Holding incense sticks, the Master chanted:

> O Lord-Teacher of Saha![35]
> The uncreate rightly taught by You
> Is Dharma most profound and wonderful.[36]
> But who is Buddha and who living being?[37]

Then the Master prostrated himself before the Buddha.

IN THE ABBOT'S ROOM

The Master entered the Abbot's room and chanted:

> I enter now the room of the late Virtuous One
> And climb up to the former Patriarch's seat.[38]
> Holding firm the horizontal sword[39]
> I give the Right Supreme Command.[40]
> This is where the Patriarch and Ancestors
> Taught the Dharma for the benefit of men.
> Today, this unworthy man comes here.
> What does he?

118

The Master snapped his fingers thrice and continued.[41]

These finger-snaps bring to perfection the 80,000 Dharma doors[42]
Ensuring 'Straight entry' to the state of the Tathagata.[43]

Then the Master prostrated himself before the statue of Buddha.

IN THE DHARMA HALL

Pointing his staff at the Dharma seat, he chanted;

The eminence of this Precious Seat
Has been handed down from Sage to Sage.[44]
There is no hindrance from all angles[45]
And all Dharmas are profound.[46]
When in the sun the head is raised,
The pressure of what can be grasped is cut off and turned away.[47]
Even eyes of iron with copper pupils
Though they look can never reach it.[48]
The coming of the mountain-monk
Is not peculiar in itself.
If long sight you want to penetrate all quarters,
To a higher storey must you climb.[49]

The Master pointed his staff at the seat and continued:

Let us ascend![50]

After ascending to the seat, he held incense sticks in his hand and
chanted:

These incense sticks
Do not descend from heaven;
How can they come from Earth?[51]
They smoke in the incense burner
As a token of my offerings
To our Teacher Sakyamuni Buddha,
To all Buddhas and Bodhisattvas
To all Patriarchs and Sages from India and of this Eastern land,
To Arya Jnanabhaisajya who founded first this monastery.[52]
To the great master the Sixth Patriach,
And to all past Masters who revived and succeeded to this sect.
May the Buddha sun shine greater,
May the Wheel of the Law for ever turn.

119

Then the Master arranged his robe and took the seat. Thereupon, the leading monk chanted:

> All elephants and dragons here assembled for the Dharma feast[53]
> Should look into the Supreme Meaning.[54]

Holding his staff, the Master said:

In this great affair,[55] it is clear that there exists not a single Dharma.[56] The causes, fundamental as well as secondary, are many and have not come to an end; after Han-shan's departure, I now come here. The restoration of this ancient monastery will depend on many contributory causes. It was set up by Arya Jnanabhaisajya who predicted that some 170 years later, a great Saint[57] would come here to expound the Dharma for the liberation of men and that those attaining sainthood would be as many as the trees in the wood. Hence, its name of 'Precious Wood'. Since the Sixth Patriarch came here to teach and convert people, one thousand and a few hundred years have passed and countless living beings have been liberated. There have been alternating periods of prosperity and decline, and in the Ming Dynasty, ancestor Han-shan rebuilt this monastery and revived the Sect. Since then, over three hundred years have elapsed and during that period, the lack of a suitable successor has caused it to fall into disuse.

When I was at Gu-shan I saw in a dream the Patriarch who thrice called me here. At the same time, the high officials and Upasakas who sponsored the reconstruction of the monastery sent their representatives to Gu-shan to invite me to take charge of it. In view of their devotion, I have been obliged to accede to their requests and am now taking this seat. I feel ashamed of my poor virtues and shallow wisdom and also am not familiar with the management of the monastery. Therefore, I must rely on the support of all of you so that the withered branch will be sprinkled with Amrta[58] and the house in flames[59] will be covered by the clouds of compassion. Together we will do our utmost to preserve the Patriarch's monastery.

> About striving to preserve it,
> What am I doing now?

With his two palms brought together, the Master turned to the right and to the left in salutation and said:

Under the corner of my robe stand the four deva kings.[60]

Then the Master got down from his seat.

Notes

1. Hui-neng (638–713) was the famous Sixth Patriarch of the Chan School after whom the doctrine of the Mind really began to flourish in China. Anciently, the Nan-hua Monastery had been called 'Bao-lin' or 'Precious Wood' after an Indian *Tripitaka* Master, Jnanbhaisajya, visited the locality early in the sixth century, suggesting that a monastery should be built there and predicting that a 'flesh and blood' bodhisattva would appear there some 170 years after the monastery was built. His body still sits in repose at Nan-hua alongside that of the Sixth Patriarch's.

2. A dream at Gu-shan came true at Cao-xi.

3. Lit: from the horizon: from distant Gu-shan. A monk calls himself a 'poor man' because he is really penniless.

4. All expediencies of the teaching school should be put aside in this place where the mind is directly pointed at for instantaneous enlightenment.

5. Even Shen-xiu was wrong when he compared a bright mirror with the Mind which is indescribable. (See Shen-xiu's gatha in the *Altar Sutra* of the Sixth Patriarch).

6. Transmission from the Fifth to the Sixth Patriarch. (See *Altar Sutra*.)

7. Lamps transmitted from one Patriarch to another to reveal the doctrine of the Mind.

8. It was originally called 'The Bao-lin Monastery'.

9. The self-nature is essentially pure and free from all impurities.

10. Dharma realm: Dharmadhatu in Sanskrit, the unifying underlying spiritual reality, regarded as the ground or cause of all things, the absolute from which all proceeds. It is neither within nor without nor between the two.

11. The one door out of mortality into Nirvana, i.e. the Chan Sect which contains all the wonders of the other schools.

12. i.e. the Chan roar of laughter to reveal the Mind which actually laughs. In China, Maitreya is represented by a statue with a broad smile and a big belly, symbolising his boundless benevolence.

13. The white lotus is a symbol of the Pure Land of every Buddha. When the self-nature is realised, the six worlds of existence are transmuted into Pure Lands.

14. In the Liang Dynasty (907–21), there was a monk who carried a cloth bag everywhere he went and was called 'the cloth-bag monk'. When he was about to pass away, he sat on a rock and chanted a *gatha* disclosing that he was an avatar of Maitreya. After his death, he reappeared in other places also carrying a cloth bag on his back. Maitreya had the power to appear everywhere because his spiritual body was as immense as space.

15. Maitreya is the Buddhist Messiah, or next Buddha, now in the Tushita heaven, and is to come 5,000 years after the Nirvana of Sakyamuni Buddha. He will attain enlightenment under a Bodhi tree called the

'Dragon Flower Tree' and will liberate all living beings.

16. One of the generals under the Southern Deva king, guardian in a temple. His vow was to protect the Buddha Dharma in the eastern, western and southern worlds, i.e. Purvavideha, Aparagodaniya and Jambudvipa (our earth) respectively.

17. i.e. the Buddha's injunction to all Protectors of the Dharma who were present when He expounded sutras. The Western exclamation 'Hey' is used here instead of the text's 'I' which is unknown in the West. This cry was uttered by enlightened masters to reveal the presence of the self-mind which uttered it in their direct pointing at the Mind for realisation of self-nature and attainment of Buddahood.

18. Bodhidharma came to the East and transmitted the robe which was handed down to five Chinese Patriarchs, hence five petals.

19. Shen-xiu and Hui-neng (the Sixth Patriarch) expounded the Chan Dharma in the North and South respectively, and handed it down to their succeeding descendants who spread it all over the country.

20. The Patriarch's birthday fell on the second day of the eighth moon. The Master inverted day and month to wipe out all trace of *Time* which has no place in the absolute Wisdom.

21. A bird leaves no tracks when flying in the air. Thus *Space* is also wiped out.

22. The self-nature is omnipresent but is imperceptible to deluded men. It cannot be named and the word 'IT' is used to indicate the inexpressible.

23. Li Lou, a man mentioned by Mencius – he was a contemporary of Huang Di and could see even a hair at a hundred paces. The self-nature cannot be seen even by the cleverest deluded men.

24. Today, thanks to the Patriarch, the self-nature can be perceived according to his method.

25. Han-shan had no rival when he had the honour of rebuilding the monastery of the Sixth Patriarch in 1602. (See *Han-shan's Autobiography.*)

26. Now Master Xu-yun also had the honour of rebuilding the same monastery; hence a competitor of Han-shan.

27. Recollection of one's restlessness caused by delusion.

28. The Master called on his followers to wipe out their views of dualism, the cause of delusion. Two clay oxen: dualism which splits our undivided self-nature into 'ego' (self) and 'other'. One should cast away one's false views of dualism in order to realise one's undivided nature.

29. Each time I offer incense sticks to Buddha, I think of deluded living beings who turn their backs on the right Dharma and my heart is full of sadness.

30. De-qing was the name Master Xu-yun used when he was young.

31. De-qing was also the name used by Han-shan before he called himself 'Han-shan' after the 'Silly Mountain'.

32. So modern and ancient De-qing meet at the same monastery which both found in the same deplorable condition and which both reconstructed although at different times. Han-shan had entered Nirvana whereas Xu-yun still appeared in human form.

122

33. The Sect was revived by Han-shan and declined again after a period of prosperity. Now the Master was doing the same thing.

34. In spite of alternation of prosperity and decline, the self-nature is always the same whether in forests or meadows, i.e. it is everywhere and unchanging.

35. Saha, a Sanskrit word: our world. The Buddha was teacher of this world.

36. The Buddha urged His disciples to strive to attain the 'endurance of the uncreate' in order to get out of this illusory Samsara of birth and death.

37. Buddha and sentient beings are of the same nature. Where is the difference? Cognisance of one's self-nature will, according to the Chan Sect ensure attainment of Buddhahood.

38. Quotation from the Lotus Sutra: the room or house and seat or throne are respectively the Tathagata-House or Compassion and Tathagata-Throne in the absolute vacuity, i.e. immutability.

39. The indestructible sword of wisdom was held horizontally to bar the passage of falsehood, i.e. to arrest all false thinking.

40. A Chan term meaning the correct command or order of the Supreme Vehicle, likened to an irrevocable order from the Commander-in-Chief.
To reveal the mind which actually snapped the fingers. 'Thrice' is to reveal the presence of the threefold body (Trikaya) in one.

42. The digit 8 symbolises the eighth consciousness or Alaya-Vijnana, or the self-nature under delusion. Many Dharmas were set up to deal with different kinds of delusion and constituted what was called the Teaching School of which the ultimate aim was enlightenment. The Chan Sect's finger-snap was also a Dharma which pointed direct at the mind for realisation of self-nature and attainment of Buddhahood. Therefore, these finger-snaps would also being about the complete perfection of all other Dharmas.

43. Chan ensures the 'Straight Entry' into the Tathagata-state, without the necessity of passing through successive stages of sainthood before final enlightenment. In Chan parlance, this is called the 'Straight or Direct Entry'.

44. Sage to Sage. Literally Ancestor to Ancestor.

45. Seen from all angles, Chan is free from all hindrances.

46. From the Chan viewpoint, all Dharmas can be correctly interpreted and are very profound.

47. When the mind wanders outside, the Chan method turns away and cuts off all discernings and graspings.

48. The mind, although disentangled from sense-organs, sense-data and consciousness, and even likened to iron eyes and copper pupils which are insensible to all externals, is still unable to perceive the self-nature. This is called a state one experiences when reaching the top of a hundred-foot pole. (See *Han-shan's Autobiography*, 'Song of the Board-Bearer'.)

49. From the top of a hundred-foot pole, one should take a step forward so that his self-nature will appear in full everywhere in the ten directions of space.

50. Let us ascend to this Transcendental Path.
51. Incense sticks are created by the mind only.
52. See *The Altar Sutra of the Sixth Patriarch*.
53. Dragons and Elephants: terms of respect applied to the whole assembly seeking enlightenment. Dharma feast: Sermon to satisfy the hunger of seekers of the truth.
54. Supreme Meaning. In the Teaching School, this term means Supreme Reality; in a Chan hall, it means: 'Please look into the self-mind for attainment of enlightenment.' This sentence is always chanted by the leader of the assembly before a master gives a sermon.
55. Revelation of mind for realisation of self-nature and attainment of Buddahood.
56. Self-nature is fundamentally pure, and no Dharma is required to realise it. It will suffice to arrest false thinking and take cognisance of the self-mind.
57. The Sixth Patriarch.
58. Ambrosial drink.
59. House in flames: Samsara, our world. A quotation from the Lotus Sutra.
60. I can surely rely also on the four deva kings whose tall statues now stand at the entrance door of the monastery and who also appeared when the Patriarch unfolded his nisidana, or cloth for sitting on. (See Fa Hai's preface to *The Altar Sutra of the Sixth Patriarch*.)

MY 96TH YEAR
(1935/36)

That spring, General Li Han-yun was transferred to the eastern district of Guangdong, so we lost his valuable support and met with growing difficulties in renovating the monastery. After the transmission of the Precepts, the Donghua group of hospitals in Hong Kong invited me there to perform rites for the welfare of the dead on earth and in water; an altar was set up for the purpose at the Dong-lian and Jue-yuan temples. After the rites, I returned to Gu-shan Monastery to tend my resignation as its Abbot and asked its superintendent, the old Master Zhong-hui, to fill the vacancy. I then returned to the Nan-hua Monastery, where I renovated the Hall of the Sixth Patriarch and built the Shrine of Avalokitesvara, plus the dormitories. In that winter, the three cedars behind the monastery which had been planted in the Song Dynasty [960–1279] which had withered away during the last few hundred years, suddenly sprang into leaf. Master Guan-ben, the assembly leader, recorded this rare occurrence in a song which was inscribed by Upasaka Cen Xue-lu on a stone tablet at the monastery.

MY 97TH YEAR
(1936/37)

After the transmission of the Precepts in the spring, the renovation of the Nan-hua Monastery was gradually completed. Mr Lin-shen, President of the Republic; Mr Chu-zheng, a cabinet minister, and General Jiang Gai-shek came to the monastery one after the other. President Lin and Minister Chu subscribed funds to rebuild the main hall and General Jiang Gai-shek made a contribution of funds to hire labour so that we could alter the course of the Cao-xi stream which ran past the monastery. However, this change of the Cao-xi's course did not require manpower in the end, but was made possible thanks to the help from spiritual guardians of the Dharma.

Note by Upasaka Cen Xue-lu
Originally the Cao-xi Stream flowed some 1400 feet away from the monastery. As it had not been dredged for a very long time, it was full of rocks and sediment and changed its course to the north, heading directly towards the monastery. To bring it back to its old bed would have required 3000 labourers and cost a very great deal. When the work was about to start, in the evening of the twentieth of the seventh month, there was suddenly a severe thunderstorm which lasted the whole night. The next morning, flood waters burst the Cao-xi's banks, forming a new bed exactly where we intended it to be. The former bed was full of sand and rocks which piled above the previous banks by several feet, so it seemed as if the divine guardians of the monastery had helped us to correct the course of the stream.

MY 98TH YEAR
(1937/38)

In the spring, after the transmission of the Precepts, I was invited by the Guangdong Buddhist Association to Canton, where I expounded the sutras and received Tibetan Lamas and their disciples. Devotees of the neighbouring town of Fu-shan asked me to inaugurate the stupa erected at the Ren-shou Temple. I then returned to Nan-hua Monastery where I supervised the renovation of the temple buildings.

MY 99TH YEAR
(1938/39)

In the spring, after the transmission of the Precepts, I went to Canton to expound the sutras and thence to Hong Kong to perform the Mahakaruna rites[1] at Dong-lian and Jue-yuan Temples. After that I returned to Nan-hua Monastery.

Notes
1. These rites usually involve recitation of the Great Compassion (Mahakaruna) Dharani of Avalokitesvara or Guanyin Bodhisattva. Sometimes, a special altar is set up with a mandala of the Garbhadhatu or 'Womb Treasury' group with a long liturgy, the purpose being to transfer concentrated spiritual energy to the sick, the dying or the dead.

MY 100TH YEAR
(1939/40)

During the transmission of the Precepts in the spring, a great number of people came to the monastery to receive them on account of hostilities breaking out in the north. I proposed that, since there were many casualties which included both soldiers and civilians, all disciples of the Buddha should do a penance for two hours each day, pray for the spirits of the dead and for an early end to all hostilities. I also proposed that everybody should eat less to save money for a relief fund. My suggestions were approved and carried out.

MY 101ST YEAR
(1940/41)

After the transmission of the Precepts in the Spring, Canton fell to the Japanese Army and all civil and military departments were moved to Qujiang, where a great number of monks gathered from all parts of the province. I repaired the Da-jian (Great Mirror) Temple and used it as part of Nan-hua Monastery to receive visitors. I also renovated the Yue-hua (Moon Flower) Monastery for the same purpose.

126

MY 102ND YEAR
(1941/42)

In the spring, after transmission of the precepts, I handed over to the provincial government the whole sum of 200,000 dollars which my disciples and other devotees had given to me during the previous two years for the relief of famine victims in the Qujiang area.

That autumn, the Guangdong Buddhist Association moved to Qujiang and elected me as President and Upasaka Zhang-lian as Vice-President.

MY 103RD YEAR
(1942/43)

During the transmission of the Precepts in the spring, a spirit which lived in a tree at the monastery came to receive them as a preceptee. Master Guan-ben, the Superintendent of the temple, recorded this unusual occurrence as follows:

At the transmission of the Precepts, a monk came and asked for the *Bhiksu* precepts. He said that he was called Zhang, had been born in Qujiang, that he was 34, but had never found anyone to shave his head. When asked if he had come with the usual ceremonial robe and articles for the occasion, he replied that he had not. As he was frank and sincere, he was provided with all the things required and given the Dharma name of Zhang-yu. Before his turn came for the transmission, he worked hard at cleaning the temple. He was reserved and did not speak to the other monks, when he was admitted to the Vinaya Hall, he faultlessly observed the rules of discipline, but after he had received the Bodhisattva Precepts, he could not be found so his robe and certificate of discipleship were kept in the Vinaya Hall and the incident was soon forgotten. . . . The following year, before the transmission of the Precepts, Master Xu-yun dreamed that the monk came and asked for the certificate. Asked where he went after the transmission, he replied that he had not gone anywhere as he lived with the earth god. . . . his certificate was then burned as an offering and thus returned to him.

In the summer and autumn, we repaired the nunnery of Wu-jin

127

to receive all the nuns coming to Qujiang. Da-jian Temple had just been rebuilt but the renovation of the Nan-hua Monastery was not yet complete. From time to time I was consulted by Gu-shan Monastery on various matters and thus kept busy all of the time. On top of all this, Japanese bombers disturbed us every day by flying over the monastery on their missions.

Note by Cen Xue-lu, Xu-yun's Editor

After the fall of Canton to the Japanese, the provincial wartime capital was set up at Qujiang and high-ranking military leaders frequently came to the Nan-hua Monastery. The Japanese Intelligence learned that the temple was used as a meeting-place for Chinese officials. In the seventh month, when a large number gathered there, eight enemy bombers came and circled over it. The Master knew of their intention and ordered the monks to return to their dormitories. After all the guests had taken refuge in the Hall of the Sixth Patriarch, the Master went to the main hall, where he burned incense and sat in meditation. A plane dived, dropping a large bomb which fell in a grove on the river bank outside the monastery without causing damage. The bombers returned and circled over it when suddenly, two of them collided and crashed to the ground at Ma-ba, some ten miles to the west. Both planes were destroyed with their pilots and gunners. Since then the enemy planes dared not come near the monastery and always avoided flying over it on their bombing missions to the hinterland.

That winter, in the eleventh month, President Lin-shen and the Government sent Upasakas Chu Ying-guang and Zhang Zi-lien to the monastery, inviting me to the wartime capital of Chongqing to hold a prayer meeting for the welfare of the country. I left Nan-hua on the sixth of the eleventh month and when I arrived at the sacred mountain of Heng-shan in Hunan Province, I offered incense at the monastery there and met Upasaka Xu Guo-zhu who had been sent by Marshall Li Ji-shen to invite me to Guilin. On arrival, I stayed at Mount Yue-ya where monks, nuns, male and female lay devotees came and asked to be disciples of mine. Next, when I reached Guizhou, I stayed at the Qian-ming Monastery where Abbot Guang-miao asked me to expound the Dharma. When I arrived in Chongqing again, I was met by government officials and the monasteries' representatives. After calling on President Lin-shen and Upasaka Dai, the chairman of the prayer meeting, we decided to hold two Dharma-assemblies at the temples of Ci-yun and Hua-yan.

MY 104TH YEAR
(1943/44)

In the first month, I performed rituals for the welfare of the country which ended on the twenty-sixth day. President Lin-shen, General Jiang Gai-shek, Minister Dai, General Ho and other high officials invited me, one after the other, to vegetarian meals. General Jiang Gai-shek enquired about the Dharma in detail, listening the various points on materialism and idealism, as well as the doctrine of Christianity. I replied to his inquiry in a letter.[1]

I then expounded the Dharma at the temples of Ci-yun and Hua-yan, where my lectures were recorded by my attendant Wei-yun. In the third month, I returned to the Nan-hua Monastery to build a stupa for the ashes of dead disciples. When the ground was dug up, we found four empty coffins, each of them 16 feet in length, and also black tiles 8 inches square with impressions of birds, animals and astrological symbols, but bearing no date.

In the sixth month we opened the Vinaya School for novices and a free school for poor children of the locality. The building of the stupa was completed in the winter.

Notes
1. This letter was published in English translation for the *World Buddhism Wesak Annual*, 1965.

Master Xu-yun in his 113th year (1952/53).
Temple of Three Buddhas, Wuchang.

CHAPTER TWELVE

YUN-MEN MONASTERY

MY 105TH YEAR
(1944/45)

In 1940, after the monastery of the Sixth Patriarch had been completely rebuilt, I went with the Bhiksu Fu-guo to Qujiang to search for the ancient monastery of Ling-shu, but we failed to find it.[1] When we arrived at Mount Yun-men, we found an old dilapidated temple in the dense thickets which contained the body of the founder of the Yun-men School.[2]

On seeing the holy site in such a condition, I was so sad that I could not refrain from tears. A monk called Ming-kong had lived there alone since 1938 and had braved hardships to continue the worship of the founder of the sect. He related his difficulties and said that if the monastery was not rebuilt, it would soon fall into ruins and be buried in oblivion. I then returned to the Nan-hua Monastery.

One day, Marshall Li Ji-shen and Chairman Li Han-yun came to see me and I told them of what I had seen at Yun-men. Later during his tour of inspection, Chairman Li passed by Mount Ru-yuan and saw the ruined monastery of Ta-jue (Great Enlightenment) on the Yun-men Peak, which was in the same dilapidated condition as the Nan-hua Monastery before its renovation. He called the Sangha and notables to a meeting during which I was asked to take charge of the monastery's reconstruction. In anticipation of the war spreading to Nan-hua, I secretly moved the bodies of the Sixth Patriarch and Master Han-shan to Yun-men.

On my arrival at Yun-men I saw that most of the temple buildings were in ruins except the Hall of Master Yun-men, which, however, was in imminent danger of collapse. I settled in a small room behind the Shrine of Avalokitesvara Bodhisattva where I planned the restoration of the holy site. In the winter, I returned to

131

Nan-hua to hold a prayer meeting for the welfare of the dead on earth and in water.

Notes
1. The Ling-shu Monastery was the temple of Master Ling-shu (d. 918), where Master Yun-men studied the Dharma before founding his own temple.
2. Master Wen-yen Yun-men (d. 949) was the founder of the Yun-men School. His monastery was west of Qujiang, anciently Shaozhou, on the peak of Mount Yun-men. (See *Chan and Zen Teaching*, second series, pp. 181–214, the Yun-men Sect.)

MY 106TH YEAR
(1945/46)

Between the spring and summer, the Japanese armies invaded Northern Guangdong and occupied all the districts, including Ruyuan. Most of the refugees fled to the monastery at Yun-men, where they shared with the community first meals of rice, then rice gruel and eventually yam-flour as the provisions decreased. Among them were carpenters, brickmakers and bricklayers numbering about a hundred skilled persons who offered to work without wages, thus greatly contributing to the reconstruction of temple buildings.

In the summer, when Chinese troops moved to another defence line, the local bandits thought that they were retreating, attacked them and seized a large quantity of their rations. Reinforcements soon arrived and planned to attack the bandits in more than forty villages. About a thousand villagers, including men and women of ages, fled with their clothes and cattle to the hills inhabited by aborigines. The elders of the villages came to the monastery and asked me to intervene. I then discussed the matter with the army commander and three days later, all the loot was returned and the army indemnified. An agreement was then signed and conditions returned to normal. Since then the villagers regarded me as compassionate as a mother to them and although the Japanese occupied the towns, they did not come to Yun-men and so avoided trouble with the hostile population of the region.

MY 107TH YEAR
(1946/47)

World War II came to an end and all government departments returned to their former locations. In the spring, I transmitted the Precepts and read the sutras as usual. In the autumn, the central government ordered all the monasteries in the land to hold prayer meetings and read sutras to comfort the spirits of those killed in the war. I was invited by officials and notables to visit Canton in November in order to hold a similar meeting for the welfare of the dead at Jin-hui Temple (also called the Liu-rong (Six Banyans) Temple. There were peach trees in the temple and while holding rites there, they suddenly blossomed, showing an exuberance of flowers. Over 100,000 people came to the temple and saw the unseasonable flowering which was really remarkable. To mark the occasion, Upasika Zeng Bi-shan made an embroidery of an ancient Buddha with peach blossoms, and Upasaka Hu Yi-sheng painted a picture of the auspicious flowers.

After the meeting, I was invited by officials and notables of the Chaozhou and Shantou area to expound the Buddhadharma in the Kai-yuan Monastery at Chaozhou, where a great number of devotees came to receive the Precepts. That winter, my senior disciple Guan-ben passed away.

MY 108TH YEAR
(1947/48)

In the spring, I went to the Nan-hua Monastery to expound the sutras and transmit the Precepts. The Donghua group of hospitals in Hong Kong invited me to hold a prayer meeting for the welfare of the Crown Colony. I went there and stayed at the Chong-lan School, where Upasika Zeng Bi-shan gave me every assistance at the meeting where a few thousand devotees became my disciples.

I was subsequently invited by my disciples at Macao (Aomen) to expound the sutras and hold a meditation week and a few thousand devotees there became my disciples. Upasaka Ma Shi-chuan invited me to Mount Zhong where I held a *Mahakaruna* meeting at which another few thousand devotees became disciples of mine.

After that I returned to the Yun-men Monastery to speed up its renovation.

MY 109TH YEAR
(1948/49)

In the spring, after the transmission of the Precepts at Nan-hua Monastery, I went to Canton to open Zhi-de's Buddhist Hospital, where I expounded the Dharma. I then proceeded to Hong Kong, where I expounded the sutras at the Temple of Ci-hang Jin-yuan at Shatin, held a week of Pure Land meditation and taught the refuge-formula and five precepts at the Temple of Zhi-lin, and held a meeting for repentance and reform at the Temple of Dong-lian Jue-yuan (Enlightenment Garden of the Eastern Lotus). After that I returned to the Yun-men Monastery, In the fifth month, Dharma-master Jia-chen passed away in Yunnan. In the autumn an American lady, Ananda Jennings, came and was given Precepts. On the occasion, a week of Chan meditation was held; she was filled with joy and eventually returned to the United States.

Note by Cen Xue-lu, Xu-yun's Editor

That year, Ananda Jennings, who had heard of the Master's erudition and saintliness, expressed a desire to visit to China to call on him. He was informed of it through the Chinese and American consular services and replied that he would be delighted to meet her. When she arrived in Hong Kong, the Master was in Canton, where she went to see him. She said that her object was to study the Dharma; that her father was a Doctor of Divinity and that she herself had studied comparative religion for twenty years. She had previously travelled in quest of the Buddha's teaching and had been in India, where she lived in seclusion, later practising the Dharma in retreat for four years in the West. After trying to help the cause of world peace for three years at the League of Nations, she felt that peace could only be found on a deeper, spiritual level. This search ultimately led her to the Highest Buddhadharma, which alone frees the mind from continually recreating the problem of war in its very attempt to solve it: 'When the mind is at peace all wrong view disappear of themselves.'

The Master then took Ananda Jennings to the Nan-hua Monastery to pay reverence to the Sixth Patriarch. After the refuge-taking ritual, she was given the Dharma-name of Kuan-hung (Great Vastness). A Chan meditation week was held on the occasion and those who came from the four quarters were numerous. When the Chan week began, the Master came to the hall and said to the meeting: 'Speaking of this "thing", it is fundamentally perfect; it neither increases in the holy state nor decreases in the worldly realm. When the Tathagata transmigrates through the six realms of existence, each realm hears of him and when Guan-yin [lit. 'Regarder of Sound'] passes through the ten species of living beings, every one of them is in the state of "thatness". If all is "thus", what do you seek and why do you search for it? An ancestor said, "As soon as there is differentiation the mind is lost in the ensuing confusion." Even before your boat was moored you already deserved to be given some strokes from my staff.[1] What a pity! Instead of opening up your own store of treasure, you come to a thatched hut to fetch worthless straw. All of this is because of a single unenlightened thought. Since your mad mind does not stop, you are just like someone searching for another head while holding his own in both hands or saying that you are thirsty while there is water in front of you. Virtuous friends, why trouble to come here? . . . Why? Since you do not grudge spending your money on rush sandals, I shall not hesitate to open my foul mouth.'

The Master then gave a Chan shout and said, 'The Grand Old Man of Shakya has come. Tsan!'[2]

Elder monks from other monasteries who were present, also spoke at the meeting, Below is a dialogue (Chin. *Wen-ta*; Jap. *Mondo*) between Ananda Jennings and a disciple of Master Xu-yun, called Qi-shi (lit. 'The mendicant'):

Qi-shi: You have crossed the ocean to come here and have thus endured danger. What is the object of your visit?

Ananda Jennings: My object is to realise the Buddhadharma.

Q: One should be clear about the question of birth and death when one studies the Dharma; what is your opinion about 'birth and death'?

AJ: Since fundamentally there is neither birth nor death, what is the use of formulating opinions which alone are 'birth and death'?

Q: If there is neither birth nor death, what is the use of studying the Buddhadharma?

AJ: Fundamentally there is no Buddhadharma, and he who realises Dharma is Buddha.

Q: The Buddha possessed thirty-two characteristic marks and when he pressed his toes to the ground, the ocean symbol radiated; can you do this?

AJ: Both the ability to do this and inability to do this pertain to phenomenalistic sophistry.

Q: Although your interpretation is profound and what you say is correct, the mere speaking of eating does not satisfy hunger, what, according to you, is the 'Ultimate Sentence'?

AJ: The Ultimate has no 'sentence' and speech also has no basis, the non-thinking nature of enlightenment being free from verbiage of opinion and ideas.

135

Q: You have spoken of it in detail and every word of yours accords well with the Patriarch's meaning. But the word 'knowledge' is the gateway to all kinds of calamity. Since you have entered by means of correct interpretation, may I ask you this: Without using words or speech, what is your fundamental face?[3]

AJ: The *Diamond Sutra* says, '*Anuttara-samyak-sambhodi* is not *anut-tara-samyak-sambhodi.*'[4]

Q: It seems to be so, but the life-root cannot be cut off by knowledge and views [consciousness]. I hope you will look into all this.

AJ: I have not had much opportunity to read the sutras. After my previous seclusion for four years, when I spoke to others, they all said that my words accorded with the Buddhadharma. In my opinion, understanding that does not derive from the mere reading of sutras seems not to belong entirely to human consciousness.

Q: That which does not derive from the reading of sutras and *shastras* but manifests during one's meditation still belongs to the former wisdom which is also consciousness.

AJ: That Buddhadharma postulates true realisation but does not rely on human or cosmic consciousness.

Q: By not being bogged down in sutras and *shastras* and by not clinging to the self-nature, the 'thusness' of the Dao is everywhere and the truth prevails anywhere one may happen to be. It can expediently be called 'This One'.

Ananda Jennings then accompanied the Master to Yun-men Monastery, where they paid reverence to the body of Master Yun-men, and where she stayed for about a fortnight. She said that she would spread the Buddhad-harma after her return to America.

Notes

1. i.e. before you left your boat to come and seek my instruction you were already wrong, because you disregarded the Buddha-nature which is inherent in you and looked for something outside. For this carelessness, you should be given thirty strokes of my staff.

2. 'Tsan' is a Chan idiom meaning 'Investigate' or 'look into your mind'. The vastness of the meditation of the Buddha, the vision of all things in totality.

3. The mendicant intended to draw the American visitor into a Chan dialogue (*wen-ta*). If she had wanted to test his ability to do so, she should have given a shout or slapped his face to reveal the 'function' of her 'fundamental face'.

4. *Anuttara-samyak-sambhodi* means 'unexcelled complete enlighten-ment'. In the *Vajracchedika*, the Buddha said that 'unexcelled complete enlightenment' is to realise the 'unattainability' of the transcendental nature, for if there be a 'realiser' and 'object' realised, how would this

differ from the world of birth and death? Thus, the discovery of *anuttara-samyak-sambhodi* is to realise the emptiness *(sunyata)* of all conditioned things, and thus be beyond all 'gain' and 'loss'. Thus it is expediently called *anuttara-samyak-sambhodi.*

MY 110TH YEAR
(1949/50)

After the transmission of the Precepts at Nan-hua Monastery, I returned to Yun-men where I supervised the gilding of over eighty statues and the making of stands for them, which took over a year. The whole monastery was thus ninety per cent renovated. Upasaka Fang Yang-qiu invited me to Hong Kong to inaugurate the opening of his Buddha-shrine. I also expounded the sutras at the Prajna Vihara there. After staying a month in Hong Kong, I returned to Yun-men. That year, I asked Upasaka Cen Xue-lu to edit the Annals of Yun-men Monastery.

Note by Cen Xue-lu, Xu-yun's Editor

The Master came to Hong Kong at the invitation of Upasaka Fang Yang-qiu. One day, I asked the Master: 'The world is changing fast, where should I go [to maintain my practice]?'

The Master replied, 'To a student of the Dao, his home is everywhere and if you only lay down everything, the place where you are is a Bodhimandala [place for realising the truth]. Please set your mind at rest.'

I asked, 'The monasteries will be greatly affected by what happens on the mainland; why don't you stay here temporarily to expound the Dharma for the benefit of living beings?'

He replied, 'There are others who can expound the Dharma here. It seems that I have a special responsibility [to the temples on the mainland]. As for myself, my mind is beyond going or staying, but on the mainland, all the temples and monasteries are in a state of uncertainty. If I stay here, who will look after the tens of thousands of monks and nuns whose plight will worsen; how can my mind be set at rest [if I stay here]? That is why I must return to the mainland.' – *Cen Xue-lu.*

MY 111TH YEAR
(1950/51)

In the spring I went to the Nan-hua Monastery to transmit the Precepts and to hold a week of Chan meditation at which some people subsequently realised spiritual awakening.

After my return to the Yun-men Monastery, I began to put in order all my manuscripts so that they could be arranged for editing. This was not easy for most of my works had been written several decades before.

MY 112TH YEAR
(1951/52)

During the transmission of the Precepts in the spring, misfortune befell me at the Yun-men Monastery.

Note by Cen Xue-lu, Xu-yun's Editor

The Master dictates his life story up to his 112th year, after which his attendants recorded subsequent events as they occurred until the time of his death.

[At this time, the Communist Revolution had taken place and the first shudders of ideological change were beginning to make themselves felt.] That spring a great many monks, nuns, male and female lay-disciples had gathered to receive the Precepts at Yun-men Monastery, where the community numbered over 120 monks. On the twenty-fourth of the second month, a band of more than a hundred thugs suddenly came and surrounded the monastery, allowing no one to enter or leave it. First, they forcibly detained the Master in the Abbot's room, leaving a few to watch him, and confined the monks to the Dharma and Meditation halls. After that, they searched the temple buildings from the roof-tiles to the flooring bricks, including the statues of the Buddhas and Patriarchs, sacred articles and the cases containing the *Tripitaka*.

Although over a hundred men searched for over two days, they found nothing illegal. Finally, they took away Bhiksu Ming-gong – the Superintendent of the monastery, and Wei-xin, Wu-hui, Zhen-kong and Wei-Zhang – the monks in charge. They also put the registers, documents, correspondence and all the Master's manuscripts of explanations and commentaries on the sutras – and his recorded saying during a whole century – in gunny bags which they carried away. They then accused the community of all sorts of crimes, but in reality they had wrongly believed groundless rumours that there were arms, ammunition, radio transmitters, gold bars and silver bullion hidden in the monastery, these items being the real object of their search.

Altogether twenty-six monks were arrested and brutally beaten in an attempt to force them into divulging the supposed cache of arms and money, but they all declared that they knew nothing of such things. Bhiksu Miao-yun was beaten to death and Bhiksus Wu-yun and Ti-zhi were so ruthlessly knocked about that their arms were broken. A few other monks went missing. As the thugs found nothing after ten days of vain searching, they visited their anger of the Master.

On the first of the third month, he was taken to another room, the doors and windows of which were sealed up. He was given nothing to eat or drink and was not even allowed to go out and ease nature. The room, dimly lit by a small lamp, resembled hell. On the third day, about ten tall men entered roughly and ordered the Master to surrender gold, silver and arms. When he said that he had none, they struck him – first with wooden sticks – and then with iron bars until his head and face bled profusely and his ribs broke.

He was interrogated while being attacked, but sat in the meditation posture to enter the state of *dhyana*. As the blows rained down mercilessly, he closed his eyes and mouth and seemed to be in the state of *samadhi*. That day they beat him brutally four times and finally, they threw him to the ground. Seeing that he was badly hurt, they thought he was dead and left the room. A little later the guards also left and the Master's attendants carried him to a bed and helped him sit in the meditation posture.

On the fifth day, when they heard that the Master was still alive, they came again and seeing that he was sitting in the meditation posture as before, they were furiously angry and struck him with wooden sticks. Dragging him to the ground, they kicked and trampled on him with their heavy leather boots. As he lay there with blood streaming from his head, they thought he was dead, laughed brutally and left. At night, his attendants again carried him to the bed and helped him to sit in the meditation posture.

On the tenth day, early in the morning, he slowly reclined on his right side (in a position similar to that of the Buddha at his Parinirvana). As he was motionless for a whole day and night, his attendant took a lamp-wick and held it close to his nostrils; he was found to be breathless and was thought to have died. However, the

Master's mien was fresh as usual and his body was still warm. His attendants, Fa-yun and Kuan-shan, kept watch by his bedside.

Early in the morning of the eleventh, the Master was heard to groan feebly. His attendants helped him sit up and told him how long he had sat in *dhyana* and lain on the bed. Slowly, the Master said: 'I thought it was just a few minutes.' He then said to Fa-yun: 'Take a pen and write down what I dictate but don't show the notes to outsiders lest they blaspheme.'

Then he said slowly, 'I dreamed that I went to the inner chamber of Maitreya Buddha in the Tushita Heaven which surpassed in beauty and majesty all that we have on earth. Maitreya Bodhisattva was seated on a throne and was expounding the Dharma to a large assembly where I saw over ten of my late acquaintances; among them were Abbot Zhi-shan of Hai-hui Monastery in Jiangxi, Dharma-master Yong-jing of Mount Tian-tai, Master Heng-zhui of Mount Qi, Abbot Bao-wu of the Baisui-gong Monastery, Abbot Sheng-xin of Mount Bao-hua, Vinaya-master Du-di, Abbot Guan-xin of Mount Jin and also Master Zi-bai.

'I brought my palms together to salute them and they pointed to the third vacant seat in the front row on the east side, telling me to sit there. Arya Ananda was the leader of the assembly and sat close to me. Maitreya was teaching meditation on the mind to still consciousness but purposely stopped to say to me, "You should go back [to your monastery]." I said, "My karmic hindrance is too great and I an unwilling to return." He said, "Your karmic link with the world has not ended yet and you must go back now so that you can return here later. He then chanted the following *gatha:*

How do consciousness and wisdom differ
When like wave and water they are one?
Distinguish not between a golden jug and bowl
For in essence the gold of both is but the same.
The capacity of self-nature is three times three.[1]
A thin string of hemp or small snail's horn
Appears like a strong-bow to the hallucinating;
This fearful illness vanishes when delusion ends.
Like a house of dreams is this human body,
An illusion to which one ne'er should cling.
When that illusion's recognised.
One keeps from it and is enlightened.[2]

Bodhi is illuminating
And perfect as it shines on all.
Saints and worldlings, good and evil, even happiness
Are illusions like flowers appearing in the sky.
Because of your great compassion you have vowed to save
All beings and are now involved in this world of dreams.
The evil karma of this aeon flourishes
So be alert, awake to all that happens.
Turn not back when from compassion
The seas of suffering you sail.
The lotus rises from the mud to flower
Bearing a Buddha seated in its centre . . .

There were many other verses which I do not remember. He also gave me advice which I must keep to myself.'

In this profound state of *dhyana-samadhi*, the Master wiped out all feelings of suffering and happiness. In the past, when they were arrested, beaten and tortured, Masters Han-shan [1546–1623] and Zi-bai [1543–1604][4] entered the same state of *samadhi* which is beyond the reach of those who have not realised the Dharma.

The thugs who had beaten and tortured the Master and who now witnessed his remarkable feat of endurance, whispered to one another and began to be afraid. A man who seemed to be their leader, asked a monk: 'Why did not the old monk succumb to our beating?'

The monk replied, 'The old Master endures suffering for the welfare of all living beings and also to help you escape from your troubles. Later, you will know why he did not succumb to your beating.'

The man trembled and never thought of torturing the Master again.

Since they did not find what they were looking for and were afraid that news of the torture might leak out, they stayed on at the monastery and searched the monks, forbidding them to speak to one another or leave their quarters. Even their food and drink were subject to their captors' rigid examination. This state of things lasted for over a month. As a result of the beating and torture, Master Xu-yun suffered great pain and felt very ill; he could neither see nor hear. Afraid that he might pass away, his disciples urged him to dictate his life-story; hence this autobiography.

In the fourth month, the news of events at the Yun-men Monastery reached Shaozhou, where the monks at Da-jian Temple at Qujiang relayed it to the Master's disciples in Beijing and to overseas Chinese Buddhists who then jointly worked to rescue him.

As a result the Beijing government telegraphed the Guangdong provincial authorities to inquire into the matter. The thugs gradually relaxed their control of the monastery, but the community's clothing and food had been seized and taken away.

After his torture, the Master did not even take rice-gruel but drank only water. When he learned that all the provisions had been confiscated, he said to the monks, 'I am sorry that you are all involved in my heavy karma. The situation being such as it is, you should leave this place to make a living somewhere else.' As his disciples refused to leave him, he urged them to gather firewood on the hills behind the monastery, sell it in the local markets, and then purchase rice for the community. Thus they had meals of rice-gruel and continued reading the sutras and practising the morning and evening meditation without interruption.

During the first fortnight of the fifth month, the Beijing government sent a few officials to Guangdong Province. On the Twenty-second they went with provincial officials to Ru-yuan and reached Yun-men Monastery the following day. They brought with them technicians, tape-recorders and cameras to make on the spot investigations. They inquired first about the Master, who was then very ill and kept in bed. He could neither see nor hear clearly and did not realise that the officials had come from Beijing.

When he recognised the local officials and policemen, he refused to speak; when asked if he had been ill-treated and if the monastery and lost anything, he replied in the negative. When the visitors revealed their identities, he only asked them to make an accurate investigation and report it to Beijing. After repeatedly comforting him, they ordered the local authorities to release all the arrested monks. Thus the misfortune that had befallen Yun-men Monastery on the twenty-fourth of the second month ended on the twenty-third of the fifth month.

In the autumn and winter, the Master rested at the monastery to recuperate, while the community of about a hundred monks earned their living by gathering and selling firewood, farming and working at handicrafts. When people in the hundred or so local villages heard that the thugs had left the monastery, they came to inquire after the Master. His disciples in Beijing and elsewhere wrote to comfort him, urging him to leave Yun-men. They also wrote, asking the provincial authorities to give him protection.

Notes

1. Lt. 'Three-three' 3 × 3 = 'nine worlds of existence'.
2. Quoted from the *Sutra of Complete Enlightenment* (See *Chan and Zen Teaching*, third series).
3. See *The Secrets of Chinese Meditation*, page 51.
4. Ibid, page 62, Master Da-guan, alias Zi-bai.

Master Xu-yun with Ven. Lai-guo. No date.

CHAPTER THIRTEEN

TWO DISCOURSES

In the spring the Master felt a little better and led the community in a vigorous course of Chan training to make the best of the uncertain circumstances. During the first three months of that year, the Government telegraphed him four times, urging him to go to Beijing. When officials came from the north to take him to the capital, the whole community advised him to wait, but he said, 'The time is now ripe. The Sangha is in a state of uncertainty all over the country and like a lot of loose sand for lack of a leader. If there is no strong organisation to protect our interests, misfortune will not be confined to Yun-men. My responsibility is to go north in order to protect the Dharma.'

The Master then selected a few elderly monks to take charge of Yun-men Monastery and after comforting the community, he prepared for the trip. Before leaving, he wrote the following on a pair of scrolls.

While I witnessed five reigns and four dynasties in turn, great changes have occurred.[1]
Untold tribulations have made me realise the world's impermanence.

On the fourth of the fourth month, the Master left Yun-men Monastery and went north with his attendants Fu-yuan, Jue-min, Kuan-tu, Fa-yun and the officials who had come to escort him. A few hundred villagers came to see him off. When he reached Shaozhou (Qujiang), over a thousand devotees welcomed him. At Da-jian Temple where he stayed, each day a great number of people crowded together to pay him reverence which showed that their faith in him had remained unchanged in spite of the altered social conditions.

On the tenth, the Master took the Canton–Hankou railway for Wuchang, where he arrived the following day, subsequently staying at the Temple of the Three Buddhas. Owing to the fatigue of the journey, the wounds throughout his body gave him great pain. Upasaka Chen Zhen-ru arranged for him to be given medical treatment and Abbot Ying-xin also looked after him. When he felt a little better, the Abbot invited him to hold a week's practice involving recitation of the mantra of Avalokitesvara Bodhisattva. Over two thousand devotees took the refuges and became disciples of the Master. After the Buddhist meeting, the Master then went on to Beijing in spite of his ill health. Before his departure, the monks at the temple took a photograph of the Master who inscribed the following poem upon it:

> The wind of karma drove me to Wuchang city
> Where my illness causes others so much trouble.
> I stayed three months at the Temple of Three Buddhas,
> Filled with shame and horror at all my misfortunes.
> Mindless of having climbed to the top of the world,
> I wait for those who have also vowed to ascend to *Bodhi*,
> Remembering that Guan Zhang-miu on Yu-zhuan Peak[2]
> Achieved Reality supreme after hearing a word or two.

On the twenty-eighth of the seventh month, with his attendants and other devotees, the Master took the train to Beijing where they were welcomed at the station by abbots and leaders of various Buddhist groups. Upasakas Li Ji-shen, Yen Xia-an and Chen Zhen-ru took the Master to the Guang-hua Monastery, which soon proved too small to receive the large crowd of devotees who came to pay him reverence. He then moved to the Guang-ji Monastery where he got in touch with officials who were either natives of Hunan like the Master or old acquaintances in Yunnan who supported his efforts to protect the Dharma.

Over a hundred delegates from Buddhist organisations all over the country were present and decided to re-establish the Chinese Buddhist Association. The Master was asked to be its President but declined on the grounds of old age and ill health. Master Yuan-ying was then elected President with Sherab Gyatso and Zhao Bo-zhu as Vice-presidents. After convening its planning committee, the Master petitioned the Government to make regulations for the freedom of religion and the preservation and maintenance of Buddhist temples and monasteries all over the country. Above all, he urged them to forbid the further demolition of temples and monasteries with the destruction of their statues and libraries, to stop compelling monks and nuns to return to lay-life, and to return them enough of their land to become self-supporting by its cultivation.

The petition was approved and the Sangha thus obtained some sort of security and, in addition, it was agreed that repairs would be made to the temples, monasteries and holy sites in all provinces.

On the thirteenth of the eighth month, the Master welcomed the Ceylonese Buddhist delegation Guang-ji Monastery on behalf of the Chinese Buddhist Association. The delegation was headed by Bhikkhu Dhammaratna who came to present a relic of the Buddha, a Pali Sutta written on pattra (palm-leaves) and a Bo-tree sapling. Over two thousand devotees were present at the reception.

In the ninth month, the abbots and leaders of Buddhist groups invited the Master to be Abbot of Guang-ji Monastery, but he declined on the grounds of old age and ill health.

In the tenth month, the Buddhists of Shanghai invited the Master to hold a Prayer Meeting for World Peace and he arrived there on the twenty-fifth. The meeting began the following day and lasted for seven weeks, at the end of which over 3,000 Chinese dollars (or over 70,000 Hong Kong dollars) had been collected in contributions and offerings to the Master by devotees, but which, however, he refused to keep for himself. With his approval, the money was distributed to four holy sites (Pu-tuo Island in Zhe-jiang; Wu-tai Shan in Shansi; Mount Emei in Sichuan;) and to eight great monasteries (Tian-tong, Ayu-Wang, Gong-zong and Qi-ta at Ningbo; the Gao-min at Yangzhou; Ling-yen at Suzhou, plus the Gu-shan and Ti-zang monasteries at Fuzhou), besides 250 other large and small temples throughout the country.

Master Xu-yun's Sermon at the Prayer Meeting in Shanghai on 17 December 1952

This Prayer Meeting for World Peace which began a few days ago is virtually unique. Today the Dharma-master Wei-fang, Abbot Miao-zhen and Upasakas Zhao Bo-zhu, Li Si-hao and Fang Cu-hao have asked me to preach the Dharma. I avail myself of this occasion to speak of the inter-relation between the Chan and Pure

Land Schools so that beginners can understand both. Today is the first day set for the Pure Land practice, which consists of reciting the Buddha's name. It was decided that Abbot Miao-zhen should be the speaker but my venerable friend has been very modest and has asked me to take his place.

This *saha* world in which we live is a bitter sea of suffering from which all of us want to escape but to do so, we must rely on the Buddhadharma. Strictly speaking, Reality as taught by the Buddhadharma cannot be spoken of for it is indescribable in word and speech. Therefore, the *Surangama Sutra* says: 'The language used has no real meaning [in itself]'.

However, to cope with the great variety of living beings' propensities, countless expedients have been devised to guide them. In China, the Buddhadharma is divided into the Chan School, the Teaching School (sutras), the Vinaya School and the Pure Land and Yogacara Schools. To learned and experienced practitioners, this division is superfluous because they are already clear about the Dharma-nature which does not admit differentiation. But beginners hold conflicting opinions and like to drive the Dharma into sects and schools which they discriminate between and thereby greatly reduce the value of the Dharma for enlightening people.

We should know that the *hua-tou* technique[3] and the repetition of the Buddha's name are only expedient methods which are not the ultimate and are useless to those who have already achieved their goals by efficient training. Why so? Because they have realised the absolute state in which movement and stillness are one, like the moon reflected in a thousand rivers in which it is bright and clear without obstructions. Obstructions come from floating clouds in the sky and the mud in water (deluded thoughts). If there are obstructions, the moon cannot appear in spite of its brightness and its reflection will not be seen in spite of the clear water.

If we practitioners of the Dharma understand this truth and are clear about the self-mind which is like the bright moon in autumn and does not wander outside in search of externals but turns back its light to illumine itself, without giving rise to a single thought and without any notion of realisation, then how can there be room for different names and terms? It is only because for countless aeons we have been clinging to wrong thoughts, and because of the strong force of habits, that the Lord Buddha held three hundred assemblies during his forty-nine years of teaching. But the aim of all expedient methods is to cure living beings of different ailments caused by desire, anger and stupidity and perverted habits. If we can keep away from all this, how can there be differences among living beings? Hence an ancient said:

'Though there are many expedients for the purpose
They are identical when returned to the source.'[4]

The most popular methods in use today are Chan and Pure Land. But it is regrettable that many members of the Sangha overlook the rules of discipline without knowing that the Buddhadharma is based on discipline *(sila)*, meditation *(dhyana)* and wisdom *(prajna)*; it is like a tripod which cannot stand if one of its legs is lacking. This is so important a thing that no students of the Buddhadharma should disregard it.

The Chan transmission began when in the assembly on Vulture Peak, the World-Honoured One held up a flower, a gesture which was acknowledged by Mahakasyapa with a smile. This is called the sealing of mind by mind and is the 'Transmission outside the Teaching'; it is the foundation of the whole Buddhadharma. The repetition of Amitabha's name, sutra-reading and concentration upon mantras are also designed to help us escape from birth and death.

Some say that Chan is a sudden method while the Pure Land and Mantrayana are gradual ones; it is so, but this is only a difference in names and terms because in reality all methods lead to the same result. Hence the Sixth Patriarch said, 'The Dharma is neither instantaneous nor gradual, but man's awakening may be slow or quick.'[5]

If all methods are good for practice and if you find one which suits you, practise it; but you should never praise one method and vilify another, thereby giving rise to discrimination. The most important thing is *sila* (discipline) which should be strictly observed. Nowadays there are corrupt monks who not only disregard the rules of discipline, but who say that to observe them is also a form of clinging; such an irresponsible statement is harmful and dangerous to beginners.

The Chan doctrine of the Mind was handed down through Mahakasyapa and his successors in India and reached China where it was eventually transmitted to Master Hui-neng, its Sixth (Chinese) Patriarch. This was the Transmission of the Right Dharma which then flourished (all over China).

The Vinaya-discipline School began with Upali, who received it from the Lord Buddha who declared that *sila* is the teacher of all living beings in the Dharma-ending-age. After Upagupta,[6] it was divided into five schools (the Dharmagupta, Sarvastivada, Mahisasaka, Kasyapiya and Vatsuputriya). In China, Dao-xuan (a celebrated monk of the Tang Dynasty) of Mount Nan studied the Dharmagupta, wrote a commentary on it and founded the Vinaya School, becoming its Chinese Patriarch.

The Tian-tai School was founded in China by Hui-wen of the Bei-qi Dynasty (550–78) after he studied Nagarjuna's *Madhyamika Shastra* and realised the Mind-ground.

Du-shun [d. 640] studied the *Avatamsaka Sutra* and subsequently founded the Hua-yan School, which was later called the Xian-shou School after its Third Patriarch.[7]

Hui-yuan [d. 416] founded the Pure Land School which was handed down through its Nine Patriarchs. Its Sixth Patriarch, Yanshou Yong-ming [d. 975] and three succeeding ones were enlightened Chan Masters who spread the Pure Land doctrine, and the two schools [Chan and Pure Land] intermingled like milk and water. In spite of the division of the Buddhadharma into different schools, these do not stray from the underlying meaning revealed by the Buddha when he held a flower aloft. Thus we realise that Chan and Pure Land are closely related and that the ancients were painstaking when they taught the Buddhadharma.

The Yogacara (Mi-zong) School was introduced in China by Vajrabodhi (who arrived there in 619). It was spread by Amogha [d. 774] and then flourished thanks to the efforts of Chan Master Yi-xing [672–717].

The above expedient methods of teaching the Buddhadharma are mutually complementary and should never be categorised as separate denominations, contrary and hostile to one another, for this would run counter to the intentions of the Buddhas and Patriarchs. An ancient said that they are but like yellow leaves given to children to prevent them from crying.

People who do not understand the real reason for sayings such as Chao-zhou's 'I do not like hearing the word "Buddha",' or 'If I mistakenly utter the Buddha's name but once, I shall rinse my mouth out for three days,' are unaware of the compassionate heart he had when teaching his disciples to disengage themselves from illusory 'Buddhas' and quote him to vilify the Pure Land method as the concern of ignorant old women. Again, some people regard the Chan practice as the occupation of heretical seekers of emptiness. In short, they pretend that they are always right whereas others are always wrong.

This sort of controversy is endless and not only contradicts the good intention of the Buddha and Patriarchs in setting up convenient methods of teaching the Dharma, but it also furnishes outsiders with a good pretext to criticise and hinder it. The consequences being so great, I especially draw the attention of experienced devotees as well as beginners to this unfortunate state of things so that they can put an end to it; if it is allowed to continue, it will strangle the Buddhadharma to death.

We should know that all methods lead to the same result. Students of Buddhism should read and reread Chan Master Yong-ming's works *Zong Jing Lu* and *Wan Shan Tong Gui Ji*.[8]

Students of the Pure Land School should read and understand well the chapter on Mahasthama's means of perfection in the *Surangama Sutra*,[7] and so recognise the self-natured Pure Land by keeping from delusion and turning to the inner reality without wandering in search of externals.

If we comprehend this truth we can, while not straying from it, speak of either Chan or Pure Land, of either East or West, both of which are reachable, and of either 'existence' or 'non-existence' which will no longer hinder us. This is the moment when either 'form' or 'smell' are but the Profound Mean, the Self-natured Amitabha and the Pure Land which is but Mind, all of which will be attainable in a place where there are not too many creepers [i.e. expedient methods which, in Chan terminology, are likened to 'creepers' which hide the trunk of the tree and should never be clung to in quest of the latter, or self-nature].

The Surangama Sutra says, 'Just wipe out all worldly feelings and passions, beyond which nothing can be interpreted as holy'. If we can do so and thereby cut off all false thoughts, attachments and habits, we shall be Bodhisattvas, Patriarchs and Buddhas; otherwise we shall continue to be living beings.

Reciters of the Buddha's name should never cling to that name for it can become as harmful as poison. We now recite the

Buddha's name because our habits are deeply rooted from time without beginning and our thoughts cannot be easily stopped. So we use his name as a prop in our striving to wipe out all rising thoughts until they eventually vanish completely and give way to the Pure Land which will then manifest itself. So why should we seek it from outside?

Master Xu-yun's Discourse on the 12th Anniversary of the Death of Dharma-Master Yin-guang, a Saint of the Pure Land on 21 December 1952.

Today is the twelfth anniversary of the death of the late Dharma-Master Yin-guang, who was reborn in the Western Paradise (of Amitabha). All of you, his disciples, have gathered in this hall to celebrate the occasion. As when one drinks water and thinks of its source, so your celebration today is in memory of your fatherly Master. In Buddhism, a Master is the father of one's *Dharmakaya*, so to commemorate the death of one's Master is to have filial thoughts of him. This filial piety is much deeper than that towards one's parents. I still remember meeting the Master on Pu-tuo Island in the twentieth year of Emperor Guang-xu [1894]. He had been asked by Abbot Hua-wen to expound the *Sutra of Amitabha* at Qian-si Temple and stayed there for over twenty years to read the *Tripitaka.* He isolated himself to practise the Pure Land method and although he was an authority on the Buddhist Sutras, he used only the word 'Amitabha', which was recited in his daily practice. He never pretended that, with his deep knowledge of the sutras, he could slight and dispense with this simple practice of the Pure Land School.

All expedient methods taught by the Buddha are good for treating worldly illnesses and the recitation of the Buddha's name is an *agada* (medicine) that cures all diseases. However, each of these methods requires a firm faith, an inflexible resolution and considerable practice in order to give good results. If you are strong in faith, you will achieve the same perfection whether you concentrate on mantras, practise Chan or repeat the Buddha's name.

If you are weak in faith and rely on your tiny good roots, little intelligence and shallow knowledge, or if you memorise a few Buddhist terms or a few *gong-ans* and then talk aimlessly, praising and censuring others, you will only increase your karma-producing habits and when death closes in, you will follow your karma to transmigrate again in *samsara*. Is it not a greaty pity?

As you commemorate the death of your Master, you should commemorate his true practice and observance of the Dharma. He was firm in his practice and kept in step with the ancients. He understood Mahasthama Bodhisattva's means of perfection, which consists of concentrating all thoughts upon the Buddha; he put it into actual practice and thereby realised the state of *samadhi* which resulted from his concentration upon Amitabha. He then spread the Pure Land Dharma for the benefit of living beings, unflinchingly and without tiring for several decades. Today, you cannot find another man like him.

A true practitioner always avoids discriminating between self and others, but concentrates and relies on the Buddha at all times and in all situations. He firmly holds on to this single thought of the Buddha, which is intimate and unbroken, until it becomes effective and causes the manifestation of Amitabha's Pure Land from which he will enjoy all benefit. In order to realise this, one's believing mind should be firm and set solely on remembering Amitabha Buddha. If one's believing mind wavers, nothing can be achieved.

For instance, if someone says that Chan is better than Pure Land, you try Chan and stop reciting the Buddha's name; then if others praise the Teaching School, you read the sutras and drop Chan meditation; or if you fail in your studies of the teachings, you concentrate upon mantras instead. If you practise the Buddha-dharma in this way, you will be confused and achieve no result. Instead of blaming yourself for this ineffectual practice, you will accuse the Buddha of deceiving living beings; by so doing, you will slander the Buddha and vilify the Dharma, thereby creating an unintermittently *(avici)* hellish karma.

Therefore, I urge all of you to have faith in the profitable practice of the Pure Land School and to follow the example set by your late Master, whose motto was, 'Only sincere recitation of the Buddha's name,' to develop and inflexible resolution, to develop a bold mind and to regard the Pure Land as the sole concern of your life.

Chan and Pure Land seem to be two different methods as seen by beginners, but are really one to experienced practitioners. The *hua-tou* technique in Chan meditation, which puts an end to the stream of birth and death, also requires a firm believing mind to be effective. If the *hua-tou* is not firmly held, Chan practice will fail. If the believing mind is strong and if the *hua-tou* is firmly held, the practitioner will be mindless of even eating and drinking and his training will take effect; when sense-organs disengage from sense data, his attainment will be similar to that achieved by a reciter of the Buddha's name when his training becomes effective and when the Pure Land manifests in front of him. In this state, noumenon and phenomenon intermingle, Mind and Buddha are not a duality and both are in the state of suchness which is absolute and free from all contraries and relativities. Then what difference is there between Chan and Pure Land?

Since you are all adherents of the Pure Land School, I hope you will rely on the Buddha's name as your support in your lifetime and that you will truly and sincerely recite it without interruption.

Notes

1. The five reigns of Dao-guang, Xian-feng, Tong-zhi, Guang-xu and Xuan-tong. The four dynasties are: Manchu, Republic of China, the Puppet regime of Wang Jing-wei during the Japanese occupation and the present Communist government of Beijing.

2. Also called Guan-gong, a well-known general in the 'Three Kingdoms' period who called on Master Zhi-yi (Zhi-zhe) of the Tian-tai School for instruction, subsequently vowing to protect the Dharma. He is still regarded as a Dharma-protector by Chinese Buddhists today, who occasionally invoke his influence when in trouble.

3. *Hua-tou* is the mind before it is stirred by a thought. The technique was devised by enlightened Masters who taught their disciples to concentrate their attention on the mind for the purpose of stopping all thought to realise singleness of mind for the perception of their self-nature.

4. Quoted from Manjusri's *Long Gatha* in the *Surangama Sutra*. (See *The Secrets of Chinese Meditation*, page 34, and *The Surangama Sutra*, pages 143–9.

5. See *Chan and Zen Teaching, Third Series*, Part I, *The Altar Sutra*.

6. The Fourth Patriarch of the Chan sect in India. See *Chan and Zen Teaching*, Second Series, page 34.

7. Otherwise known as Fa-zang (643–712). He was a prolific commentator on the Hua-yan.

8. Both works explain the inter-relationship of all methods of practice and their common aim, i.e. the realisation of Bodhi, despite their classification into different schools.

Master Xu-yun on Mount Yun-ju, Jiangxi Province, 1959.
Yun-ju was the site of the Zhen-ru Monastery, the last to be restored
in his lifetime. Xu-yun was 120 when this picture was taken.

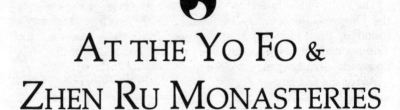

CHAPTER FOURTEEN

AT THE YO FO & ZHEN RU MONASTERIES

XU-YUN'S 114TH YEAR
(1953/54)

At the end of the Prayer Meeting, as the Master intended to leave Shanghai, monks and lay devotees invited him to hold a week of Chan meditation to revive the Chan tradition at the Temple of the Jade Buddha (Yu Fu Monastery) where there was a large meditation hall. Headed by Abbot Wei-fang, a delegation which consisted of Upasakas Jian Yu-jie, Li Si-hao and other well-known devotees, called on the master, who accepted their request. The meditation began on 22 February 1953, and when it ended, they asked him to continue for another week. At both meetings, the Master delivered sermons which were duly recorded.[1]

Daily Lectures at a Chan Week
given at the Jade Buddha Monastery, Shanghai, in 1953
(from the Xu Yun He Shang Nian Pu)

THE FIRST WEEK

The First Day

The Venerable Wei-fang, Abbot of this monastery, is very compassionate indeed, and the chief monks are also earnest in their efforts to spread the Dharma. In addition, all the laymen *(upasakas)* here are keen in their studies of the truth and have come to sit in meditation during this Chan week. All have asked me to preside over the meeting and this is really an unsurpassable co-operating cause. However, for the last few years, I have been ill and am, therefore, unable to give long lectures.

The World-Honoured One spent over forty years in expounding the Dharma, exoterically and esoterically, and his teaching is found in the twelve divisions[2] of the Mahayana canon in the *Tripitaka*. If I am asked to give lectures, the most I can do is to pick up words already spoken by the Buddha and Masters.

As for the Dharma of our sect, when the Buddha ascended to his seat for the last time, he held up and showed to the assembly a golden flower of sandalwood, offered to him by the king of the eighteen Brahmalokas (Mahabrahma Devaraja). All men and gods *(devas)* who were present did not understand the Buddha's meaning. Only Mahakasyapa acknowledged it with a broad smile. Thereupon the World-Honoured One declared to him: 'I have the treasure of the correct Dharma eye, Nirvana's wonderful mind and the formless reality which I now transmit to you.' This was the transmission outside of teaching, which did not make use of scriptures and was the unsurpassed Dharma door of direct realisation.

Those who came afterwards got confused about it and wrongly called it Chan (*Dhyana* in Sanskrit and *Zen* in Japanese). We should know that over twenty kinds of Chan are enumerated in the *Mahaprajna-paramita Sutra*, but none of them is the final one.

The Chan of our sect does not set up progressive stages and is, therefore, the unsurpassed one. Its aim is the direct realisation leading to the perception of the self-nature and attainment of Buddhahood. Therefore, it has nothing to do with the sitting or not sitting in meditation during a Chan week. However, on account of living beings' dull roots and due to their numerous false thoughts, ancient masters devised expediences to guide them. Since the time of Mahakasyapa up to now, there have been sixty to seventy generations. In the Tang and Song Dynasties [619–1278], the Chan sect spread to every part of the country and how it prospered at the time! At present, it has reached the bottom of its decadence and only those monasteries like Jin-shan, Gao-min and Bao-guan, can still manage to present some appearance. This is why men of outstanding ability are now so rarely found and even the holding of Chan weeks has only a name but lacks its spirit.

When the Seventh Ancestor[3] Xing-si of Qing-yuan Mountain asked the Sixth Patriarch: 'What should one do in order not to fall into the progressive stages?'[4] the Patriarch asked: 'What did you practise of late?' Xing-si replied: 'I did not even practise the Noble

Truths.[5] The Patriarch asked: 'Then falling into what progressive stages?' Xing-si replied: 'Even the Noble Truths are not practised, where are the progressive stages?' The Sixth Patriarch had a high opinion of Xing-si.

Because of our inferior roots, the great Masters were obliged to use expediencies and to instruct their followers to hold and examine into a sentence called *hua-tou*. As Buddhists of the Pure Land School who used to repeat the Buddha's name in their practice were numerous the great Masters instructed them to hold and examine into the *hua-tou*: 'Who is the repeater of the Buddha's name?' Nowadays, this expedient is adopted in Chan training all over the country. However, many are not clear about it and merely repeat without interruption the sentence: 'Who is the repeater of the Buddha's name?' Thus they are repeaters of the *hua-tou*, and are not investigators of the *hua-tou's* meaning. To investigate is to inquire into. For this reason, the four Chinese characters *zhao gu hua-tou* are prominently exhibited in all Chan halls. '*Zhao*' is to turn inward the light, and *gu* is to care for. These (two characters together) mean 'to turn inward the light on the self-nature'. This is to turn inward our minds which are prone to wander outside, and this is called investigation of the *hua-tou*. 'Who is the repeater of the Buddha's name?' is a sentence. Before this sentence is uttered, it is called *hua-tou* [lit. sentence's head]. As soon as it is uttered it becomes the sentence's tail *(hua-wei)*. In our inquiry into the *hua-tou*, this word 'who' should be examined: What is it before it arises? For instance, I am repeating the Buddha's name in this hall. Suddenly someone asks me: 'Who is repeating the Buddha's name?' I reply: 'It is I.' The questioner asks again: 'If you are the repeater of the Buddha's name, do you repeat it with your mouth or with your mind? If you repeat it with your mouth, why don't you repeat it when you sleep? If you repeat it with your mind, why don't you repeat it after your death?' This question will cause a doubt to arise in your minds and it is here that we should inquire into this doubt. We should endeavour to know where this 'Who' comes from and what it looks like. Our minute examination should be turned inward and this is also called 'the turning inward of the hearing to hear the self-nature'.

When offering incense and circumnambulating in the hall, one's neck should touch the back of the wide collar of the robe, one's feet should follow closely the preceding walker, one's mind should be set at rest and one should not look to the right or to the left. With a single mind, the *hua-tou* should be well cared for.

When sitting in meditation, the chest should be pushed forward. The *prana* (vital energy) should neither be brought upward nor pressed down, and should be left in its natural condition. However, the six sense organs should be brought under control, and all thoughts should be brought to an end. Only the *hua-tou* should be gripped and the grip should never loosen. The *hua-tou* should not be coarse for it will float up and cannot be brought down. Neither should it be fine, for it will become blurred with the resultant fall into the void. In both cases, no result can be achieved.

If the *hua-tou* is properly looked after, the training will become easier and all former habits will be brought automatically to an end. A beginner will not find it easy to hold the *hua-tou* well in his mind, but he should not worry about it. He should neither hope for awakening nor seek wisdom, for the purpose of this sitting in meditation in the Chan week is already the attainment of awakening and wisdom. If he develops a mind in pursuit of these ends, he puts another head upon his own head.[6]

Now we know that we should give rise only to a sentence called *hua-tou* which we should care for. If thoughts arise, let them rise and if we disregard them, they will vanish. This is why it is said: 'One should not be afraid of rising thoughts but only of the delay in being aware of them.' If thoughts arise, let our awareness of them nail the *hua-tou* to them. If the *hua-tou* escapes from our grip, we should immediately bring it back again.

The first sitting in meditation can be likened to a battle against rising thoughts. Gradually the *hua-tou* will be well gripped and it will be easy to hold it uninterruptedly during the whole time an incense stick takes to burn.[7] We can expect good results when it does not escape from our grip any more.

The foregoing are only empty words; now let us exert our efforts in the training.

The Second Day

To sit in meditation during a Chan week is the best method which sets a time limit for realising the truth by personal experience. This method was not used in ancient times for the ancients had sharp roots (and did not require it). It has gradually been put into use since the Song Dynasty [fell in 1278]. In the Qing Dynasty [1622–1910], it was brought into vogue and the Emperor Yong Cheng used to hold frequent Chan weeks in the imperial palace. He entertained the highest regard for the Sect and his attainment of Chan *samadhi* was excellent. Over ten persons realised the truth under the imperial auspices and Master Tian Hui-che of the Gao-min monastery at Yangzhou attained enlightenment during these meetings in the palace. The emperor also revised and improved for observance the rules and regulations of the Sect, which flourished and produced so many men of ability. The strict observance of rules and regulations is, therefore, of paramount importance.

This method of setting a time-limit for personal experience of the truth is likened to a scholars' examination. The candidates sit for it and write their compositions according to the subjects, for each of which a time-limit is set. The subject of our Chan week is Chan meditation. For this reason, this hall is called the Chan hall. Chan is *dhyana* in Sanskrit and means 'unperturbed abstraction'. There are various kinds of Chan, such as the Mahayana and Hinayana Chans, the material and immaterial Chans, the Sravakas' and the Heretics' Chan. Ours is the unsurpassed Chan. If one succeeds in seeing through the doubt (mentioned yesterday) and sitting on and cracking the life-root,[8] one will be similar to the Tathagata.

For this reason, a Chan hall is also called a Buddha's selecting place. It is called a Prajna hall. The Dharma taught in this hall is the Wu Wei Dharma[9]. Wu Wei means 'not doing'. In other words, not a single thing can be gained and not a single thing can be done. If there be doing *(samskrta)*,[10] it will produce birth and death. If there is gain, there will be loss. For this reason, the sutra says: 'There are only words and expressions which have no real meaning.' The recitation of sutras and the holding of confessional services pertain to doing *(samskrta)* and are only expediencies used in the teaching school.

As to our Sect, its teaching consists in the direct self-cognisance for which words and expressions have no room. Formerly, a student called on the old Master Nan-quan and asked him: 'What is Dao?' Nan-quan replied: 'The ordinary mind[11] is the truth.' Every day, we wear robes and eat rice; we go out to work and return to rest; all our actions are performed according to the truth.[12] It is because we bind ourselves in every situation that we fail to realise that the self-mind is Buddha.

When Chan-Master Fa-chang of Da-mei Mountain called for the first time on Ma-zu, he asked the latter: 'What is Buddha?' Ma-zu replied: 'Mind is Buddha.' Thereupon, Da-mei[13] was completely enlightened. He left Ma-zu and proceeded to the Si-ming district, where he lived in a hermitage formerly belonging to Mei Zu-zhen.

In the Zhen-yuan reign [785–804] of the Tang Dynasty, a monk who was a disciple of Yan-guan and went to the mountain to collect branches of trees for making staffs, lost his way and arrived at the hut. He asked Da-mei: 'How long have you stayed here?' Dai-mei replied: 'I see only four mountains which are blue and yellow.'[14] The monk said: 'Please show me the mountain track so that I can get out of here.' Da-mei replied: 'Follow the stream.'[15]

Upon his return the monk reported what he saw in the mountain to Yan-guan, who said: 'I once saw a monk in Jiangxi province but I have had no news of him since. It is not that monk?'

Then Yan-guan sent the monk to the mountain to invite Da-mei to come to his place. In reply, Da-mei sent the following poem:

> A withered log in the cold forest
> Does not change heart for several springs,
> The woodcutter will not look at it.
> How can a stranger hunt it?
> A lotus pond yields boundless store of clothing:
> More fir cones drop from pines than you can eat.
> When worldly men discover where you live
> You move your thatched hut far into the hills.[16]

Ma-zu heard of Da-mei's stay on the mountain and sent a monk to ask him this question: 'What did you obtain when you called on the great Master Ma-zu and what prompted you to stay here?' Da-mei replied: 'The great Master told me that mind was Buddha and that is why I came to stay here.' The monk said: 'The great Master's Buddha Dharma is different now.' Da-mei asked: 'What is it now?' The monk replied: 'He says it is neither mind nor Buddha.'[17] Da-mei said: 'The old man is causing confusion in the minds of others and all this will have no end. Let him say that it is neither mind nor Buddha. As far as I am concerned, Mind is Buddha.'

When the monk returned and reported the above dialogue to Ma-zu the latter said: 'The plum is now ripe.'[18]

This shows how the ancients were competent and concise.

Because of our inferior roots and perverted thinking, the Masters taught us to hold a *hua-tou* in our minds and they were obliged to use this expedient. Master Yong-jia said: 'After the elimination of the ego and Dharma, the attainment of reality will destroy the *Avici* hell in a moment *(ksana)*. If I tell a lie to deceive living beings, I will consent to fall into the hell where the tongue is pulled out (as punishment for my verbal sin).'[19]

Master Yuan-miao of Gao-feng said: 'Chan training is like throwing into a deep pond a tile which sinks to the bottom.' When we hold a *hua-tou*, we must look into into it until we reach its 'bottom' and 'crack' it. Master Yuan-miao also swore: 'If someone holding a *hua-tou* without giving rise to a second thought, fails to realise the truth, I will be ready to fall into the hell where the tongue is pulled out.' The sole reason why we do not succeed in our practice is because our faith in the *hua-tou* is not deep enough and because we do not put an end to our wrong thinking. If we are firmly determined to escape from the round of births and deaths, a sentence of the *hua-tou* will never escape from our grip. Master Gui-shan said: 'If in every reincarnation we can hold it firmly without backsliding, the Buddha stage can be expected.'

All beginners are inclined to give rise to all kinds of false thoughts; they have a pain in the legs and do not know how to undergo the training. The truth is that they should be firm in their determination to escape from the round of births and deaths. They should stick to the *hua-tou* and no matter whether they walk, stand, sit or lie, they should grasp it. From morning to evening, they should look into this word 'Who' until it becomes as clear as 'the autumn moon reflected in a limpid pool'. It should be clearly and closely inquired into and should be neither blurred nor unsteady. If this can be achieved why worry about the Buddha stage which seems unattainable?

If the *hua-tou* becomes blurred, you can open your eyes wide and raise your chest gently; this will raise your spirits. At the same time, it should not be held too loosely, nor should it be too fine, because if it is too fine, it will cause a fall into emptiness and dullness. If you fall into emptiness, you will perceive only stillness and will experience liveliness. At this moment, the *hua-tou* should not be allowed to escape from your grip so that you can take a step forward after you have reached 'the top of the pole'.[20] Otherwise, you will fall into dull emptiness and will never attain the ultimate.

If it is loosely gripped, you will be easily assailed by false thoughts. If false thoughts arise, they will be difficult to suppress.

Therefore, coarseness should be tempered with fineness and fineness with coarseness to succeed in the training and to realise the sameness of the mutable and immutable.

Formerly I was at Jin-shan and other monasteries and when the Karmadana[21] received the incense sticks which he had ordered previously, his two feet ran[22] with great speed as if he flew in the air and the monks who followed him were also good runners. As soon as the signal was given, all of them looked like automata. Thus how could wrong thoughts arise in their minds? At present although we also walk after sitting in meditation, what a great difference there is between then and now!

When you sit in meditation, you should not push up the *hua-tou* for this will cause its dimness. You should not hold it in your chest for it causes pain in the chest. Neither should you press it down, for it will expand the belly and will cause your fall into the realm of the five aggregates *(skandhas)*[23] resulting in all kinds of defect. With serenity and self-possession, only the word 'Who' should be looked into with the same care with which a hen sits on her egg and a cat pounces on a mouse. When the *hua-tou* is efficiently held, the life-root will automatically be cut off.

This method is obviously not an easy one for beginners, but you must exert yourselves unceasingly. Now I give you an example. Self-cultivation is likened to making fire with a piece of flint. We must know the method of producing a fire and if we do not know it, we will never light a fire even if we break the flint in pieces. The method consists in using a bit of tinder and a steel. The tinder is held under the flint and the steel strikes the upper part of the flint so as to direct the spark to the tinder which will catch it. This is the only method of starting a fire with a flint.

Although we know quite well that Mind is Buddha, we are still unable to accept this as a fact. For this reason, a sentence of the *hua-tou* has been used as the fire-starting-steel. It was just the same when formerly the World-Honoured One became thoroughly enlightened after gazing at the stars at night. We are not clear about the self-nature because we do not know how to start a fire. Our fundamental self-nature and the Buddha do not differ from each other. It is only because of our perverted thinking that we are still not liberated. So the Buddha is still Buddha and we are still ourselves. Now as we know the method, if we could inquire into it, it would indeed be an unsurpassing co-operating cause! I hope that everyone here will, by exerting himself, take a step forward from the top of a hundred-foot pole and will be elected Buddha in this hall so that he can pay the debt of gratitude he owes to the Buddha high above and deliver living beings here below. If the Buddha Dharma does not produce men of ability, it is because no one is willing to exert himself. Our heart is full of sadness when we talk about this situation. If we really have deep faith in the words uttered under oath by Masters Yong-jia and Yuan-miao, we are sure we will also realise the truth. Now is the time to exert yourselves!

The Third Day

Time passes quickly indeed; we have only just opened this Chan week and it is already the third day. Those who have efficiently held the *hua-tou* in their minds have been able to clear up their passions and wrong thoughts; they can now go straight home.[24] For this reason, an ancient Master said:

> Self-cultivation has no other method;
> It requires but knowledge of the way.
> If the way only can be known,
> Birth and death at once will end.

Our way consists in laying down our baggage[25] and our home is very near. The Sixth Patriarch said: 'If the preceding thought does not arise, it is mind. If the following thought does not end, it is Buddha.[26]

Fundamentally, our four elements are void and the five aggregates *(skandhas)* are non-existent. It is only because of our wrong thoughts which grasp everything that we like the illusion of the impermanent world and are thereby held in bondage. Consequently, we are unable to perceive the voidness of the four elements and to realise the non-existence of birth and death. However, if in a single thought, we can have an experience of that which is not born, there will be no need for those Dharma doors expounded by Sakyamuni Buddha. If so can it still be said that birth and death cannot be brought to an end? On that account, the brightness of our Sect's Dharma really illumines the boundless space in the ten directions.

Master De-shan was a native of Jianzhou town in Sichuan. His lay surname was Zhou. He left home at the age of 20. After being fully ordained, he studied the *Vinaya-pitaka*[27] which he mastered. He was well-versed in the teaching of the noumenal and phenomenal as expounded in the sutras. He used to teach the Diamond Prajna and was called 'Diamond Zhou'.

Said he to his schoolmates:

> When a hair swallows the ocean[28]
> The nature-ocean[29] loses naught.
> To hit a needle's point with mustard seed
> Shakes not the needle's point.[30]
> Of *saiksa* and *asaiksa*[31]
> I know and I alone.

When he heard that the Chan Sect was flourishing in the South, he could not keep his temper and said: 'All who leave home take a thousand aeons to learn the Buddha's respect-inspiring deportment[32] and ten thousand aeons to study the Buddha's fine deeds; in spite of this they are still unable to attain Buddhahood. How can those demons in the south dare to say that the direct indication of the mind leads to the perception of the self-nature and attainment of Buddhahood? I must go to the south, sweep away their den and destroy their race to repay the debt of gratitude I owe the Buddha.'

He left Sichuan province with Qing-long's Commentary[33] on his shoulders. When he reached Li-yang, he saw an old woman selling dian-xin (lit. mind-refreshment)[34] on the roadside. He halted, laid down his load and intended to buy some pastries to refresh his mind. The old woman pointed at the load and asked him: 'What is this literature?' De-shan replied: 'Qing-long's Commentary.' The old woman asked: 'Commentary on what sutra?' De-shan replied: 'On the *Diamond Sutra*.' The old woman said: 'I have a question to ask you; if you can answer it, I will offer you mind refreshment. If you cannot reply, please go away. The *Diamond Sutra* says: "The past, present and future mind cannot be found." What do you want to refresh?'

De-shan remained speechless. He left the place and went to the Dragon Pond (Long-tan) Monastery. He entered the Dharma hall and said: 'I have long desired to see the Dragon Pond, but as I arrive here, neither is the pond seen nor does the dragon appear.' Hearing this, Master Long-tan came out and said: 'You have really arrived at the Dragon Pond.[35] De-shan remained speechless; he then made up his mind to stay at the monastery.

One night, while he was standing as an attendant by Long-tan, the latter said to him: 'It is late now, why don't you go back to your quarters?' After wishing his master good night, he withdrew but returned and said: 'It is very dark outside.' Long-tan lit a paper-torch and handed it to him. When De-shan was about to take the torch, Long-tan blew out the light.[36]

Thereupon De-shan was completely enlightened and made his obeisance to the Master to thank him. De-shan asked him: 'What have you seen?' De-shan replied: 'In future, I will entertain no more doubt about the tips of the tongues of the old monks all over the country.'[37]

The following day, Long-tan ascended to his seat and said to the assembly: 'There is a fellow whose teeth are like sword-leaf trees and whose mouth is like a blood bath.[38] He receives a stroke of the staff but does not turn his head.[39] Later, he will set up my doctrine on the top of a solitary peak.'[40]

In front of the Dharma hall De-shan laid on the ground all the sheets of the Qing-long Commentary in a heap and raising a torch said: 'An exhaustive discussion of the abstruse is like a hair placed in the great void and the exertion to the full of all human capabilities is like a drop of water poured into the great ocean.' Then he burned the manuscript. He bade farewell to his master and left the monastery.

He went straight to Gui-shan Monastery and, carrying his baggage under his arm, he entered the Dharma hall which he crossed from its east to its west side and then from its west to its east side. He looked at the Abbot (Master Gui-shan) and said: 'Any-thing? Anything?' Gui-shan was sitting in the hall but paid no attention to the visitor. De-shan said: 'Nothing, nothing,' and left the hall.[41]

When he reached the front door of the monastery, he said to himself: 'Be that as it may, I should not be so careless.' Then, he turned back and again entered the hall in full ceremony. As he crossed its threshold, he took out and raised his cloth rug (nisi-

dana),[42] calling: 'Venerable Upadhyaya![43] As Gui-shan was about to pick up a dust-whisk,[44] De-shan shouted[45] and left the hall.

That evening, Gui-shan asked the leader of the assembly: 'Is the newcomer still here?' The leader replied: 'When he left the hall, he turned his back to it, put on his straw sandals and went away.' Gui-shan said: 'That man will later go to some lonely peak where he will erect a thatched hut; he will scold Buddhas and curse Patriarchs.'[47]

De-shan stayed thirty years at Li-yang. During the persecution of Buddhists by the Emperor Wu-zong (841–8) of the Tang Dynasty, the Master took refuge in a stone hut on the Du-fou mountain (in 847). At the beginning of Da-zhong's reign, Prefect Xie-ting Wang of Wu Ling restored the veneration of De-shan monastery and named it Ge-de Hall. He was looking for a man of outstanding ability to take charge of the monastery when he heard of the Master's reputation. In spite of several invitations, De-shan refused to descend the (Du-fou) mountain. Finally, the Prefect devised a stratagem and sent his men falsely to accuse him of smuggling tea and salt in defiance of the law. When the Master was brought to the prefecture, the Prefect paid obeisance to him and insistently invited him to take charge of the Chan hall where De-shan eventually spread widely the Sect's teaching.

Later, people talked about De-shan's shouting and Lin-ji's[48] caning. If we can discipline ourselves like these two Masters, why should we be unable to put an end to birth and death? After De-shan came Yan-tou and Xue-feng. After Xue-feng, came Yun-men and Fa-yan[49] and also State Master De-shao and ancestor Yan-shou of the Yong-Ming (monastery). They were all 'produced' by (De-shan's) staff.

During the past successive dynasties, the Sect was kept going by great ancestors and Masters. You are here to hold a Chan week and you understand very well this unsurpassed doctrine which will enable us without difficulty to attain direct self-cognisance and liberation from birth and death. However, if you trifle with it and do not train seriously, or if from morning to evening, you like to behold the 'demon in the bright shadow' or to make your plans inside 'the den of words and expressions', you will never escape from birth and death.[50] Now, all of you, please exert yourselves diligently.

The Fourth Day

This is the fourth day of our Chan week. You have exerted

yourselves in your training; some of you have composed poems and *gathas* and have presented them to me for verification. This is not an easy thing but those of you who have made efforts in this manner must have forgotten my two previous lectures. Yesterday evening, I said:

> Self-cultivation has no other method;
> It requires but knowledge of the way.

We are here to inquire into the *hua-tou* which is the way we should follow. Our purpose is to be clear about birth and death and to attain Buddhahood. In order to be clear about birth and death, we must have recourse to this *hua-tou* which should be used as the Vajra King's[51] precious sword to cut down demons if demons come and Buddhas if Buddhas come[52] so that no feelings will remain and not a single thing (Dharma) can be set up. In such a manner, where could there have been wrong thinking about writing poems and *gathas* and seeing such states as voidness and brightness?[53] If you made your efforts so wrongly, I really do not know where your *hua-tou* went. Experienced Chan monks do not require further talks about this, but beginners should be very careful.

As I was apprehensive that you might not know how to undergo your training, I talked during the last two days about the purpose of sitting in meditation in a Chan week, the worthiness of this method devised by our Sect and the way of making efforts. Our method consists in concentrating pointedly on a *hua-tou* which should not be interrupted by day or night in the same way as running water. It should be spirited and clear and should never be blurred. It should be clearly and constantly cognisable. All worldly feelings and holy interpretations should be cut down by it. An ancient Master said:

> Study the truth as you would defend a citadel
> Which, when besieged, at all costs must be held.
> If intense cold strikes not to the bone,
> How can plum blossom fragrant be?

These four lines came from Master Huang-bo and have two meanings. The first two illustrate those who undergo the Chan training and who should hold firm the *hua-tou* in the same manner as the defence of a citadel which no foe must be allowed to enter. This is the unyielding defence of the citadel. Each of us has a mind which is the eighth consciousness *(vijnana)*, as well as the seventh, sixth and the first five consciousnesses. The first five are the five thieves of the eye, ear, nose, tongue and body. The sixth consciousness is the thief of mind *(manas)*. The seventh is the deceptive consciousness *(klista-mano-vijnana)* which from morning to evening grasps the eighth consciousness, 'subject' and mistakes it for an 'ego'. It incites the sixth to lead the first five consciousnesses to seek external objects such as form, sound, smell, taste and touch. Being constantly deceived and tied the eighth consciousness-mind is held in bondage without being able to free itself. For this reason we are obliged to have recourse to this *hua-tou* and use its 'Vajra King's Precious Sword' to kill all these thieves so that the eighth consciousness can be transmuted into the Great Mirror Wisdom, the seventh into the Wisdom of Equality, the sixth into the Profound Observing Wisdom and the first five consciousnesses into the Perfecting Wisdom.[54] It is of paramount importance first to transmute the sixth and seventh consciousnesses, for they play the leading role and because of their power in discriminating and discerning. While you were seeing the voidness and the brightness and composing poems and *gathas*, these two consciousnesses performed their evil functions. Today, we should use this *hua-tou* to transmute the discriminating consciousness into the Profound Observing Wisdom and the mind which differentiates between ego and personality into the Wisdom of Equality. This is called the transmutation of consciousness into wisdom and the transformation of the worldly into the saintly. It is important not to allow these thieves who are fond of form, sound, smell, taste, touch and dharma, to attack us. Therefore, this is likened to the defence of a citadel.

The last two lines:

> If intense cold strikes not to the bone
> How can plum blossom fragrant be?

illustrate living beings in the three worlds of existence[55] who are engulfed in the ocean of birth and death, tied to the five desires,[56] deceived by their passion, and unable to obtain liberation. Hence

169

the plum blossom is used as an illustration, for these plum trees spring into blossom in snowy weather. In general, insects and plants are born in the spring, grow in summer, remain stationary in autumn and lie dormant in winter. In winter, insects and plants either die or lie dormant. The snow also lays the dust which is cold and cannot rise in the air. These insects, plants and dust are likened to our mind's wrong thinking, discerning, ignorance, envy and jealousy resulting from contamination with the three poisons.[57] If we rid ourselves of these impurities, our minds will be naturally comfortable and plum blossom will be fragrant in the snow. But you should know that these plum trees blossom in the bitter cold and not in the lovely bright spring or in the mild breeze of charming weather. If we want our mind-flowers to bloom, we cannot expect this flowering in the midst of pleasure, anger, sorrow and joy or when we hold the conception of ego, personality, right and wrong. If we are confused about these eight kinds of mind, the result will be unrecordable.[58] If evil actions are committed, the result will be evil. If good actions are performed, the results will be good.

There are two kinds of unrecordable nature; that of dreams and of dead emptiness. The unrecordable nature of dreams is that of illusory things appearing in a dream and unconnected with usually well-known daily activities. This is the state of independent mind-consciousnesses *(mano-vijnana)*.[59] This is also called an independent unrecordable state.

What is unrecordable dead emptiness? In our meditation, if we lose sight of the *hua-tou*, while dwelling in stillness, there results an indistinctive voidness wherein there is nothing. The clinging to this state of stillness is a Chan illness which we should never contract while undergoing our training. This is the unrecordable dead emptiness.

What we have to do is throughout the day to hold without loosening our grip the *hua-tou*, which should be lively, bright, undimmed and clearly and constantly cognisable. Such a condition should obtain no matter whether we walk or sit. For this reason, an ancient Master said:

'When walking, naught but Chan; when sitting, naught but Chan.
Then the body is at peace whether or no one talks or moves.'

Ancestor Han-shan said:

High on a mountain peak
Only boundless space is seen.
How to sit in meditation, no one knows.
The solitary moon shines o'er the icy pool,
But in the pool there is no moon;
The moon is in the night-blue sky.
This song is chanted now,
But there's no Chan in the song.

You and I must have a co-operating cause, which is why I have this opportunity of addressing you on the Chan training. I hope you will exert yourselves and make steady progress, and will not wrongly apply your minds.

I will tell you another story, a *gong-an* (or *koan* in Japanese). After the founder of the Xi-tan (*Siddham* in Sanskrit) Monastery on the Cock's Foot (Ji-zu) mountain had left home, he called on Enlightened Masters for instruction and made very good progress in his training. One day, he stopped at an inn, and heard a girl in a bean-curd shop singing this song:

Bean-curd Zhang and Bean-curd Li![60]
While your heads rest on the pillow,
You think a thousand thoughts,
Yet tomorrow you will sell bean-curd again.

The master was sitting in meditation and upon hearing this song, he was instantaneously awakened.[61] This shows that when the ancients underwent the training, there was no necessity of doing it in a Chan hall for experiencing the truth. The self-cultivation and training lie in the One-Mind. So, all of you, please don't allow your minds to be disturbed in order not to waste your time. Otherwise, you will be selling bean-curd again tomorrow morning.[62]

The Fifth Day

About this method of self-cultivation, it can be said that it is both easy and difficult. It is easy because it is really easy and it is difficult because it is really difficult.

It is easy because you are only required to lay down every

thought, to have a firm faith in it [the method] and to develop a lasting mind. All this will ensure your success.

It is difficult because you are afraid of enduring hardships and because of your desire to be at ease. You should know all worldly occupations also require study and training before success can be achieved. How much more so when we want to learn wisdom from the sages in order to become Buddhas and Patriarchs. Can we reach our goal if we act carelessly?

Therefore, the first thing is to have a firm mind in our self-cultivation and performance of the truth. In this, we cannot avoid being obstructed by demons. These demoniacal obstructions are the external karmic surroundings caused by our passions for all form, sound, smell, taste, touch and dharma as enumerated in my talk yesterday. This karmic environment is our foe through life and death. For this reason, there are many sutra-expounding Dharma-Masters who cannot stand firm on their own feet while in the midst of these surroundings because of their wavering religious mind.[63]

The next important thing is to develop an enduring mind. Since our birth in this world, we have created boundless karmas and if we now wish to cultivate ourselves for the purpose of escaping from birth and death, can we wipe out our former habits all at once? In olden times, ancestors such as Chan Master Chang-qing, who sat in meditation until he had worn out seven mats, and Chan Master Chao-zhou who wandered from place to place soliciting instruction at the age of 80 after having spent forty years in meditating on the word 'Wu' (lit. No) without giving rise to a thought in his mind. They finally obtained complete enlightenment, and the princes of the Yan and Zhao states revered them and made offerings to them. In the Qing Dynasty, Emperor Yong-Zheng (1723–35) who had read their sayings and had found these excellent, bestowed upon them the posthumous title of 'Ancient Buddha'. This is the resultant attainment after a whole life of austerity. If we can now wipe out all our former habits to purify our One-thought, we will be on an equality with Buddhas and Patriarchs. The *Surangama Sutra* says:

It is like the purification of muddy water stored in a clean container; left unshaken in complete calmness, the sand and mud will sink to the bottom. When the clear water appears, this is called the first suppression of the intruding evil element of passion.[64] When the mud has been removed leaving behind only the clear water, this is called the permanent cutting off of basic ignorance.[65]

Our habitual passions are likened to mud and sediment, which is why we must make use of the *hua-tou*. The *hua-tou* is likened to alum used to clarify muddy water in the same manner as passions are brought under control. If in his training, a man succeeds in achieving the sameness of body and mind with the resultant appearance of the condition of stillness, he should be careful and should never abide in it. He should know that it is only an initial step but that ignorance caused by passions is still not wiped out. This is only the deluded mind reaching the state of purity, just like muddy water which, although purified, still contains mud and sediment at the bottom. You must make additional efforts to advance further. An ancient Master said:

> Sitting on a pole top one hundred feet in height[66]
> One will still perceive that which is not real.
> If from the pole top one then takes a step
> One's body will appear throughout the Universe.

If you do not take a step forward, you will take the illusion-city for your home and your passions will be able to rise again. If so, it will be difficult for you to become even a self-enlightened person.[67] For this reason, the mud must be removed in order to retain the clear water. This is the permanent wiping out of the basic ignorance and only then can Buddhahood be attained. When ignorance has been permanently wiped out, you will be able to appear in bodily form in the ten directions of the Universe to expound the Dharma, in the same manner as Avalokitesvara Bodhisattva, who can appear in thirty-two forms and who, in manifesting to teach the Dharma, can choose the most appropriate form to liberate a responsive living being. You will be free from restraint and will enjoy independence and comfort everywhere, even in a house of prostitution, a public bar, the womb of a cow, a mare or a mule, in paradise or hell.

On the other hand, a discriminating thought will send you down to the turning wheel of births and deaths. Formerly, Qin-guai,[68] who had in a former life made offerings of incense and candles to

Ksitigarbha Bodhisattva but did not develop an enduring mind in his training because of his failure to wipe out his ignorance caused by passions, was the victim of his hatred-mind in his following reincarnation. This is just an example.

If your believing-mind is strong and your enduring-mind does not retrograde, you will, in your present bodily form, be able to attain Buddhahood, even if you are only an ordinary man.

Formerly there was a poor and miserable man who joined the order *(sangha)* at a monastery. Although he was keen to practise self-cultivation, he did not know the method. As he did not know whom to ask about it, he decided to toil and moil every day. One day, a wandering monk came to the monastery and saw the man toiling. The monk asked him about his practice and the man replied: 'Every day, I do this kind of hard work. Please show me that method of self-cultivation.' The monk replied: 'You should inquire into the sentence: "Who is the repeater of Buddha's name?"' As instructed by the visiting monk, the man managed to bear the word 'Who' in mind while he did his daily work. Later, he went to stay in a grotto on an islet to continue his training, using leaves for clothing and plants for food. His mother and sister who were still living, heard of his retreat in a grotto on an islet where he endured hardships in his self-cultivation. His mother sent his sister to take him a roll of cloth and some provisions. When she arrived, she saw him seated in meditation. She called him but he did not reply, and she shook him but he did not move. Seeing that her brother neither looked at nor greeted her but continued his meditation in the grotto, she was enraged, left the roll of cloth and provisions there and returned home. Thirteen years later, his sister went again to visit him and saw the same roll of cloth still lying in the same place.

Later a hungry refugee came to the grotto wherein he saw a monk in ragged garments; he entered and begged for food. The monk got up and went to the side of the grotto to pick some pebbles, which he placed in a pot. After cooking them for a while, he took them out and invited the visitor to eat them with him. The pebbles looked like potatoes and when the visitor had satisfied his hunger, the monk said to him: 'Please do not mention our meal to outsiders'.

Some time later, the monk thought to himself: 'I have stayed here so many years for my self-cultivation and should now form propitious causes for the welfare of others.' Thereupon, he proceeded to Xiamen,[69] where, on the side of a road, he built a thatched hut offering free tea to travellers. This took place in Wanli's reign (1573–1619) about the time the Empress mother passed away. The Emperor wanted to invite eminent monks to perform Buddhist ceremonies for the welfare of his deceased mother. He first intended to invite monks in the capital but at the time, there were no eminent monks there. One night the Emperor saw in a dream his mother, who said that there was one in the Zhang-zhou prefecture of Fujian province. The Emperor sent officials there to invite local monks to come to the capital for the ceremonies. When these monks with their bundles set out on their journey to the capital, they passed by the hut of the poor monk, who asked them: 'Venerable Masters, what makes you so happy and where are you going?' They replied: 'We have received the Emperor's order to proceed to the capital to perform ceremonies for the spirit of the Empress mother.' The poor monk said: 'May I go with you?' They replied: 'You are so miserable, how can you go with us?' He said: 'I do not know how to recite sutras but I can carry your bundles for you. It is worth while to pay a visit to the capital.' Thereupon, he picked up the bundles and followed the other monks to the capital.

When the Emperor knew that the monks were about to arrive, he ordered an official to bury a copy of the *Diamond Sutra* under the doorstep of the palace. When the monks arrived, they did not know anything about the sutra, crossed the doorstep and entered the palace one after another. When the miserable monk reached the threshold, he knelt upon his knees and brought his palms together but did not enter the palace. In spite of the door-keepers who called him and tried to drag him in, he refused to enter. When the incident was reported to the Emperor, who had ordered the burial of the sutra, he realised that the holy monk had arrived and came personally to receive him. He said: 'Why don't you enter the palace?' The monk replied: 'I dare not, because a copy of the *Diamond Sutra* has been buried in the ground.' The Emperor said: 'Why don't you stand on your head to enter it?' Upon hearing this, the monk placed his hands upon the ground and somersaulted into the palace. The Emperor had the greatest respect for him and invited him to stay in the inner palace.

When asked about the altar and the ceremony, the monk replied: 'The ceremony will be held tomorrow morning, in the fifth watch of the night. I will require only one altar with one leading[70] banner and one table with incense, candles and fruit for offerings to Buddha.' The Emperor was not pleased with the prospect of an unimpressive ceremony and was at the same time apprehensive that the monk might not possess enough virtue to perform it. To test his virtue, he ordered two maids of honour to bathe the monk. During and after the bath, his genital organ remained unmoved. The maids of honour reported this to the Emperor, whose respect for the monk grew the greater for he realised now that the visitor was really holy. Preparation was then made according to the monk's instruction and the following morning, the monk ascended to his seat to expound the Dharma. Then he ascended to the altar, joined his palms together to salute and, holding the banner, went to the coffin, saying:

> In reality I do not come;
> But in your likes you are one-sided.
> In one thought to realise there is no birth
> Means that you will leap o'er the *deva* realms.

After the ceremony, the monk said the the Emperor: 'I congratulate you on the liberation of Her Majesty the Empress Mother.' As the Emperor was doubting the efficiency of a ceremony which ended in such a manner, he heard in the room the voice of the deceased saying: 'I am now liberated; you should bow your thanks to the holy master.'

The Emperor was taken aback, and his face beamed with delight. He paid obeisance to the monk and thanked him. In the inner palace, a vegetarian banquet was offered to the Master. Seeing that the Emperor was wearing a pair of coloured trousers, the monk fixed his eyes on them. The Emperor asked him: 'Does the Virtuous One like this pair of trousers?' and taking them off he offered them to the visitor, who said: 'Thank your Majesty for his grace.' Thereupon, the Emperor bestowed upon the monk the title of State Master Dragon Trousers. After the banquet, the Emperor led the monk to the imperial garden, where there was a precious stupa. The monk was happy at the sight of the stupa and stopped to admire it. The Emperor asked 'Does the State Master like this stupa?' The visitor replied: 'It is wonderful!' The Emperor said: 'I am willing to offer it to you with reverence.' As the host was giving orders to remove the stupa to Chang Chou, the monk said: 'There is no need, I can take it away.' After saying this, the monk placed the stupa in his long sleeve, rose in the air and left. The Emperor, stunned and overjoyed at the same time, praised the unprecedented occurrence.

Dear friends, it is a wonderful story indeed and it all came about simply because from the time he left his home, the monk never used his discriminating mind and had a lasting faith in the truth. He did not care for his sister who came to see him, paid no attention to his ragged garments, and did not touch the roll of cloth lying thirteen years in the grotto. We must now ask ourselves if we can undergo our training in such a manner. It would be superfluous to talk about our inability to follow the monk's example when our sisters come to see us. It is enough to mention the attitude we take after our meditation when, while walking, we cannot refrain from gazing at our leader when he offers incense or at our neighbour's movements. If our training is done in this manner, how can our *hua-tou* be firmly held?

Dear friends, you have only to remove the mud and retain the water. When the water is clear, automatically the moon will appear. Now it is time to give rise to your *hua-tou* and to examine it closely.[71]

The Sixth Day

The ancients said: 'Days and months pass quickly like a shuttle and time flies like an arrow.' Our Chan week began only the other day and will come to an end tomorrow. According to the standing rule, an examination will be held tomorrow morning, for the purpose of a Chan week is to set a time-limit for experiencing the truth. By experiencing, it means awakening to and realisation of the truth. That is to say, the experiencing of one's fundamental self and the realisation of the Tathagata's profound nature. This is called the experiencing and realisation of the truth.

Your examination is for the purpose of ascertaining the extent to which you have reached attainment during these seven days and you will have to disclose your achievement to the assembly. Usually this examination is called the collection of the bill of fare[72] from all of you. This means that you must all appear for this examination. In other words, all of you must be awakened to the truth so that you can expound the Buddha Dharma for the liberation of all the living. Today, I am not saying I expect that you must all be awakened to the truth. If even one of you is awakened, I can still collect this bill of fare. That is to say, one person will pay the bill for the meals served to the whole assembly. If all of us develop a skilful and progressive mind in quest of the truth, we will all be awakened to it. The ancients said:

> It is easy for a worldly man to win Buddahood,
> But hard indeed is it to bring wrong thinking to an end.

It is only because of our insatiable desires since the time without beginning that we now drift about in the sea of mortality, within which there are 84,000 passions and all sorts of habits which we cannot wipe out. In consequence, we are unable to attain the truth and to be like Buddhas and Bodhisattvas who are permanently enlightened and are free from delusion. For this reason, Master Lian-chi said:

> It is easy to be caught up in the causes of pollution,[73]
> But to earn truth producing karma is most hard.[74]
> If you cannot see behind what can be seen,
> Differentiated are concurrent causes,
> Around you are but objects which, like gusts of wind,
> Destroy the crop of merits you have sown.[75]
> The passions of the mind e'er burst in flames,
> Destroying seeds of Bodhi in the heart.
> If recollection[76] of the truth be as intense as passion,
> Buddahood will quickly be attained.
> If you treat others as you treat the self,
> All will be settled to your satisfaction.
> If self is not right and others are not wrong,
> Lords and their servants will respect each other.
> If the Buddha-dharma's constantly before one,
> From all passions this is liberation.

How clear and how to the point are these lines! The word pollution means the act of making unclean. The realm of worldly men is tainted with desires of wealth, sensuality, fame and gain as well as anger and dispute. To them, the two words 'religion' and 'virtue' are only obstacles. Every day, they give way to pleasure, anger, sorrow and joy and long for wealth, honour, glory and prosperity. Because they cannot eliminate worldly passions, they are unable to give rise to a single thought of the truth. In consequence, the grove of merits is ruined and all seeds of Bodhi are destroyed. If they are indifferent to all worldly passions; if they give equal treatment to friends and foes; if they refrain from killing, stealing, committing adultery, lying and drinking intoxicating liquors; if they are impartial to all living beings; if they regard other people's hunger as their own; if they regard other people's drowning as if they get drowned themselves; and if they develop the Bodhi mind, they will be in agreement with the truth and will also be able to attain Buddhahood at a stroke. For this reason, it is said: 'If recollection of the truth be as intense as passions, Buddhahood will be quickly attained.' All Buddhas and saints appear in the world to serve the living, by rescuing them from suffering, by bestowing happiness upon them and by aiding them out of pity.

We can practise self-denial as well as compassion for others, thus forgoing all sorts of enjoyment. If we can do so, no one will have to endure suffering and there will remain nothing that cannot be accomplished. It will follow that we will be able to obtain the full fruit of our reward, in the same manner as a boat rises automatically with the tide. When dealing with others, if you have a compassionate and respectful mind, and are without self-importance arrogance and deception, they will certainly receive you with respect and courtesy. On the other hand, if you rely on your abilities and are unreasonable, or if you are double-faced aiming only at your own enjoyment of sound, form, fame and wealth, the respect with which they may receive you will not be real. For this reason, Confucius said: 'If you respect others, they will always respect you. If you have sympathy for others, they will always have sympathy for you.'

The Sixth Patriarch said:

Although there faults are theirs and are not ours, should we discriminate, we too are wrong.[77]

Therefore, we should not develop a mind which discriminates between right and wrong and between self and others. If we serve other people in the same manner as Buddhas and Bodhisattvas did, we will be able to sow Bodhi seeds everywhere and will reap the most excellent fruits. Thus, passions will never be able to hold us in bondage.

The twelve divisions of the Mahayana's *Tripitaka* were expounded by the World-Honoured One because of our three poisons, concupiscence, anger and stupidity. Therefore, the aims of the twelve divisions of this *Tripitaka* are: discipline *(sila)* imperturbability *(samadhi)* and wisdom *(prajna)*. Their purpose is to enable us to wipe out our desires, to embrace (the four infinite Buddha states of mind): kindness *(maitri)*, pity *(karuna)*, joy *(mudita)*[78] and indifference *(upeksa)*[79] and all notes of salvation,[80] to eliminate the delusion of ignorance and the depravity of stupidity, to achieve the virtue of complete wisdom and to embellish the meritorious *Dharmakaya*. If we can take such a line of conduct, the Lotus treasury[91] will appear everywhere.

Today, most of you who have come for this Chan week are virtuous laymen *(upasakas)*. You should subdue your minds in an appropriate manner and get rid of all bondages. I will now tell you another *gong-an* so that you can follow the example given by those mentioned in it. If I do not tell it, I am afraid you will not acquire the Gem and will go home empty-handed, and at the same time I will be guilty of a breach of trust. Please listen attentively;

In the Tang Dynasty, there was an *upasaka* whose name was Pang-yun, alias Dao-xuan, and whose native town was Heng Yang in Hunan province. He was originally a Confucian scholar and since his youth, he realised the futility of passions and was determined in his search for the truth.

At the beginning of Zhen-yuan's reign (785-804), he heard of Master Shi-tou's learning and called on him for instruction. (When he saw the Master), he asked him: 'Who is the man who does not take all dharmas as his companions?'[82] Shi-tou stretched out his hand to close Pang-yun's mouth and the visitor immediately understood the move.[83]

One day, Shi-tou asked Pang-yun: 'Since you have seen this old man [i.e. men], what have you been doing each day?' Pang-yun replied: 'If you ask me what I have been doing, I do not know how to open my mouth (to talk about it).' Then he presented the following poem to Shi-tou:

There is nothing special about what I do each day;

180

I only keep myself in harmony with it,[84]
Everywhere I neither accept nor reject anything.
Nowhere do I confirm or refute a thing.
Why do people say that red and purple differ?[85]
There's not a speck of dust on the blue mountain.[86]
Supernatural powers and wonder-making works
Are but fetching water and the gathering of wood,[87]

Shi-tou approved of the poem and asked Pang-yun: 'Will you join the Sangha order or will you remain a layman (upasaka)?' Pang-yun replied: 'I will act as I please', and did not shave his head.[88]

Later, Pang-yun called on Master Ma-zu and asked him: 'Who is the man who does not take all dharmas as his companions?' Ma-zu replied: 'I will tell you this after you have swallowed all the water in the West River.[89] Upon hearing this, Pang-yun was instantaneously awakened to the profound doctrine. He stayed two years at the monastery (of Ma-zu).

Since his complete realisation of his fundamental nature, the Upasaka gave up all worldly occupations, dumped into the Xiang River his whole fortune amounting to 10,000 strings of gold and silver coins and made bamboo-ware to earn his living.

One day, while chatting with his wife on the doctrine of the unborn, the Upasaka said: 'Difficult! Difficult! Difficult! It is like unpacking and distributing ten loads of sesame seeds on the top of a tree.[90]

His wife interjected: 'Easy! Easy! Easy! A hundred blades of grass are the Master's indication.'[91]

Hearing their dialogue, their daughter Ling-zhao said laughingly: 'Oh, you two old people! How can you talk like that?' The Upasaka said to his daughter: 'What, then, would you say?' She replied: 'It is not difficult! And it is not easy! When hungry one eats and when tired one sleeps.[92]

Pang-yun clapped his hands, laughed and said: 'My son will not get a wife; my daughter will not have a husband. We will all remain together to speak the language of the un-born.[93] Since then, his dialectic powers became eloquent and forcible and he was admired everywhere.

Where the Upasaka left Master Yo-shan the latter sent ten Chan monks to accompany him to the front door (of the monastery).

Pointing his finger at the falling snow, the Upasaka said to them: 'Good snow! The flakes do not fall elsewhere.' A Chan monk named Quan asked him: 'Where do they fall?' The Upasaka slapped the monk in the face, and Quan said: 'You can't act so carelessly.' The Upasaka replied: 'What a Chan monk you are! The god of the dead will not let you pass.' Quan asked: 'Then what does the Venerable Upasaka mean?' The Upasaka slapped him again and said: 'You see like the blind and you talk like the dumb.'[94]

The Upasaka used to frequent places where sutras were explained and commented on. One day, he listened to the expounding of the *Diamond Sutra*, and when the commentator came to the sentence on the non-existence of ego and personality, he asked: 'Venerable Sir, since there is neither self nor other, who is now expounding and who is listening?' As the commentator could not reply, the Upasaka said: 'Although I am a layman, I comprehend something.' The commentator asked him: 'What is the Venerable Upasaka's interpretation?' The Upasaka replied with the following poem:

> There is neither ego nor personality,
> Who is distant then and who is intimate?
> Take my advice and quit your task of comment
> Since that cannot compare with the direct quest of the truth.
> The nature of the Diamond Wisdom
> Contains no foreign dust.[95]
> The words 'I hear', 'I believe' and 'I receive'
> Are meaningless and used expediently.

After hearing the poem, the commentator was delighted (with the correct interpretation) and praised (the Upasaka).

One day, the Upasaka asked Ling-zhao: 'How do you understand the ancients' saying: "Clearly there are a hundred blades of grass; clearly these are the Patriarchs' indications?"' Ling-zhao: 'Oh you old man, how can you talk like that?' The Upasaka asked her: 'How would you say it?' Ling-zhao replied: 'Clearly there are a hundred blades of grass; clearly these are the Patriarchs' indications.[96] The Upasaka laughed approvingly.

When he knew that he was about to die, he said to Ling-zhao: 'Go out and see if it is early or late; if it is noon, let me know.' Ling-zhao went out and returned, saying: 'The sun is in mid-heaven, but unfortunately it is being swallowed by the heaven-dog.[97] Father why don't you go out to have a look?' Thinking that her story was true, he left his seat and went outside. Thereupon, Ling-zhao (taking advantage of her father's absence) ascended to his seat, sat with crossed legs, brought her two palms together, and passed away.

When the Upasaka returned, he saw that Ling-zhao had died and said, with a sigh: 'My daughter was sharp-witted and left before me.' So he postponed his death for a week in order to bury his daughter.

When Magistrate Yu-ti came to inquire after his health, the Upasaka said to him:

> Vow only to wipe out all that is;
> Beware of making real what is not.[98]
> Life in this (mortal) world
> A shadow is, an echo.

After saying this, he rested his head on the magistrate's knees and passed away. As willed by him, his body was cremated and the ashes were thrown into the lake.

His wife heard of his death and went to inform her son of it. Upon hearing the news, the son stopped his work in the field, rested his chin on the handle of his hoe and passed away in a standing position. After witnessing these three successive events, the mother retired to an unknown place to live in seclusion.

As you see, the whole family of four had supernatural powers and could do works of wonder and these laymen who were also upasakas like you, were of superior attainments. At present, it is impossible to find men of such outstanding ability not only among you upasakas (and upasikas) but also among monks and nuns who are no better than myself, Xu-yun. What a disgrace!

Now let us exert ourselves again in our training!

The Seventh Day

Dear friends, allow me to congratulate you for the merits you have accumulated in the Chan week which comes to an end today. According to the standing rule, those of you who have experienced and realised the truth should come forward in this hall as did candidates who sat for a scholar's examination held previously in the imperial palace. Today, being the day of posting the list of successful graduates, should be one for congratulations. However, the venerable abbot has been most compassionate and has decided to continue this Chan meeting for another week so that we can all make additional efforts for further progress (in self-cultivation).

All the Masters who are present here and are old hands in this training, know that it is a wonderful opportunity for co-operation and will not throw away their precious time. But those who are beginners should know that it is difficult to acquire a human body[99] and that the question of birth and death is important. As we have human bodies, we should know that it is difficult to get the chance to hear the Buddha Dharma and meet learned teachers. Today you have come to the 'precious mountain'[100] and should take advantage of this excellent opportunity to make every possible effort in your self-cultivation in order not to return home empty-handed.

As I have said, our Sect's Dharma which was transmitted by the World-Honoured One when he held up a flower to show it to the assembly, has been handed down from one generation to another. Although Ananda was a cousin of the Buddha and left home to follow him as an attendant, he did not succeed in attaining the truth in the presence of the World-Honoured One. After the Buddha had entered Nirvana, his great disciples assembled in a cave (to compile sutras) but Ananda was not permitted by them to attend the meeting. Mahakasyapa said to him: 'You have not acquired the World-Honoured One's Mind Seal, so please pull down the banner-pole in front of the door.' Thereupon, Ananda was thoroughly enlightened. Then Mahakasyapa transmitted to him the Tathgata's Mind Seal, making him the second Indian Patriarch. The transmission was handed down to following generations, and after the Patriarchs Asvaghosa and Nagarjuna, Chan Master Hui-wen of Tian-tai mountain in the Bei-qi Dynasty (550–78) after reading (Nagarjuna's) Madhyamika Shastra, succeeded in realising his own mind and founded the Tian-tai School.[101] At the time, our Chan Sect was very flourishing. Later, when the Tian-tai School fell into decadence, State master De-shao (a Chan Master) journeyed to Korea (where the only copy of Zhi-yi's works existed), copied it and returned to revive the Sect.

Bodhidharma who was the twenty-eighth Indian Patriarch, came to the East where he became the first Chinese Patriarch. From his transmission of the Dharma until the time of the Fifth Patriarch, the Mind-lamp shone brilliantly. The Sixth Patriarch had forty-three successors, among whom were the eminent Chan Master Xing-si and Huai-rang. Then came Chan Master Ma-zu who had eighty-three successors. At the time, the Right Dharma reached its zenith and was held in reverence by emperors and high officials. Although the Tathagata expounded many Dharmas, the Sect's was the unsurpassed one.

As to the Dharma which consists in repeating only the name of Amitabha Buddha, it was extolled by (Chan Patriarchs) Asvoghosa and Nagarjuna,[102] and after Master Hui-yuan,[103] Chan master Yan-shou of the Yong-ming monastery became the Sixth Patriarch of the Pure Land Sect (Jin-tu Zong), which was subsequently spread by many other Chan Masters.

After being propagated by Chan master Yi-xing, the Esoteric Sect[104] spread to Japan but disappeared in China where there was no one to succeed to the Master.

The Dharmalaksana Sect[105] was introduced by Dharma-Master Xuan-zang but did not last very long.

Only our Chan Sect is like a stream which is still flowing from its remote source, bringing *devas* into its fold and subduing dragons and tigers.[106]

Lu Dong-bin, alias Shun-yang, a native of Jing-chuan, was one of the famous group of eight immortals.[107] Towards the end of the Tang Dynasty, he stood thrice for the scholar's examination but failed each time. Being disheartened, he did not return home, and one day, he met by chance in a wine-shop at Chang-an, an immortal named Zhong Li-chuan who taught him the method of lengthening his span of life infinitely. Lu Dong-bin practised the method with great success and could even become invisible and fly in the air at will over the country. One day, he paid a flying visit to the Hai Hui Monastery on Lu Shan Mountain; in its bell tower, he wrote on the wall:

After a day of leisure when the body is at ease,
The six organs[108] now in harmony, announce that all is well.
With a gem in the pubic region[109] there's no need to search for truth,
When mindless of surroundings, there's no need for Chan.

Some time later, as he was crossing the Huang-long Mountain, he beheld in the sky purple clouds shaped like an umbrella. Guessing that there must be some extraordinary person (in the monastery there), he entered. It happened at the same time that in the monastery, after beating the drum, Chan Master Huang-long was ascending to his seat (to expound the Dharma). Lu Dong-bin followed the monks and entered the hall to listen to the teaching.

Huang-long said to the assembly: 'Today there is here a plagiarist of my Dharma; the monk (i.e. I) will not expound it.' Thereupon, Lu Dong-bin came forward and paid obeisance to the Master, saying: 'I wish to ask the Venerable Master the meaning of these lines:

> A grain of corn contains the Universe:
> The hills and rivers fill a small cooking-pot.'

Huang-long scolded him and said: 'What a corpse-guarding devil you are'. Lu Dong-bin retorted: 'But my gourd holds the immortality-giving medicine.' Huang-long said: 'Even if you succeed in living 80,000 aeons,[110] you will not escape from falling into the dead void.' Forgetting all about the fortitude advocated in his own line:

> When mindless of surroundings there's no need for Chan.

Lu Dong-bin burned with anger and threw his sword at Huang-long. Huang-long pointed his finger at the sword which fell to the ground and which the thrower could not get back. With deep remorse, Lu Dong-bin knelt upon his knees and inquired about the Buddha Dharma. Huang-long asked: 'Let aside the line: "The hills, and rivers fill a small cooking-pot" about which I do not ask you anything. Now what is the meaning of: "A grain of corn contains the Universe"?[111] Upon hearing this question, Lu Dong-bin instantaneously realised the profound (Chan) meaning. Then, he chanted the following repentance-poem:

> I throw away my gourd and smash my lute.
> In future I'll not cherish gold in mercury.
> Now that I have met (the master Huang-long),
> I have realised my wrong use of the mind.[112]

This is the story of an immortal's return to and reliance on the

Triple Gem and his entry into the monastery *(Sangharama)* as a guardian of the Dharma. Lu Dong-bin was also responsible for reviving the Daoist Sect at the time and was its Fifth (Dao) Patriarch in the North. The Daoist Zi-yang also realised the mind after reading the (Buddhist) collection 'Zu Ying-ji' and became the Fifth (Dao) Patriarch in the South.[113] Thus the Dao faith was revived thanks to the Chan Sect.

Confucius' teaching was handed down until Mencius after whom it came to an end. In the Song Dynasty Confucian scholars (also) studied the Buddha Dharma, and among them we can cite Zhou Lian-qi who practised the Chan training and succeeded in realising his mind, and others such as Cheng-zi, Zhang-zi and Zhu-zi (all famous Confucians). Therefore, the Chan Sect contributed in no small measure to the revival of Confucianism.

Nowadays, there are many people who despise the Chan Dharma and who even make slanderous remarks about it, thus deserving hell.[114] Today, we have this excellent opportunity of being favoured with a co-operating cause which gathers us here. We should feel joy and should take the great vow to become objects of reverence for dragons and *devas* and to perpetuate the Right Dharma for ever. This is no child's play; so please make strenuous efforts to obtain more progress in your self-cultivation.

The Master was then invited to Hangzhou where Buddhist organisations sent Upasaka Du-wei to welcome him. Arriving on the nineteenth of the second month, he stayed at the Jin-ci Temple, where he held a Dharma-meeting at which several thousand people became his disciples. The local authorities invited him to be Abbot of the Ling-yin Monastery but he declined on the grounds of old age and ill health.

At the invitation of Abbot Miao-zhen and Dharma-Master Wu-ai of Ling-yen Monastery, the Master went to Suzhou to hold a Dharma-meeting there, after which he visited Hu-qiu (Tiger Hill) in order to pay reverence to the stupa of Chan Master Shao-long (a Dharma-descendant of Lin-ji. On arrival there, he found that people had encroached on the holy site, the stupa and stone tablet bearing the customary inscriptions had disappeared. He had previously visited the spot during the reign of Emperor Guang-xu [1875–1909] and still remembered the holy site, which was now a heap of tiles and bricks, removal of which revealed that it was indeed the ancient site. The Master then discussed the matter with local officials and notables and also conferred with protectors of the Dharma at Shanghai, who raised funds to rebuild the stupa. Abbots Miao-zhen and Chu-guang who were at Tiger Hill were asked to supervise the restoration of the holy site.

On his way to Suzhou, the Master visited the Shou-sheng Temple at Ban-tang where he paid reverence to the stupa of Master Yuan Shan-ji. After that he was invited by the devotees of Nan-tong to visit Mount Lang where he held a Dharma meeting at which several thousand people became his disciples. After the meeting he returned to Shanghai, arriving there at the end of the third month.

In the fourth month, the Master received a telegram asking him to the capital, where he stayed at the Guang-ji Monastery. After representatives of the Sangha from all parts of the country had arrived, the new Chinese Buddhist Association was formally inaugurated and proceeded to discuss and pass several important resolutions. When some degenerate monks proposed the abolition of the standing rules of discipline and morality, the Master reprimanded them and wrote a statement entitled the 'Degeneration of the Sangha in the Dharma-ending age'.[115]

Afterwards, the Master went to Da-tong in Shansi Province in order to pay reverence at the Great Stone Buddha in Yungang Grotto. When he expressed a desire to leave Beijing area, the local authorities advised him to convalesce at Mount Lu in Jiang-xi. In the fifth month, the Master went south with his attendant, Jue-min. On arrival at Han-kou, Abbot Yuan-cheng of Bao-tong Monastery asked the Master to hold two weeks of Chan meditation, after which he proceeded to Mount Lu, where Upasaka Chen Zhen-ru was awaiting him, subsequently staying there at the Da-lin Temple.

In the sixth month, a few Chan monks came from Mount Yun-ju[116] in Jiangxi and said that during the Japanese occupation, the invaders had set fire to the Zhen-ru Monastery to prevent Chinese guerrillas from using it as a hiding place. The whole temple had been destroyed except for a large bronze statue of Vairocana,[117] which remained intact amid the desolation of the grass-covered site. The Master was sad when he heard of this and thought of the holy site which had been founded in the Yuan-ho reign [806-820] of the Tang Dynasty, and where many eminent Chan Masters had stayed. If it was not rebuilt, it would be buried in oblivion. The Master vowed to rebuild the monastery and applied to the local authorities for permission to go there. Upasaka Zhu Hua-bing and a few others offered to accompany the Master who left for Jun-ju on the fifth of the seventh month.

In the ninth month, when a few *bhiksunis* in Canton who were disciples of the Master heard of his arrival at Yun-ju, they came to see him. After travelling by boat and train, they arrived at the monastery, where they saw only ruined walls. They met a monk, asking as to the Master's whereabouts. He pointed to a cowshed. They bent down to enter its low doorway but could not see him at first. After a pause to look round, they found him seated in meditation posture on a bench. Slowly, he opened his eyes and said, 'Why have you taken the trouble to come here?' After they had spoken about the object of their visit, he said, 'When I came here, there were only four monks present and I therefore decided to set up a thatched hut for them. But numerous other monks came along later. Within a month or so, their number increased to fifty. Apart from this cowshed, there are only a few ruined buildings which you have seen. But since you have called, please be content with what is available and stay for a few days.

Although the cowshed was half a *li* north-west of the monastery, the Master liked this remote location and also intended to have the nearby soil tilled to obtain food for the monks. After the tenth month, yet more monks came. The provisions were down to an ounce of stale food at meals, but fortunately Upasaka Jian Yu-jia in Shanghai contributed funds so that those on the mountain could pass the winter. The Master planned to clear the land for cultivation and to repair the halls of the monastery. That winter, the Master was invited to transmit the precepts in Qujiang and at the Nan-hua Monastery.

Notes

1. See *Chan and Zen Teaching, First Series,* pages 49–109.
2. The 12 divisions of the Mahayana canon are: (1) *sutra,* the Buddha's sermons; (2) *geya,* metrical pieces; (3) *gatha,* poems or chants; (4) *nidana,* sutras written by request or in answer to a query, because certain precepts were violated and because of certain events; (5) *itivrttaka,* narratives; (6) *jataka,* stories of former lives of Buddha; (7) *adbhuta-dharma,* miracles; (8) *avadana,* parables, metaphors, stories, illustrations; (9) *upadesa,* discourses and discussions by question and answer; (10) *udana,* im-

promptu or unsolicited addresses; (11) *vaipulya*, expanded sutras; (12) *vyakarana*, prophecies.

3. Xing-si inherited the Dharma from the Sixth Patriarch and was called the Seventh Ancestor because his two Dharma-descendants Dong-shan and Cao-shan founded the Cao-dong sect, which was one of the five Chan sects in China.

4. Of the method of gradual enlightenment which took many aeons to enable an adherent to attain the Buddha-stage.

5. The four Noble Truths are: misery; the accumulation of misery, caused by passions; the extinction of passions, being possible; and the doctrine of the Path leading to extinction of passions.

6. A Chan term which means an unwanted thing which hinders self-realisation.

7. Usually one hour. The longer sticks take an hour and a half to burn.

8. Life-root. A root, or basis for life, or reincarnation, the nexus of Hinayana between two life-periods, accepted by Mahayana as nominal but not real. The Chinese idiom 'to sit on and to crack' is equivalent to the Western term 'to break up'.

9. Wu Wei. *Asamskrta* in Sanskrit, anything not subject to cause, condition or dependence; out of time, external, inactive, supramundane.

10. *Samskrta*. Yu Wei in Chinese, active, creative, productive, functioning, causative, phenomenal, the process resulting from the laws of karma.

11. Ordinary mind = undiscriminating mind.

12. Without discrimination, the acts of wearing clothes and eating and all our activities are nothing but the functions of the self-nature; and One reality is all reality. On the other hand if the mind discriminates when one wears one's robe or takes one's meal, everything around one will be the phenomenal.

13. Da-mei. In deference to him, the Master was called after the name of the mountain where he stayed.

14. The mountains are immutable and symbolise the unchanging self-nature, whereas their colours (blue and yellow) change and symbolise appearance, i.e. the phenomenal. The reply meant that his self-nature was the same and beyond time.

15. If your mind wanders outside, it will follow the stream of birth and death.

16. When the mind is free from passions, it is like a withered log which is indifferent to its surroundings and does not 'grow' any more in spite of the spring, the season of the year in which trees begin to grow after lying dormant all winter. A mind free from delusion remains unchanged and indifferent to all changes in its surrounding and to those who hunt after it.

17. Because his disciples clung to his saying: 'Mind is Buddha,' Ma-zu said to them: 'It is neither mind nor Buddha' so that they ceased to cling, which was the cause of their delusion.

18. Da-mei means 'Big Plum', Ma-zu confirmed that Master Da-mei was ripe, i.e. enlightened.

19. Quotation from Yong-jia's 'Song of Enlightenment'. *Avici* is the last and deepest of the eight hot hells, where sinners suffer, die, and are

instantly reborn to suffering, without interruption. *Ksana* is the shortest measure of time, as *kalpa* is the longest.

20. The instant one perceives only stillness and experiences liveliness; it is called in Chan parlance 'reaching the top of a hundred-foot pole'. All Masters advised their disciples not to abide in this state, which was not real. Master Han-shan composed 'The Song of the Board-bearer' to warn his followers against 'silent immersion in stagnant water'. This state is called 'life' and is the fourth of the four signs *(laksana)* mentioned in the *Diamond Sutra*.

21. Karmadana: the duty-distributor, second in command of a monastery.

22. After a meditation, the monks used to march quickly in single file to relax their legs, preceded by the Karmadana and followed by the Abbot.

23. Realm of five *skandhas:* the present world as the state of the five aggregates. The best place in which to hold the *hua-tou* is between the pit of the stomach and the navel. A meditator may have all kinds of visions before his attainment of enlightenment, and these visions belong to the realm of the five *skandhas*, i.e. are creations of his mind. His master would instruct him to remain indifferent, neither to 'accept' or 'reject' these visions which will disappear before the meditator makes further progress in the right direction.

24. To go straight home. A Chan idiom meaning the return to the self-nature, i.e. realisation of the real. 'Home' is our self-natured Buddha.

25. Baggage: our body, mind and the seeming which we hold dear.

26. That which has no birth and death, i.e. the eternal self-nature.

27. *Vinaya-pitaka*. One of the three divisions of the Canon or *Tripitaka*. It emphasises the discipline. The other two divisions are: sutras (sermons) and *shastras* (treatises).

28. The two forms of Karma resulting from one's past are: (1) the resultant person, symbolised by a *hair*, and (2) the dependent condition or environment, e.g. country, family, possessions, etc., symbolised by the *ocean*. These two forms being illusory only, the penetrate each other without changing the self-nature, or the nature-ocean (see footnote 29) which is beyond time and space.

29. Nature-ocean. The ocean of the *Bhutatathata*, the all-containing, immaterial nature of the *Dharmakaya*.

30. The appearance of a Buddha is as rare as the hitting of a needle's point with a fine mustard-seed thrown from a *devaloka*. Even an accurate hit does not move the immutable needle's point.

31. *Saiksa*, need of study; *asaiksa*, no longer learning, beyond study, the state of arhatship, the fourth of the *sravaka* stages; the preceding three stages requiring study. When the arhat is free from all illusion, he has nothing more to study.

32. Dignity in walking, standing, sitting and lying.

33. A Commentary on the *Diamond Sutra* by Dao-yin of the Qing-long Monastery.

34. Dian-xin, pastry, snack, refreshment to keep up one's spirits.

35. Long-tan was an Enlightened Master. The sentence: 'You have really

arrived at the Dragon Pond' means; 'You have really attained the state of Long-tan or enlightenment for the real is invisible and does not appear before the eyes of the unenlightened'. De-shan did not understand its meaning and remained speechless. This was the second time he remained speechless, the first being when the old woman asked him about the past, present and future mind. He was still unenlightened but became later an eminent Chan Master after his awakening.

36. Long-tan was an eminent Master and knew the moment was ripe to enlighten De-shan. The latter perceived the Master's self-nature through its function which blew out the torch. At the same time, De-shan perceived also that which 'saw' the torch blown out, i.e. his own nature.

37. Old monks all over the country: a Chinese idiom referring to eminent Chan Masters who were intransigent and exacting when teaching and guiding their disciples. Readers may learn about these masters by studying their sayings, which seem ambiguous but are full of deep meaning.

38. A fellow who was awe-inspiring like the two hells where there are hills of swords or sword-leaf trees and blood baths as punishments for sinners. Long-tan foretold the severity with which De-shan would receive, teach and train his disciples. Those wishing to familarise themselves with these awe-inspiring things should read Dr W. Y. Evans-Wentz's *The Tibetan Book of the Dead* (Oxford University Press).

39. Chan Masters frequently used their staffs to strike their disciples to provoke their awakening. The stroke of the staff here referred to De-shan enlightenment after 'seeing' the torch blown out by his master. De-shan did not turn his head, because he was really enlightened and did not have any more doubt about his self-nature.

40. Will be an outstanding Chan Master.

41. This walk from east to west and then from west to east meant the 'coming' and 'going' which were non-existent in the Dharmadhatu wherein the Dharmakaya remained immutable and unchanging. De-shan's question: 'Anything? Anything?' and the reply: 'Nothing, Nothing,' served to emphasise the nothingness in space.

42. *Nisidana,* a cloth for sitting on.

43. *Upadhyaya,* a general term for a monk.

44. The duster used by the ancients consisted of long horse hairs attached to the end of its handle. It was used to reveal the function of the self-nature.

45. The shout was to reveal that which uttered it, i.e. the self-nature.

46. De-shan took out and raised his *nisidana,* calling: 'Venerable Upadhyaya to show the function of that which took out and raised the *nisidana* and called Gui-shan. When the latter was about to take the duster to test the visitor's enlightenment, De-shan shouted just to indicate the presence of the substance of that which called on the host. De-shan left the hall and went away to show the return of function to the substance. Thus Gui-shan's enlightenment was complete, because both function and substance, or *prajna* and *samadhi* were on a level. Therefore, he did not require any further instruction and any test of his attainment would be superfluous. For this reason, Gui-shan praised the visitor, saying: 'That man will later

go to some solitary peak . . . will scold Buddhas and curse Patriarchs.'

47. De-shan would 'scold' unreal Buddhas and 'curse' unreal Patriarchs who existed only in the impure minds of deluded disciples, for the latter's conditioned and discriminating minds could create only impure Buddhas and impure Patriarchs. De-shan's teaching was based only on the absolute *prajna* which had no room for wordly feelings and discernings, the cause of birth and death.

48. Lin-ji was the founder of the Lin-ji Sect, one of the five Chan Sects of China.

49. Yun-men and Fa-yan were respective founders of the Yun-men and Fa-yan Sects, two of the five Chan Sects in China.

50. If while sitting in meditation one only takes delight in false visions or in the wrong interpretation of sutras and sayings, one will never attain the real.

51. The strongest or sharpest precious sword.

52. i.e. false visions of demons and Buddhas in one's meditation.

53. Beginners usually see the voidness and brightness as soon as all thoughts are discarded. Although these visions indicate some progress in the training, they should not be taken as achievements. The meditator should remain indifferent to them as they are only the creation of the deluded mind and should hold firm the *hua-tou*.

54. Cf. Sutra of the Sixth Patriarch.

55. World of desire, world of form and formless world.

56. The five desires arising from the objects of the five senses, things seen, heard, smelt, tasted and touched.

57. The three poisons are: Concupiscence or wrong desire, hate or resentment, and stupidity.

58. i.e. neutral, neither good nor bad, things that are innocent or cannot be classified under moral categories.

59. i.e. when the sixth consciousness is independent of the first five.

60. Zhang and Li are the Chinese equivalents of Smith and Brown.

61. In his meditation, the Master had already discarded all thoughts and upon hearing the song, he instantly perceived that which heard the song, i.e. the self-nature. This is called Avalokitesvara's complete enlightenment by means of hearing, or the successful turning inward of the faculty of hearing to hear the self-nature. – Cf. *Surangama Sutra*.

62. Bean-curd is made of soy-bean and is very cheap, so that only poor people make it for sale. For this reason, they are never satisfied with their lot and always want to do something more profitable.

63. The mind which is bent on the right way, which seeks enlightenment.

64. *Agantu-klesa* in Sanskrit, the foreign atom, or intruding element, which enters the mind and causes distress and delusion. The mind will be pure only after the evil element has been removed.

65. Water is the symbol of self-nature and mud of ignorance caused by passions.

66. A state of empty stillness in which all thoughts have ceased to arise and *prajna* is not yet attained.

67. In contrast with a Bodhisattva, who seeks self-enlightenment to

enlighten the multitude.

68. A statesman of the Song Dynasty, through whom Yue-fei, a good commander, was executed; he is universally execrated for this and his name is now synonymous with traitor.

69. Xiamen, Amoy, a town on the south coast of Fujian province.

70. To lead the spirit of the deceased to the Pure Land.

71. Water is the symbol of self-nature and the moon of enlightenment.

72. Lit. cost of the dumplings.

73. Nidana or cause of pollution, which connects illusion with the karmic miseries of reincarnation.

74. Good karma which leads to enlightenment.

75. Accumulation of merits leading to realisation of the truth.

76. Smrti in Sanskrit.

77. Quotation from a hymn chanted by the Sixth Patriarch (Cf. *Altar Sutra*, Chapter II).

78. Joy on seeing others rescued from suffering.

79. Rising above these emotions, or giving up all things, e.g. distinctions of friend and foe, love and hate, etc.

80. The Six *Paramitas* are: *dana* (charity), *sila* (discipline), *ksanti* (patience or endurance), *virya* (zeal and progress), *dhyana* (meditation) and *prajna* (wisdom).

81. Lotus treasury: Lotus store, or Lotus world, the Pure Land of all Buddhas in their *Sambhogakaya*, or Reward bodies.

82. In plain English the question means: Who is the man who has no more attachments to things, or the phenomenal?

83. In Shi-tou's move, Pang-yun perceived that which stretched out the hand to close his mouth and became awakened to the self-nature which was invisible and manifested itself by means of its function.

84. After enlightenment one attends to one's daily task as usual, the only difference being that the mind no longer discriminates and harmonises with its surroundings.

85. Mind is now free from all conceptions of duality.

86. The blue mountain symbolises that which is immutable and free from dust, or impurities. A misprint occurs in the printed text, so I have followed the ancient version of the story of Upasaka Pang-yun.

87. Carrying water and fetching wood are the functions of that which possesses supernatural powers and accomplishes wonderful works; in other words, the self-nature which is immaterial and invisible can be perceived only by means of its functions which are no longer discriminative.

88. He did not join the Sangha order.

89. The one who has no more attachment to worldly things is the enlightened self-nature which is beyond description. Ma-zu gave this reply, because when one attains enlightenment, his body or substance pervades everywhere and contains everything, including the West River which is likened to a speck of dust inside the immense universe; he knows everything and does not require any description of himself. – A misprint in the text has been corrected.

90. The Patriarchs' doctrine was very profound and was as difficult to teach as the unpacking and distributing of sesame seeds on the top of a tree, an impossible thing for an unenlightened man.

91. In order to wipe out the conception of difficulty, the wife said the doctrine was easy to expound for even the dewdrops on blades of grass were used by eminent masters to give the direct indication of *that which* saw these dewdrops. This was only easy for enlightened people.

92. If it is said that the doctrine is difficult to understand, no one will try to learn it. If it is said that it is easy to understand, people will take it as easy and never attain the truth. So the daughter took the middle way by saying that it was neither difficult nor easy. Her idea was that one who is free from discrimination and who eats when hungry and sleeps when tired, is precisely the one meant by eminent masters. Therefore, the doctrine is not difficult for an enlightened man and not easy for an unenlightened man, thus wiping out the two extremes which have no room in the absolute.

93. This sentence is omitted in the Chinese text and is added here to be in accord with Master Xu-yun's lecture.

94. All Chan Masters had compassion for unenlightened people and never missed a chance to enlighten them. Yo-shan sent ten Chan monks to accompany the eminent visitor to the front of the monastery so that they could learn something from him. Out of pity, the Upasaka said: 'Good snow! The flakes do not fall elsewhere!', to probe the ability of the monks and to press them hard so that they could realise their self-minds for the attainment of Buddhahood. However, the monks seemed ignorant and did not realise that since the mind created the snow, the snow could not fall outside the mind. If they could only perceive *that which* slapped the unenlightened monk in the face, they would realise their self-nature. A serious monk would, under the circumstances, devote all his attention to inquiring into the unreasonable conduct of the visitor and would at least make some progress in his training.

95. i.e. free from external impurities.

96. The daughter seemed at first to criticise her father and then repeated the same sentence to confirm what he had said. Similar questions and answers are found frequently in Chan texts where Chan Masters wanted to probe their disciples' abilities by first criticising what they said. Any hesitation on the part of the disciples would disclose that they only repeated others' sayings without comprehending them. This was like a trap set to catch unenlightened disciples who claimed that they had realised the truth. When a disciple was really enlightened, he would remain undisturbed and would ask back the question. When the Master was satisfied that the disciple's understanding was genuine, he would simply repeat the same sentence to give more emphasis to what the disciple had said.

97. i.e. eclipse of the sun.

98. Existence and non-existence are two extremes which should be wiped out before one can attain the absolute reality.

99. i.e. to be reborn in the human world. The realm of human beings is

difficult of attainment; it is one of suffering and is the most suitable for self-cultivation, for human beings have more chance to study the Dharma in order to get rid of their miseries. The other five worlds of existence either enjoy too much happiness (*devas* and *asuras*) or endure too much suffering (animals, hungry ghosts and hells), thus having no chance to learn the Dharma.

100. *The Sutra of Contemplation of Mind* says: 'Like a handless man who cannot acquire anything in spite of his arrival at the precious mountain, one who is deprived of the "hand" of Faith, will not acquire anything even if he finds the Triple Gem.'

101. The Nine Patriarchs of the Tian-tai sect are: (1) Nagarjuna, (2) Hui-wen of the Bei-qi Dynasty, (3) Hui-si of Nan-yue, (4) Zhi-zhe, or Zhi-yi, (5) Guang-ting of Zhang-an, (6) Fa-hua, (7) Tian-gong, (8) Zuo-qi and (9) Zhan-ran of Jing-qi. The tenth, Dao-sui, was considered a patriarch in Japan, because he was the teacher of the Japanese Dengyo Daishi who brought the Tendai system to the country in the ninth century. The Tian-tai (or Tendai in Japanese) Sect bases its tenets on the *Lotus, Mahaparinirvana* and *Mahaprajnaparamita Sutras.* It maintains the identity of the Absolute and the world of phenomena, and attempts to unlock the secrets of all phenomena by means of meditation.

102. The twelfth and fourteenth Patriarchs of the Chan sect respectively. Readers will notice that these two Patriarchs and many other Chan Masters were not sectarian and extolled also the Pure Land School which was also a Dharma door expounded by the Buddha.

103. Hui-yuan was an eminent Master of the Pure Land Sect.

104. Zhen-yan Zong, also called 'True Word' Sect, or Shingon in Japanese. The founding of this Sect is attributed to Vairocana, through Bodhisattva Vajrasattva, then through Nagarjuna to Vajramati and to Amoghavajra.

105. The Dharmalaksana Sect is called Fa-xiang in Chinese and Hosso in Japanese. This school was established in China on the return of Xuanzang, consequent on his translation of the Yogacarya works. Its aim is to understand the principle underlying the nature and characteristics of all things.

106. Maleficent beings.

107. The immortals practise Daoism and sit in meditation with crossed legs. Their aim is to achieve immortality by putting an end to all passions, but they still cling to the view of the reality of ego and things. They live in caves or on the tops of mountains and possess the art of becoming invisible. A Chinese *bhiksu* who is a friend of mine went to North China when he was still young. Hearing of an immortal there, he tried to locate him. After several unsuccessful attempts, he succeeded finally in meeting him. Kneeling upon his knees, my friend implored the immortal to give him instruction. The latter, however, refused, saying that the visitor was not of his line, i.e. Daoism. When the young man got up and raised his head, the immortal had disappeared and only a small sheet of paper was seen on the table with the word 'Good-bye' on it.

108. According to the ancients, the six viscera are: heart, lungs, liver, kidney, stomach and gall-bladder.

109. Pubic region, two and a half inches below the navel, on which concentration is fixed in Daoist meditation.

110. The digit 8 in 80,000 symbolises the eighth Consciousness (Vijnana) which is an aspect of the self-nature under delusion. The sentence means that Lu Dong-bin was still unenlightened in spite of his long life.

111. The grain of corn is created by the mind and reveals the mind which is immense and contains the whole Universe, also a creation of the mind. Being hard pressed, Lu Dong-bin instantly realised his self-mind and was awakened to the real.

112. In ancient times, Daoists in China claimed to be able to 'extract quicksilver by smelting cinnabar', i.e. they knew the method which enabled them to become immortals, or Rsis, in Sanskrit, whose existence was mentioned by the Buddha in the *Surangama Sutra*. Their meditation aimed at the production of a hot current pervading all parts of the body and successful meditators could send out their spirits to distant places. They differed from Buddhists in that they held the conception of the reality of ego and of dharmas, and could not attain complete enlightenment. They used to wander in remote places, equipped with a gourd, a guitar and a 'divine' sword to protect themselves against demons. Today, adherents of the Daoist Sect are still found in great number in the Far East.

113. Zi-yang was an eminent Daoist who was well-versed in the Chan Dharma and his works attested his realisation of the mind. Emperor Yong-zheng considered him a real Chan Buddhist and published his works in 'The Imperial Selection of Chan Sayings'.

114. An evil karma which causes the sinner to be reborn in the *Avici* hell. Lit: committing the *Avici-karma*.

115. According to the Mahayana, the Buddha predicted that the Dharma would go through three phases of unfoldment after his *parinirvana*: (1) The correct period, when the Dharma is reliably interpreted in both theory and practice; (2) The 'semblance period' when the Dharma would become more formalised and less spiritual; and finally (3) The 'Dharma-ending-age', when even the formal traces of the Dharma begin to vanish.

116. Yun-ju became a famous Cao-dong centre after the arrival there of Dao-ying [d. 902], joint-heir of the Cao-dong transmission with Cao-shan Ben-ji [d. 901], both disciples of Dong-shan Liang-Jie [d. 869]. Ben-ji's line disappeared after four generations, leaving Dao-ying's as the main Cao-dong centre. Yun-ju also saw Lin-ji Masters of note. When the Song capital fell in 1126, the imperial retinue fled south and the Emperor invited Yuan-wu [d. 1135] to reside at Yun-ju. He was shortly joined by the great Da-hui [d. 1163]. Also at this time, the eminent Cao-dong Master Hong-zhi [d. 1157] stayed on Yun-ju.

117. The image of Vairocana symbolises the sun of wisdom, the Dharmakaya or essential Buddha-body.

XU-YUN'S 115TH YEAR
(1954/55)

In the spring, the Master planned to rebuild the main hall for the great bronze statue of Vairocana Buddha which was sixteen feet high and had been cast in the reign of Wan-li [1573–1619] of the Ming Dynasty by order of the then Empress-dowager. The roof of the previous hall had been made of iron tiles because earthenware ones could not resist the strong winds on top of the mountain. So the Master decided to have iron tiles cast together with four big iron cooking-pots and two large bronze bells.

At the time, the number of monks and laymen on the mountain exceeded a hundred and included many artisans and skilled workmen. When devotees both in the mainland and overseas heard of the Master's plan, they sent funds for the project. Since the site, labour and money were available, the Master's plan was easy to achieve. He divided the community into two groups, assigning one to reconstruct the monastery buildings and the other to clear the land for tillage.

Since everybody was willing to work, in the fifth and sixth months the Dharma-hall was completely rebuilt with, above it, a library for two editions of the *Tripitaka.* At the same time, the equivalent of ten acres of arable land was made available to grow rice for the community, thus carrying out the rules laid down by the ancient Chan Master Bai-zhang.[1]

In the seventh month, over twenty dormitories, a brick-kiln, latrines and rice-pounding rooms were rebuilt, but the Master continued to stay at the cowshed as before. When Abbot Ben-huan of the Nan-hua Monastery, Bhiksuni Guan-ding of the Tai-bing Lotus Hall and four others came to the mountain to pay obeisance to the Master, they saw a cracked bell on the grass and asked him why it had been left there. He said, 'It is an ancient bell of this mountain and used to be called the "Self-ringing bell" because in the past whenever enlightened Masters came, it rang by itself. When the Japanese Army set fire to this monastery, the tower was destroyed and the bell dropped to the ground, but its crack will mend by itself.' When they examined the bell closely, they found that the upper part of the crack seemed to have been patched by itself. The Master then said, 'I shall wait until the crack disappears completely and then hang the bell in the newly built tower.'

The Master then led them on a visit to other parts of the monastery.

In the eleventh month, the cowshed caught fire and when the monks urged the Master to move into the newly rebuilt temple, he said, 'I liked its primitive charm' and had the cowshed rebuilt. That year, the Master received several telegrams from Beijing asking him to go there but he declined on the grounds of old age and ill health. At the end of the year he held a week of Chan meditation.

Notes

1. Bai-zhang Hui-hai [720–814], successor Ma-zu Dao-Yi. Though both Masters are known for their seemingly 'eccentric' behaviour quite typical of Chan adepts in the Tang, they were both strict disciplinarians. Their apparently 'uncouth' gestures were in fact necessary to help drive away dualistic views held by their disciples and visitors. Bai-zhang is also famous for drawing up the first set of disciplinary rules for Chan monks. They were called 'Bai-zhang's pure rules' (Bai-zhang Jing-gui). Bai-zhang's dictum, 'A day without work, a day without food,' was adequately met by Master Xu-yun's plans for the Zhen-ru Monastery.

XU-YUN'S 116TH YEAR
(1955/56)

In the spring, the additional temple buildings and kitchens, a hall for the fivefold-meditation,[1] storehouses, guest halls and other meditation halls were built and completed one after the other.

In the summer, when the Chinese Buddhist Association met in Beijing, the Master was very busy and could not go north to attend its proceedings.

In the autumn, several dozen monks came from other parts of China. Those who had not received the full Precepts asked the Master to ordain them but he thought it unwise to do so under the prevailing circumstances; on the other hand, he did not think it was appropriate to refuse their request. Thus he decided to ordain only those already present at the monastery and forbade them to tell outsiders. With a view to transmitting the precepts in the tenth month and to ordaining the monks on the fifteenth of the eleventh month, the Master applied for permission from the Government and the Chinese Buddhist Association in Beijing.

When the monks in other places heard news of this, they came to be ordained by the Master. At first about a hundred arrived, but soon two hundred more followed so that there were now five hundred monks on the mountain, all seeking ordination, and it was difficult to look after them with food and lodgings. Moreover, the Roman Catholic Church, the Buddhist Youth Association and the Diamond Bodhimandala at Shanghai had been in trouble for one reason or another during the last few months – and, to make matters worse – the provincial authorities of Gansu telegraphed those in Jiangxi, saying that unscrupulous leaders of deviant sects had been coming to Mount Yun-ju to ask for ordination. When the Master heard of this allegation, he took every precaution to avoid trouble. The local authorities discussed this matter with him and offered to send police for the maintenance of peace and order on the mountain. At the time those seeking full ordination were already at the monastery and to have rejected their demands would have broken the Buddha's commandment to help others, whereas to accept would have been absolutely impossible because of present conditions what with the lack of food and accommodation. Thus the Master followed the relevant chapter in the *Brahma-Net Sutra*[2] on the expedient of self-administered ordination.

The Master expounded the ten prohibitions[3] to the monks, all the Vinaya rules and the three cumulative commandments,[4] something he did at great pains for ten consecutive days. He then urged them to return to their native locations and to act as instructed on a date fixed by himself, giving them certificates of discipleship, keeping with him only the hundred monks whom he had arranged to ordain on the appointed day and thus the trouble came to an end. Afterwards, he held a week of Chan meditation.

That year more than 140 *mou* [21.2 acres] of land were reclaimed to raise rice and millet and numerous plots were cleared in order to plant tea and fruit trees. No sooner had these wastelands become fit for tillage than outsiders began to covet them. The local authorities set up an office of the Agriculture and Forestry Department on the mountain to take over all the land reclaimed by the monastery on the pretext of increasing its productive capacity. The Master bore this patiently but when they also took over his cowshed and forced him away, he telegraphed Beijing to report the incident. The provincial authorities were then ordered to return the Master's cowshed to him along with the reclaimed land. Although the local officials obeyed this order, they bore a grudge against the Master and later caused him a great deal of trouble.

Monks from other places came to the mountain in great numbers and about 1,500 of them stayed at the monastery in thatched huts built to lodge them. Day and night they inquired about the Dharma without interruption but in order to avoid putting strain on the Master, he was asked to fix the time for daily interviews. From the eleventh of the third month, he began to give daily lectures which were duly recorded.

Notes

1. That is, meditation (1) upon the real to accord with the noumenon; (2) on purity to wipe out transient phenomena; (3) on all-embracing wisdom to accord with the Mean; (4) on compassion for the liberation of all living beings; and (5) On kindness for their happiness.

2. The *Brahmajala-sutra* or *Fan-wang-jing* was translated into Chinese by Kumarajiva in 406. It became very popular as a basic text concerning the bodhisattva-rules and commandments.

3. The 'ten prohibitions' (Saksapada) are: (1) Not to take life; (2) Not to steal; (3) Not to commit adultery; (4) Not to lie; (5) Not to take intoxicating liquor; (6) Not to take food out of regulated hours; (7) Not to use garlands or perfumes; (8) Not to sleep on high or broad beds; (9) Not to take part in singing or dancing or witness the same; (10) To refrain from handling minted or unminted gold.

It is apparent that the Northern Buddhist tradition has introduced variants of the above for practical purposes. For instance, the handling of money has been allowed in Chinese monasteries where many monks have been responsible for raising subscriptions, managing temple affairs, reprinting books, etc.

4. The 'three cumulative commandments' are (1) To do no evil; (2) To do good; (3) To benefit all sentient beings. In practice, the 'three cumulative commandments' are given prior to the 'ten prohibitions' mentioned above.

XU-YUN'S 117TH YEAR
(1956/57)

In the spring the Master began building the main hall, the shrine of the four *deva*-kings (guardians of the monastery), the Tower of Humility, the Tower of Boundless Sight, the bell tower, shrine halls, and dormitories, which were completed one after the other. They were copied from the Gu-shan, Nan-hua and Yun-men Monasteries.

Thus in less than three years after the Master's arrival, new temple buildings sprang up again to restore the ancient splendour of the holy site from the Tang and Song Dynasties. Those staying at the monastery now numbered two thousand people, among whom were technicians, building contractors and people experienced in agriculture and forestry. They contributed to the speedy renovation of the holy site and reclamation of wasted land.

In rebuilding the Zhen-ru Monastery, the Master did not appeal for funds but contributions came nevertheless from all quarters. For instance, Bhiksuni Kuan-hui of Hong Kong held a Dharma-meeting there and succeeded in raising 10,000 Hong Kong dollars, which she sent to him, and Upasaka Zhan Li-wu of Canada, who had never met the Master, contributed 10,000 Canadian dollars. Upasaka Wu Xing-cai of Shanghai, who had left that year for Yun-ju via Hong Kong in order to pay reverence at the holy site, went by way of the Zhang-gong Jetty and found the mountain track rough and difficult to negotiate. He vowed to repair it and the work, which required an expenditure of 100,000 dollars, was now under way. The Master had rebuilt a score of temples and monasteries all over the country. When he originally came to the holy site in ruins at Yun-ju, he had only a staff with him and after its renovation, he handed the newly rebuilt temple to another monk and left with that same staff as his sole possession. Now that the monastery on Mount Yun-ju[1] had been rebuilt, it seemed that he had been assisted by *devas* and everybody hoped that he would stay there.

In the ninth month, when the Pool of the Bright Moon and Blue Stream were being dredged on the mountain, a large rock was dug up which bore mainly indecipherable inscriptions except for a few characters here and there which mentioned that the ancient Chan-Master Fu-yin ('Buddha Seal'), the then Abbot of the monastery, and the great poet, Su Dong-bo, had frequently sat on the stone which was close to the stream. A bridge had later been built nearby to commemorate the occasion, the rock then being called the 'Mind Chat Rock', and the bridge 'Buddha-seal Bridge'. Master Xu-yun now built a porch for the rock at the end of a new bridge to preserve the historic site and wrote the following poem on the occasion:

> In fulfilment of a vow to worship Buddha
> Su Dong-bo crossed mountains and rivers without end.
> On a rock near the Blue Stream Bridge he chatted on about
> The Mind until it vanished, won over by the rock.

In those days at Jin-shan[2] he wore his belt of jade;[3]
Thus dull in spirit he could not forsake the world.
A cloud[4] now rolls up the Mind Chat Rock
To rebuild a bridge, commemorate a poet's name.

That winter about two hundred monks and laymen cleared over 180 *mou* [27.2 acres] of marshy land to grow rice and over 70 *mou* [10.6 acres] of dry land to plant other cereals, thus providing adequate food for a community of five hundred monks.

On the seventh of the twelfth month the Master held two weeks of Chan meditation. After that, the monks at Nan-hua Monastery, the Temple of Six Banyans in Canton, Ding-guan Monastery at Zhang-ding and the Fa-lun Temple in Ning-hua requested the Master to transmit the Precepts to their devotees expediently from a distance.

Notes
1. Yun-ju means 'Abode of the Cloud' and the master's name, Xu-yun, means 'Empty Cloud.' Yun-ju was the Master's last abode on earth.
2. Mount Jin, the site of a famous monastery.
3. Symbol of the official's high rank which showed the poet's inability to forsake worldly things.
4. The 'cloud' stands for master Xu-yun.

XU-YUN'S 118TH YEAR
(1957/58)

As requested by Upasaka Wu Xing-zai, repairs to the mountain track had begun the previous year. In the spring, the eighteen *li* of track from Zhang-gong Jetty to the monastery was widened six feet. It consisted of paths winding up steep mountains and precipitous peaks, and bridges were built over all the mountain torrents. The whole work was completed in the autumn and inscriptions in large Chinese characters such as 'Zhao-zhou Gate', 'Rainbow Bridge', etc., were carved on the rocks along the track. The Master recorded the event in a *gatha* which was carved on a stone tablet.

In the sixth month, the local Department of Agriculture and Forestry, seeing that the community had reclaimed wasteland, cancelled the 1953 agreement which authorised the monastery to do such work, set up their own organisation on the mountain and sent a few dozen men to the monastery to take over all its land. The monks in charge vainly petitioned the local authorities seven times to abide by the agreement. When the men took over the Master's cowshed and ordered him to leave it, he reported the matter to the Beijing government, who immediately instructed the provincial authorities to stop interfering with the monastery's reclamation works. Although they obeyed Beijing's orders, they bore a grudge against the Master for reporting the matter to their superiors. This was the cause of endless troubles that ensued. As a result the Master was compelled to hand over all the reclaimed land to the local Department of Agriculture and Forestry to appease them. About the same time, Abbot Hai-deng of the monastery expounded the *Lotus Sutra*, after which he selected thirty young monks to form a Buddhist Study Centre to train the novices.

XU-YUN'S 119TH YEAR
(1958/59)

In the spring, the purge of 'rightist' elements in the country affected temples and monasteries. A group of so-called Buddhists convened a general meeting in Hankou at which the abbots and the monks in charge of designated temples and monasteries were required to be present. The Master excused himself on the grounds of old age and ill health.

Abbot Beh-huan of Nau-hua Monastery, Master Chuan-shi, Director of Guests at Zhen-ru Monastery, Abbot Fu-yuan and Master Jian-xing and Yin-kai of Yun-men Monastery were accused of being 'rightists' but were given a chance to turn witness in order to denounce, incriminate and purge the Master. They narrowly escaped misfortune when they refused to do so. Finally, a small group of accusers indicted the Master on ten charges, such as corruption, reactionarism, gangsterism, extravagent transmission of the Precepts, etc., the most unbelievable one being that he shared his cowshed with young novices to practise homosexuality.

At the monasteries of Nan-hua, Yun-men and Zhen-ru, news-bulletins were posted on the walls denouncing the Master who, however, took no notice of them. When his disciples wanted to reply to these groundless charges, he prevented them from doing so. One, then two months passed without any news from Hankou, where the meeting also came to an end. However, the Master's most helpful attendants and those monks who had followed him for many years were ordered to leave him and sent to places designated by the local authorities.

Another couple of months passed without any action being taken against the Master. Then, one day he received a letter from Beijing and learned that the Hankou meeting had not dared to purge him because of his well-known lofty virtues, but had only sent a list of indictments to the highest authority who, after glancing at it, only laughed and ordered them not to purge him. Thus the Master escaped from misfortune.

On the fifteenth of the ninth month, the Police Chief, Zhang Jian-min, came with his senior assistants to the Master's cowshed, searched it and dug up the ground without finding anything. They then took away all the letters which the Master had received from Beijing, documents, sutras, accounts books, etc., which they refused to return in spite of repeated requests.

On the sixteenth of the ninth month, the Master gathered the community in the main hall to inform them of recent happenings. As a consequence of these troubles, the Master fell very ill. Before, when he paid reverence to the Buddha, he could prostrate but how he had to be supported by his assistants. The community knew that his causal life was coming to an end. One day he called in two attendants and entrusted them with his last will. On the nineteeth of the tenth month, he delivered his final sermon to the community.

相德秩八人老公印

The Pure Land Master Yin Guang (d. 1940).
See Xu-yun's Discourse, 21 December, 1952.

CHAPTER FIFTEEN

THE FINAL YEAR

XU-YUN'S 120TH YEAR
(1959)

In the spring, since the Master had entered his 120th year, temples, monasteries and all his disciples both in China and abroad were jubiliant about him reaching the same age as the ancient Master Zhao-zhou[1] and informed him of their desire to celebrate his birthday. He immediately replied to them as follows:

I myself do not know how long I shall live and my birthday is still far off. However, the Upasaka Wu Xing-zai has expressed a desire to send me birthday scrolls and I have thanked him, requesting him not to do so. My former karma has caused my present life to be full of troubles. I am like a candle in the wind and have achieved nothing; when I think of this I am ashamed of my empty reputation. A century of worldly troubles is like a dream and an illusion and is not worth any attachment. Moreover, since birth leads to death, a wise man should be on the alert and set his mind on the Dao, like one who loses no time to save his burning head. How can I indulge in following a worldly custom? I thank you for your kindness from the bottom of my heart but sincerely regret that I am unable to accept your present. I still grieve over the untimely death of my mother and would request that you stop this unprofitable plan to celebrate my birthday in order not to aggravate my sins.

In the third month, as the Master saw that the dredging of the 'Pool of the Bright Moon' and building of the stupa were not yet completed, he personally supervised the work which was finished a few months later.

As early as 1956 after Mrs Zhan Wang Shen-ji had become the Master's disciple, she and her husband, Zhan Li-wu, a Chinese merchant in Canada, had intended to contribute to the rebuilding of the main hall, but since all the temple buildings had by then been renovated, the husband expressed a desire to erect a stupa for the relics of the Buddha and a Chan hall, to be called 'Liu Yun' (lit. 'Retaining the Cloud', i.e. the Master) with a wish that he should remain in the world.

The Master replied that since the monasteries of Nan-hua and Yun-men each had a stupa for the ashes of dead monks, it would be advisable to construct one for Zhen-ru, which still lacked a stupa so that the remains of ancient Abbots and Masters of the monastery, which had been buried elsewhere, could all be brought to and preserved in one stupa where they would be well looked after so that devotees could come to the mountain and pay reverence to them. As to the Liu-yun Hall that was proposed, he was deeply moved by the patron's thought, but since had had never used a single beam or tile contributed by others for his own account during his whole life, he politely declined the offer.

Zhan Li-wu wrote to the Master saying that, besides 10,000 Hong Kong dollars which he had already remitted, he would send him another 50,000 (or 10,000 Canadian dollars in all) for building the stupa. The Master accepted the contribution and in the winter of that year [1956] began the construction of a stupa similar to that of Nan-hua Monastery and a few more sutra-reading rooms for the monks. The work was completed in the seventh month of this year [1959] and was the last work to be done in his lifetime.

In the same month, the Master received remittances from Upasikas Wang Shen-ji of Canada and Zeng Kuan-bi of Hong Kong, each requesting him to make a statue of Ksitigarbha Bodhisattva to celebrate his 120th birthday. He immediately ordered the two statues, which were finished within two months; one was placed in a shrine in the bell tower and one in the stupa. They were the last statues made in his lifetime.

The Master had gradually grown weaker after his grave illness in the third month. At first he could still manage to attend to his duties and to supervise all the unfinished works, but in the seventh month he suffered from chronic indigestion and could not take rice and other solid food; so at breakfast and midday, he only took a small bowl of *congee* [a thin rice soup].

The Beijing government ordered the provincial authorities to arrange for him to be treated by a doctor but he declined, saying, 'My causal link with this world is coming to an end.' He then wrote to his disciples who had contributed to the rebuilding of the monastery, informing them that its renovation had been completed and enjoining them to send no more remittances to him; he also urged them to take good care of themselves and to strive to practise the Dharma.

As the Master was very ill, one day the Abbot of the monastery and the monks in charge came to see him at the cowshed. Xu-yun said, 'There is a causal affinity between us so that we gather together at the same place and, thanks to your greatly developed minds, we have been able to restore this holy site in the space of a few years during which I was deeply moved by your suffering and hardship. I regret that my causal life is coming to an end and will be unable to look after this monastery, so it is incumbent upon you to take good care of it. After my death, please have my body dressed in my yellow robe and garments, placed in a coffin a day later and cremated at the foot of the hill to the west of the cowshed. Please then mix my ashes with sugar, flour and oil, knead all this into nine balls and throw them into the river as an offering to living beings in the water. If you help me to fulfil my vow, I shall be eternally grateful.'

They comforted the Master who then chanted the following three *gathas:*

First Gatha

Taking pity upon ants a shrimp jumps not into the water;[2]
To benefit watery beings throw my ashes in the river.
If they accept this last offering of my body,
I hope they will win *Bodhi* and labour for salvation.

Second Gatha

I urge my Dharma friends to think
Deeply and with care about
The karma of birth and death
As silkworms spin their cocoons.
Endless desires and thoughts
Increase all trouble and suffering.
If you would escape from this,
First practise almsgiving and the threefold study

209

Of wisdom, meditation, discipline,
Then hold firm the four correct thoughts.[3]
Suddenly you awaken and perceive
Clearly that all is like dew and lightning,
You realise that in the absolute
Myriads of things have the same substance,
The created and the uncreated
Are like water and its waves.

Third Gatha

Alas, in my declining years
My debt of gratitude is still unpaid,
As my debt is still outstanding, shallow
Is my wisdom and yet deep my karma.
I blush at my failure [in my Dharma practice],
At my stupidity while staying on Yun-ju.
Like one who still clings to words when he recites the sutras,[4]
I am ashamed to meet the World-Honoured One and the
Assembly that is still gathered on Vulture's Peak.
It is now your duty to protect the Dharma,
For you are now Wei-tuo in this age reborn[5]
To revive the true tradition of Vaisali
Which reveals the oneness of self and others.
Look up to and respect Vimalakirti,
A rock that in midstream ever stands unmoved,
One on whose words men for deliverance rely.
They endure endless ills in this Dharma-ending-age
In which scarce are they who on Truth rely.
I am involved in trouble since my reputation is not true;
You should, therefore, awaken and from the right path no longer
    stray.
Rejoice to hear of the Buddha's land
And with it strive to be in tune.
These last words are left behind
To reveal my inmost thought.

In the eighth month, as the Master's birthday drew near, the
Abbots of other monasteries and his disciples came to the mountain to offer their congratulations. He felt a little better. A few

disciples headed by Bhiksuni Kuan-hui came from Hong Kong and had several long talks with him.

At the beginning of October, as the Master was critically ill, he ordered that the statues of the Buddhas and the sutras be placed in good order in the stupa where a few monks should stay to recite the Buddha's name in the morning and evening sessions.

On 7 October, when the Master received a telegram from Beijing announcing the death of Marshall Li Ji-shen, he exclaimed, 'Li Ji-shen, why have you gone before me? I must go too.' His attendants were taken aback at these words. As the Master had lain in bed for several days during which he breathed with difficulty and slept most of the time, an attendant came to watch by his side. Each time the Master saw him, he told the latter to leave him alone, saying, 'I can take care of myself.'

On 12 October at noon, the Master ordered his attendants to take the statue of the Buddha in the niche to another room for worship. The monks felt something unusual and reported to the Abbot and the monks in charge of the monastery who came to see him in the evening and implored him to stay for the sake of the Dharma. He said, 'Why do you still take this worldly attitude at such a moment! Please recite the Buddha's name in the main hall for me.' As they asked for his last instruction and will, he said, 'A few days ago I told you what to do after my death; there is no need to repeat it all over again. As to my last words, they are: 'Practise *sila*, *dhyana* and *prajna* to wipe out desire, anger and stupidity.'

After a pause, he continued, 'Develop the right thought and right mind to create the great spirit of fearlessness for the deliverance of men and the whole world. You are tired, please retire to rest.' It was midnight when they withdrew.

Yun-ju was a high mountain and in the height of autumn, the cold from biting winds caused the leaves in the thicket to drop in abundance. The sky was hidden by tall trees which cast their confusing shadows. In the room, the flame of a tiny lamp was as small as a bean and outside dewdrops were like pearls. In his distant cowshed, the solitary old Master lay in his bed, far away from the main hall where the sutra reading and sacred music continued to bid him farewell.

Early in the morning of 13 October, two attendants entered the room, where they saw the Master seated in meditation posture as usual, the only exception being the reddish colour of his cheeks.

211

They dared not disturb him and went outside to watch. At noon, through the window, they saw him descend from his bed, drink some water and stand up to pay reverence to the Buddha. Fearing that he was too weak and might fall to the ground, they entered the room. The Master then sat down and said slowly, 'I just saw in a dream a cow trample on and break the Buddha-seal Bridge; I also saw the stream stop flowing.'[6] He then closed his eyes and said no more.

At 12.30 p.m., he called his attendants and then looked around, paused and said, 'You have been with me for years and I have been deeply moved by your hardship and suffering. It is useless to speak of past events but in the last ten years I have drunk from the cup of bitterness and have been shocked by distrust and peril. I have endured slander and injustice so that the holy sites in this country can be maintained, the best traditions and rules of pure living can be preserved and the Sangha robe kept intact. I have risked my life to fight for this Sangha robe! You are my close disciples and know all that has happened. Later on if you stay in thatched huts or go to other monasteries, you should always keep this Sangha robe as a symbol of our faith, but how to preserve it? The answer is in the word *sila*.' After saying this, he brought his palms together and enjoined upon his assistants to take good care of themselves. They refrained from tears and went outside to watch.

At 1.45, the two attendants entered the room and saw the Master reclining on his right side. Seeing that he had passed away, they immediately informed the Abbot and the whole community who gathered to read sutras to bid farewell to the Master and then took turns to recite the Buddha's name by day and night.

The Master's body was encoffined on the 18th and when it was cremated on the 19th, the air was filled with a rare fragrance and a white smoke went up into the sky. In the ashes were found over a hundred large relics of five different colours and countless small ones which were mostly white; all of them were clean and brilliant in appearance. On the 21st, the ashes were placed in the stupa.

The Master passed away in his 120th year at the Dharma-age of 101.[7]

Notes
1. Master Zhao-zhou (778–897), well known for his *gong-an Wu* (Jap. *Mu*).

2. This life refers to Xu-yun being offered the chance to leave the troubled conditions in mainland China but because of his compassion he declined.
3. The four correct thoughts: (1) That the body is impure; (2) That suffering comes from sensation; (3) That mind is impermanent; (4) That there is no ego-self in phenomena.
4. One who recites the sutras aimlessly without trying to understand their meaning.
5. A general under the Southern Deva-King, one of the guardians in a monastery.
6. This means release from the last link with the world of illusion.
A monk's 'Dharma-age' means the number of years he has been in the Sangha.

THE SONG OF THE SKIN BAG

WRITTEN BY MASTER XU-YUN
IN HIS 19TH YEAR

The Song of the Skin Bag,[1] the skin bag is sung.Before the empty aeon[2]
    it had neither name nor form,
After the Buddha with awe-inspiring voice[3] it became a hindrance.
Three hundred and sixty tendons are linked within the body[4]
Enclosed by four and eighty thousand pores.[5]
Divided it splits into heaven, earth and man,
United it combines the four elements.
It supports heaven, props up earth,
But what of its mettle?
Understand cause and effect, discern the times
Survey the stupidity of past and present.
Because of wrong clinging to illusory forms,
Parents are involved and wife and children loved.
By vain indulgence in delusion karma is left behind,
The Song of the Skin Bag, the skin bag is sung.
Drinking wine and eating meat upset the mind-nature,
Indulgence in pleasure and desire leads to utter ruin.
When officialdom is strong to oppress the innocent[6]
And traders artful against their consciences, how long
Will their wealth and power last, their pride and their extravagance?
The poor and lowly will not so last while there is cruelty and violence.
Discrimination between self and others leads to inequality,
Destroying living beings as worthless things.
Thinking and discerning cause desire, stupidity and hatred,
While becoming lost in heresies invites self-destruction.
Killing, stealing, adultery and lying have no end,
And rude behaviour to others increases attachment and aversion.
To scold the wind and curse the rain is desrespectful to the gods,
While depression comes from ignorance of birth and death.
When leaving a cow's womb to enter a mare's belly

THE SONG OF THE SKIN BAG

Who will sing of or lament your change of form?
Many evil acts without a good deed will make
Aimless and toilsome your transmigration.
Entering the three evil realms, falling into hell[7]
Causes suffering to animals and hungry ghosts.
The ancient sages would oft repeat their warning,
Likewise the morning bell and drum at eve are to change your heart.
Good and evil karma bring certain retribution,
Escape then, worldly men, from the five periods of impurity.[8]
The Song of the Skin Bag, the skin bag is sung;
If the owner of form is not entangled by it,
For illusory matter to interdependence owes its name –
He can readily turn his mind within
To contemplate in sovereign ease.
With no desire for fame and for wealth no craving,
Cut off all liking and from the world retire.
With no love for wife and no affection for children
Enter a monastery to keep the discipline.
Look for learned teachers, seek out their teaching
On Chan practice and meditation to O'er-leap the three worlds.[9]
Store what you see and hear, forsake all causal clingings
To escape for ever from the worldly way.
By taming the six senses and stopping all your thoughts,
With neither self nor other, no trouble will remain,
Unlike worldly men who sigh when mist and dew disperse.[10]
With one robe to cover you and food enough
To satisfy your hunger, keep yourself in shape.
Give wealth away, sacrifice your body and life
Without a second thought as when you spit or sneeze.
Keep pure the discipline, be without fault
And correct in your deportment.[11] Be not angry
When insulted, bear no hatred when you are beaten,
Forget all derison by enduring the unendurable.
Without deviation, without interruption
Hold for ever the one thought of Amitabha.
Let there be no dullness, no confusion,
But like the fir and cypress defy the bitter cold.
Doubt no more the Buddha, doubt no more the Dharma;
With innate wisdom look clearly into what you see and hear,
Bore the paper, cut the hide[12] and go back

To the source, for self-liberation means
Returning to the spring and source of reality.
There is neither 'non-existence' nor emptiness
Exposed is the potentiality divine, wondrous and inconceivable.
When you reach here all grievance ends.
Hurrah, for now you realise the goal.
With the ten titles of Buddha[13] you will teach a myriad worlds.
Aha, that same leaking shell [14] is now
The omnipresent Buddha-body.[15]
Clearly good and evil karmas are infallible, so why
Rely on falsehood instead of practising the truth?
When the absolute is split the two extremes appear,
The spiritual mind turns into heaven and earth.
Kings and ministers are noble owing to their past karmas,
None are rich or noble, poor or humble without previous cause.
Where there is birth – there will be death,
Why grumble since this is known to everyone?
For wife, children (and self), for happiness and wealth
All prospects are spoiled by anger and desire.
For what fame or gain did I trifle
Away my last nineteen springs?[16]
Frustrations of a thousand, nay ten thousand kinds
Harass and make your life yet more unbearable.
When you grow old with failing sight and snow-white hair
You will have vainly passed a lifetime ignorant of virtue.
From day to month, from month to year in vain will you
Regret that months and years turn like a wheel.
Who is an immortal in this world of ours?
'Tis better to revere once more the cloud of compassion[17]
And on a famous mountain or in some renowned place
To live at ease in transcendental bliss.
Do not you know how fast the temporary flies?
Respectfully ponder a few expedient sentences,
Recite Amitabha's name, see clearly into birth and death,
Then enjoy happiness beyond the reach of others.
Practise Chan, seek out its aim; the pure
And the spiritual are only this.
With clear tea and vegetarian food the mind
Errs not enjoying Dharma night and day.
Forsake both self and other, relinquish 'you' and 'I',

Treat friend and foe alike forgetting praise and censure.
When the mind is free from hindrance and disgrace
Do Buddhas and Patriarchs regards its Oneness as being without use?
The World-Honoured One renounced his love to climb the snowy
    mountains,[18]
While Avalokitesvara left home to become a son of the Buddha.[19]
In the days of Yao and Shun[20] lived Zhao and Yu,[21]
When the throne was offered to Zhao he washed his ears.[22]
Remember Zhang Zi-fang and Liu Cheng-Yi
Who cast away their glory, retiring from the world.
In this period of termination when troubles lie ahead,[23]
Why do you not awaken to vie with the ancestors?
To indulge in ignorance, committing the ten evils
Exhausts your ingenuity and wins the world's contempt.
Wars, epidemics, droughts and floods are frequent,
Dearth, famine and strife succeed each other and
When weird tales prevail misfortune follows.
'Midst earthquakes, landslides and tidal waves
What will you do in order to escape?
Evil acts in past transmigrations
Cause present falsehood and frustration.
When poor and in trouble virtue should first be cultivated,
Then in a monastery worship with virtuous heart the King of the Law,
Repentance and reform from past wrong deeds improve your lot.
Call on learned teachers, seek your experience to seal,
First learn, then leave both birth and death to realise the Mind-nature,
Impermanence exposed reveals eternity.
Path lies in path within your practice.
The saints and sages left clear sayings to reform the world,
Slight not then the teaching of the *Tripitaka.*
With earnestness and deep sincerity
I urge all human beings to be righteous
Take not my words as idle nor forget them,
For self-cultivation leads to perception of self-nature.
Hasten your practice, be ever zealous,
For the sowing of *Bodhi* is the direct cause of awakening.
The nine stages after rebirth in the Lotus are testified by the Buddha,
An Amitabha will take you to the Western Paradise.
Lay down your bag of skin, leap on the Vehicle Supreme.
This is the Song of the Skin Bag, hearken to it friends!

Notes

1. The human body is likened to a skin-bag which obstructs our realisation of the truth.

2. The empty aeon is regarded as coming after that of the destruction of the world systems and preceding that of their formation, the latter being followed by that of 'existence'.

3. *Bhimsa-garjita-ghosa-svara-raja* (short form *Bhimsa-raja*) or the King with awe-inspiring voice, the name of countless Buddhas, successively appearing during the aeon free from misery, decay, calamities, epidemics, etc.

4. The digit 3 symbolises the past, present and future, or time. The digit 6 stands for the six worlds of existence and the six directions north, south, east, west, the zenith and nadir, or space.

5. The digit 8 stands for the eight consciousnesses and the digit 4 for the four elements: earth, water, fire and air which constitute the human body.

6. The Master's father was an official.

7. The three evil realms: hungry ghosts, animals and hells.

8. The five periods of impurity: (1) The aeon in decay when it suffers deterioration giving rise to form; (2) Deterioration of views, selfishness etc., arising; (3) Passions and delusions arising from desire, anger and stupidity in which pride and doubt prevail; (4) The subsequent increase in human miseries and decrease in happiness and (5) The gradual shortening of human life to ten years.

9. The 'Triple realms' of Desire, form and formlessness.

10. All worldly men are grieved about the impermanence of things which are likened to mist and dew.

11. That is, while walking, standing, sitting and reclining.

12. Bore the paper of the sutras to extract the correct meaning and pierce the ox-hide of ignorance to realise the truth.

13. The ten titles of a Buddha are: (1) *Tathagata*, He who comes thus as do all other Buddhas; the absolute 'coming'; (2) *Arhat* or one worthy of worship; (3) *Samyak-sambuddha*, Omniscient; (4) *Vidyacarana-sampanna*, perfect knowledge and conduct; (5) *Sugata*, the well-departed; (6) *Lokavid*, knower of the world; (7) *Anuttara*, the peerless lord; (8) *Purusadamya-sarathi*, the tamer of passions; (9) *Sasta deva-manusyanam*, teacher of gods and men; (10) *Bhagavat* or *Lokanatha*, the World-Honoured One.

14. The illusory human body.

15. The spiritual body appearing in full.

16. Xu-yun complained that he had wasted his time until his 19th year before succeeding in escaping from home.

17. The over-spreading, fructifying cloud of compassion, the heart of the Buddha.

18. The Himalayas. According to the Chinese Buddhist tradition, this symbolises the Buddha's renunciation ascent on the Bodhi-path.

19. A bodhisattva, son of 'the Buddha's family'.

20. The golden age of Chinese history when the country was ruled by the wise Emperors Yao and Shun.

21. Yao knew that Zhao and Yu were two sages and offered to abdicate in their favour but both declined.
22. When Zhao heard of Yao's offer of the throne to him, he went to the river bank to wash his ears from the 'impurity' of the offer.
23. The present period of the Dharma-ending-age.
24. The nine stages of progression as described in the *Sutra of Amitabha*.

GLOSSARY

ABHIDARMA (Chin. Lun-zang): One of the three divisions of the *Tripitaka* or 'Three Baskets' *(San-zang)*. It consists of systematic treatises and commentaries, usually attributed to disciples of the Buddha or eminent scholars who lived in the centuries after the Buddha's *parinirvana*.

ALAYA VIJNANA (Chin. A-le-ye-shi): The 'eighth consciousness' or 'store consciousness', so-called because it is held to contain the seeds of all dharmas, physical and mental. As such, it occupies an ambivalent role in Buddhist psychology. While screened by inborn and discriminative attachments it is the source of delusion, but when these are eradicated, it is the source of enlightenment. Cf. *The Surangama Sutra*.

AMITABHA BUDDHA (Chin. Amito-fo): The Buddha of Boundless Light of the Western Pure Land or Sukhavati, the central figure of the Pure Land tradition. Appears in sutras and mandala groups with Avalokitesvara on his left and Mahasthamaprapta on his right. He vowed to bring all sentient beings to his 'Pure Land' and aherents of this school recite his name in order to be reborn there. Cf. *The Sutra of Amitabha, Sutra of Amitayus*, etc.

ANANDA (Chin. A-nan): Young brother of Devadatta and cousin of the Buddha. Said to have accompanied the Buddha for twenty years. Famous for his keen learning and memory. Regarded as the Second Indian Chan Patriarch by Chinese Buddhists.

ANUTTARA-SAMYAK-SAMBHODI (Chin. A-nu-duo-lo-san-miao-san-pu-ti): Supreme and unexcelled enlightenment. Short form: *anubodhi*.

ARHAT (Chin. Lohan): The saint or highest type of the Hinayana tradition who has reached the fourth *dhyana*-stage but only

220

pursues self-enlightenment, in contrast with the Bodhisattva or highest type of the Mahayana who pursue self-enlightenment for the sake of others. The term is sometimes used more broadly to denote any Buddhist saint or sage.

ARYA (Chin. Sheng): a noble saint, an honoured *bhiksu;* one who follows the royal path to attainment. Noted for wisdom and insight.

ASHVAGOSHA (Chin. Ma-ming): Known as the 'Neighing Horse'. A Brahmin converted to Buddhism in the first century c.e. Said to have been an advisor to King Kanishka. Eventually settled in Benares. His most famous contribution is the *Awakening of Faith,* a commentary which has exerted wide influence in the Far East.

AVALOKITESVARA (Chin. Guan-yin): Known as the 'Goddess of Mercy' in China and as 'She who looks down upon the cries of the world'. A Bodhisattva linked with the compassion aspect of mind. Attained enlightenment by looking into the hearing faculty. The name means 'sound regarder'. Cf. the *Surangama Sutra.* Guan-yin's bodhimandala is at Pu-tuo.

AVATAMSAKA SUTRA (Chin. Hua-yan Jing): Said to have been the first long sermon expounded by the Buddha. It teaches the Four Dharma-realms: (1) the phenomenal realm, with differentiation; (2) the noumenal realm, with unity; (3) the phenomenal and noumenal as interdependent; and (4) the phenomenal as interdependent. There are three Chinese translations: Buddhabhadra's 60-fascicle work (418–20); Siksananda's 80-fascicle work (695–9) and Prajna's 40-fascicle work on the Gandhavyuha portion (759–62).

AVIDYA (Chin. Wu-ming): Ignorance or unenlightenment. First of the '12 Nidanas' or links in the chain of existence.

AVYAKRITA (Chin. Wu-ji): Unrecordable, either as good or bad; things that are innocent and cannot be classified under moral categories. Also used in Chan and Mahayana to indicte a blank or torpid state of mind which is simply a lack of awareness and not to be confused with the 'non-dual wisdom' which is beyond all categories and opposites. *Sila* (discipline) is a precondition for the awakening of wisdom.

AWAKENING OF FAITH SHASTRA (Chin. Da-cheng-qi-xin-lun): A famous commentary attributed to Ashvagosha. Its Sanskrit title is the *Mahayana-sraddhotpada-shastra.* It explains the Mahayana viewpoint in relation to universal enlightenment. The Sanskrit original has been lost but the Chinese translations are attributed to Paramartha (554) and Siksananda (695–700). This shastra has exerted extensive influence upon Far Eastern Buddhism, including all the Mahayana schools, such as the Chan, Pure Land and Tian-tai.

BAI-ZHANG: Bai-zhang Hui-hai (d.814). Successor to Ma-zu Dao-yi and teacher of Gui-shan and Huang-bo. Famous for his *Treatise on the Essential Gateway to the Truth by Means of Instantaneous Awakening.* His temple was on Mount Bai-zhang in Hung-zhou, the modern-day Nanchang, not far from Mount Lu in Jiangxi Province.

BHIKSU, BHIKSUNI (Chin. Bi-qiun, Bi-qiu-ni): Male and female disciples respectively, who observe at least the Ten Precepts as monks or nuns, but frequently many more rules and commandments besides.

BHUTATATHATA (Chin. Zhen-ze): *Bhuta* means 'substance' or that which exists; *tathata* means 'thusness' or 'suchness'. Thus *Bhutatathata* means 'That which exists in suchness', the always-so, the eternal or immutable mind-ground as contrasted with form. It is the Buddhist 'absolute'.

BODHI (Chin. Pu-ti): Enlightenment, awakening. Realisation of the absolute or unborn nature.

BODHIDHARMA (Chin. Pu-ti-ta-ma): The 28th Indian Patriarch and First 'Chinese' Patriarch of the Chan lineage. Said to have been a Brahmin from southern India who took up the Mahayana and Chan Transmission, introducing it to China in about 520. His doctrine was called 'empty-handed' for it consisted of direct pointing to the Mind without fixed methods. Teacher of Hui-ke. Also recognised as a Master of the Lankavatara School with which the Chan tradition had early associations.

BODHIMANDALA (Chin. Pu-ti-dao-chang): Truth plot, holy site or any place where the Dharma is taught, practised or realised.

Used for monasteries in general, but also to denote the genius-loci of certain bodhisattvas, e.g. Manjusri on Mount Wu-tai, Avalokitesvara at Pu-tuo, etc.

BODHISATTVA (Chin. Pu-sa): A Mahayanist who seeks enlightenment for the sake of others and who is devoid of egotism. The Mahayana also recognises the liberating power of past bodhisattvas through the strength of their vows, so that if a devotee links his or her mind with the qualities or characteristics of a given bodhisattva (e.g. compassion, wisdom, etc.), the same qualities can be aroused in that devotee's mind. Seen from a deeper level, such bodhisattvic energy is but a reflex of the innate wisdom-nature of the mind and does not come from outside.

BRAHMAJALA SUTRA (Chin. Fan-wang-jing): Very popular in Chinese Buddhism as a basic text for the bodhisattva commandments. It is really the tenth chapter of a larger work, the *Bodhisattva-sila-sutra*. Translated into Chinese by Kumarajiva as a two-fascicle work in about 406.

BRAHMALOKAS (Chin. Fan-tian): the eighteen *Brahmalokas* of the *rupadhatu* or form realms. Divided into four *dhyana*-heavens.

BUDDHA (Chin. Fo/Fo-ta): (1) The historical Buddha, Shakyamuni; (2) First of the 'three gems' in the refuge formula, in which the term then means the innate Buddha-potentiality in all, and (3) Any enlightened one who reaches the same stage as Shakyamuni. The Mahayana recognises a plurality of Buddhas for all have the Buddha-nature, and all will eventually attain Buddhahood.

CAO-DONG-ZONG: One of the Five Chan Schools; see under Cao-shan and Dong-shan.

CAO-SHAN: Chan Master Cao-shan Ben-ji (840–901). Enlightened successor of Dong-shan Liang-jie and co-founder with him of the Cao-dong School. Famous for its 'Five Ranks' teaching to indicate the correct understanding of the phenomenal and noumenal or 'guest' and 'host' as one undivided whole. Cao-shan was the name given to the mountain in Jishui where Ben-ji taught his followers in Jiangxi, its title being a tribute to the Cao-xi area where Hui-neng's teaching had flourished.

CAO-XI: The 'Cao-stream'. Name of a river and district in

Guangdong Province. The monastery of the Sixth Patriarch was built there after the visit of the Indian *Tripitaka* Master Jnanabhaisajya in about 502. He liked the forests in the vicinity, which reminded him of the woods in western India, suggesting that a monastery should be built there called 'Precious Wood' (Bao-lin), predicting that a living bodhisattva would later appear at the site and liberate countless living beings. Hui-neng subsequently appeared and made the monastery famous as a great centre of Chan Buddhism. The bodies of Jnanabhaisajya and Hui-neng still sit in repose at Cao-xi. The temple was later called 'Nan-hua'. Master Xu-yun restored this temple in his lifetime, among many others.

CHAN: This is often translated as *Dhyana* (Chin. Chan-na) in other contexts, but in the 'Transmission of the Mind' or Chan School proper, it has a wider meaning. Though Chan adherents do indeed cultivate *dhyana* and *prajna* or stillness and wisdom, the Chan school understands this in a dynamic and not static way. Bodhidharma's mission was to 'point directly to the Mind' for outright cognisance of the Dharmakaya or Buddha-body without passing through the gradual stages mentioned in the teaching school. His Chinese successors also 'pointed to the Mind' without fixed methods and in early times they had only to hint about the presence of this immutable Mind for their disciples to awaken to it without further ado, then understanding the difference between this essentially still Mind and their previous thinking and comparing which alone held them in bondage. For expediency's sake, such direct awakening was called Chan. Eventually, because people found it harder to lay down their false thinking, the Masters were compelled to use strange-seeming tactics such as shouts, blows, etc., with the introduction of the *gong-an* and *hua-tou* methods, but all along they had only wished to indicate this Mind.

The Chan School has thus specialised in a direct and abrupt awakening, instead of its adherents having to pass through the gradual stages mentioned in the teaching school. Five main Chan schools appeared in China, these being the Gui-yang, Lin-ji, Cao-dong, Yun-men and Fa-yan schools.

DANA (Chin. Tan-na): First of the six *paramitas;* almsgiving, charity, whether of goods or doctrine.

DAO: This term means the way, path, truth, etc. Originally coined in ancient Chinese books like the *Yi-jing* or Lao-zi's *Dao-de-jing* and Daoist doctrines anteceding Lao-zi, this term was borrowed by Chinese Buddhists as a convenient way to convey the essentially inexpressible nature of ultimate reality. In Chinese thought, it is inseparable from the 'de' or 'hidden virtue' traditionally associated with it, appropriate because to 'attain the Dao' and its virtue is not so much 'do-gooding' as it is a silent accordance with the inner nature of things.

DAO-YING: Chan Master Dao-ying Yun-ju (d. 902). Eminent Master of the Cao-dong School based at the Zhen-ru Monastery on Mount Yun-ju in Jiangxi Province. One of the famous sites restored by Master Xu-yun.

DE-SHAN: (d. 865). Chan Master Xuan-jian of Mount De in Western Hunan. Enlightened successor of Long-tan and teacher of Xue-feng. Famous for his *gong-an* 'thirty-blows'.

DE-SHAO: (d. 972). National Master De-shao of Mount Tian-tai in Zhejiang Province. Successor of Fa-yan. Revived the Tian-tai School after visiting Korea to retrieve the lost works of Master Zhi-yi.

DEVA (Chin. Ti-wa/tian): The highest incarnations in the six realms of existence. Variously regarded as gods, nature spirits, etc.

DEVADATTA (Chin. Ti-wa-ta-duo): Cousin of the Buddha, of whom he was an enemy and rival.

DHARMA (Chin. Fa): (1) Law, doctrine, ultimate truth, the Dharmata or Dharma-nature itself; (2) Anything Buddhist; (3) Any discrete or particular thing (pl. *dharmas*).

DHARMADHATU (Chin. fa-jie): (1) A term for things in general as they constitute the phenomenal universe; (2) The unifying or underlying spiritual reality regarded as the ground of all things. The Mahayana also accounts for them as 'The Ten Dharma Realms' viz. (1) Buddhas; (2) Bodhisattvas; (3) Pratyeka Buddhas; (4) Sravakas; (5)Devas; (6) Humans; (7) Asuras; (8) Demons; (9) Animals and (10) Hades or the hells. Also interpreted in terms of the 'eighteen realms of sense' (3 × 6) or six sense-organs, six sense-objects and six sense-data. The Mahayana view is summed up in

225

the saying: 'The Ten Dharma Realms are not beyond a single thought'.

DHARMAKAYA (Chin. Fa-shen): The Buddha-body or essential nature as such. It is immaterial and only Buddhas can see it, in contrast to the *Nirmanakaya* (transformation body), which is perceptible to men.

DHUTA (Chin. Tou-ta): Ascetic practices and precepts to purify body and mind. Anyone who practises them is a *Dhuta*.

DHYANA (Chin. Chan-na): See Chan above. Otherwise it means abstract contemplation, or rather, the stillness resulting therefrom. Hui-neng said that *dhyana* is like a lamp and that *prajna* or wisdom is like its light. In Chan, these two must be perfectly balanced. *Dhyana* does not mean 'trance' as some of the old dictionaries suggested, but a state of spiritual equilibrium which remains unhindered amid the rise and fall of phenomena.

DHYANA HEAVENS: See *Brahmaloka*.

DONG-SHAN: (807–69). Chan Master Liang-jie. Disciple of Yun-yan and teacher of Cao-shan. Joint founder – with the latter – of the Cao-dong Chan School. His teaching of the 'Five Positions of Prince and Minister' was devised in order to clarify the relationship between the phenomenal and noumenal or 'guest' and 'host' so that disciples would realise their interdependence and integration as one undivided whole. His monastery was on Mount Dong, Yun-zhou, Jiangxi Province. Master Xu-yun also revived the Cao-dong transmission line.

DUHKHA (Chin. Ku): Suffering, misery born of conditioned existence. First of the 'Four Noble Truths'.

EGO AND DHARMA (Chin. Wo/Fa): The *Vajracchedika* or *Diamond Sutra* mentions two aspects of delusion involving 'ego' and 'dharma'. The first is the coarse view held by worldly men who believe that there is a real or fixed 'self' in the body of four elements confronting a world of objective things (dharma) independent of the mind which creates them. After this coarse view has been eliminated, there still remains the subtle view of 'ego and dharma' which is caused by the mind grasping its own activity and realisation. This last, subtle dualism is hard to spot and overcome, as pointed out by Masters like Han-shan and Xu-yun.

EMEI SHAN: The *bodhimandala* of Samantabhadra Bodhisattva, situated in Sichuan. Samantabhadra or 'Pu Xian' (Universal Worthy) is revered as a protector of *dhyana* and the practice of all the Buddhas. He is depicted in Buddhist iconography seated on a white elephant. He is regarded as a patron of the *Lotus Sutra* and its devotees, besides having links with the *Avatamsaka Sutra* (Hua-yan Jing). In this latter connection, he is known to many Far Eastern Buddhists for the 'ten vows' set out in the 'Xing Yuan Pin', a devotional epilogue.

FA-HUA/FA-HUA-ZONG: Fa-hua means 'Dharma-flower', one of the titles given to the *Lotus Sutra*. As the Tian-tai school bases itself on the *Lotus Sutra* it is often referred to as the 'Dharma Flower School'.

FA-XIANG-ZONG: The Dharmalakshana School. Founded in China by the monk Kui-ji (632–82). It aims at discovering the ultimate reality underlying the phenomenal world by meditating upon the relationship between the characteristic marks *(Lakshana)* of things and the aspects of consciousness *(vijnana)*, its main tenet being all is 'Mind Only' as taught in the idealist doctrines of Maitrayanatha, Asanga, Vasubandhu, etc., as brought back to China by Xuan-zang.

FA-RONG: (584–657): An enlightened successor of Dao-xin, the Fourth Chan Patriarch. His school was known as the 'Ox-head School' because his temple was located on Mount Niu-tou or 'Ox-head Mountain' south of Nanjing.

FA-YAN: (885–958). Chan Master Wan-yi, alias Fa-yan. The founder of the Fa-yan Chan School at the Qing-liang Monastery in Shengzhou district, modern-day Nanjing. Disciple of Gui-chen. Had many successors, some of the most notable being De-zhao, Hui-zhu, Long-guang and Tai-qin. This School was revived by Master Xu-yun. It urges its disciples to identify all phenomena with the absolute, teaching that the three worlds of 'desire, form and formlessness' arise within the One Mind.

GATHA: (Chin. Ji-ta): Poems, metrical chants, usually of four lines. The Chinese devised their own forms but still chanted them when transmitting the Dharma or on other appropriate occasions like their Indian peers. Master Xu-yun composed many *gathas*.

GONG-AN: More commonly known in the Japanese form as *koan* in the west. The tem originally meant a dossier, case record, public document, etc. It was borrowed by Chan Masters as a convenient term and came into use when ancient Masters quoted from instances of enlightenment found in Chan records, these being typical 'concurrent causes' in the process of enlightenment, their sayings and instruction being as valid as the law. By extension, any statement, gesture or action which helps to provoke enlightenment came to be called a *'gong-an'*. Often called 'riddles' or 'nonsensical' sayings in modern books, such enigmatic *gong-an* will never be understood without recognising that the direct cause of enlightenment lies in a disciple's 'inner potentiality' which has first to be aroused by Chan training. Without this, a *gong-an* only reveals its 'dead' or literal meaning.

GU-SHAN: The mountain in Fuzhou where Master Xu-yun took refuge at the Yung-quan Monastery and where many years later, he served as Abbot for a while.

GUEST/HOST: (Chin. Bin/Zhu): Two terms skilfully used by Chinese Masters to help their disciples realise the identity of the phenomenal and noumenal or mutable world of particulars with the immutable Mind. These two terms were coined by Ajnata-kaundinya in the *Surangama Sutra*, when he likened the changing phenomenal to a 'guest' who has nowhere permanent to stay and the unchanging Mind to the 'host' who is free from all coming and going. He also used the further analogy of 'floating dust' in 'clear sunlight' to indicate this identity, the dust always moving while the clear-light remains motionless. See *Surangama Sutra*.

GUNABHADRA: An Indian Dharma Master and member of the Lankavatara School who went to China in the Song Dynasty (420–77) and built an altar at Cao-xi in Guangdong, setting up a stone tablet predicting that a 'flesh and blood' bodhisattva would later be ordained there. Hui-neng (d. 713) was eventually ordained there in 676, in keeping with this prophecy.

GUI-SHAN: (771–853). Master Ling-yu of Mount Gui. Enlightened successor of Bai-zhang and teacher of Yan-shan Hui-ji. Co-founder with the latter of the Gui-yang Chan School. The Gui-shan Monastery was located at Tan-zhou, near the modern-day Changsha in Hunan. Master Xu-yun also revived the Gui-yang School, which teaches the correct understanding of 'substance' *(ti)* and 'function' *(yong)* or the identification of all phenomena with the essential body of the Buddha, which is immaterial.

HAN-SHAN (Cold Mountain) 627–49. An eccentric Buddhist and poet who lived in Mount Tian-tai during the Tang Dynasty. Han-shan and his 'lunatic' friend Shi-de (the 'foundling') are often pictured as a couple of mad vagabonds. They are said to have lived by scrounging leftovers from the temples on Tian-tai. Han-shan was a prolific poet and his poems remain famous to this day, not only in China but also in Japan. The Buddhists regard Han-shan as a 'transformation-body' or Manjusri.

HAN-SHAN: (Silly Mountain) 1546–1623. The name adopted by Chan Master De-qing, who revived the Chan tradition in the Ming Dynasty and wrote many famous commentaries on Chan training, *sutras, shastras,* etc., after his own enlightenment. During one retreat with a companion, both Masters sat in *samadhi* for forty days and nights without eating or sleeping. Han-shan rebuilt many temples in his lifetime.

HETUVIDYA SHASTRA (Chin. Ying-ming Lun): One of the five *pancavidya shastras* explaining causality or the law of causation. The Indian school was founded by Aksapada. According to its formula, it sets out a kind of syllogism involving: (1) the proposition *(pratijna)*; (2) the reason *(hetu)*; (3) the example *(drstanta)*; (4) the application *(upanaya)* and; (5) the conclusion *(nigamana)*.

HINAYANA (Chin. Xiao-cheng): Lit. 'Small vehicle', the preliminary teaching given by the Buddha according to the Northern School. Its 'nirvana' is described in the *Lotus Sutra* as an 'illusion city' or temporary abode until disciples mature enough to receive the complete teaching of the Mahayana or 'Greater Vehicle'.

HUA-TOU: Lit. 'Word-head'. A Chan term. It originally meant the main gist or topic of a literary passage, so it was borrowed by Chan Masters to indicate the living meaning in a Chan phrase or saying. In this context, it is understood quite differently from its literal sense, for in Chan practice the *hua-tou* means the mind before it is stirred, and it is thus the equivalent of 'ante-word' or 'ante-thought'. For this reason, it is not quite correct to render this term as 'head of speech', for a Chan *hua-tou* should be looked into whether there is speech or silence, words or no words. In short, *hua-tou* is the mind before it is disturbed by a thought, that is before the mind bifurcates. In practice, it is inseparable from another term, called *yi-qing* or 'feeling of doubt', meaning doubt about 'who' is looking into the *hua-tou*. Without this 'feeling of doubt' the *hua-tou* cannot become effective. See *Xu-yun's Discourses and Dharma Words*.

HUA-WEI: Lit. 'Word-tail' or 'tail of thought'. As *hua-tou* means the 'head of thought', 'ante-word' or point before the mind stirs to discriminate, *hua-wei* means the mind after it has bifurcated, forming concepts. Most practitioners find that at the beginning of their training, their minds initially give rise to discrimination about the *hua-tou* instead of looking into it. This is what is meant by *hua-wei* or the 'tail of thought'.

HUAI-RANG: (677–744). Enlightened successor of Hui-neng and teacher of Ma-zu. Famous for his 'tile polishing' episode when enlightening the latter. Huai-rang lived and taught at the Chuan-fa Monastery on Mount Heng in the Nan-yue region of Hunan, hence his line of succession was called the 'Nan-yue lineage'.

HUANG-BO (d. 849). Master Xi-yun of the Guang-tang Monastery on Mount Huang-bo, Fujian. Enlightened successor of Bai-zhang and teacher of Lin-ji. His teaching was very strict and consisted of driving away all dualistic conceptions held by his disciples, be they about 'worldly' or 'saintly' views, including the very notion of 'attainment' and 'realisation' so that their minds would become still and passionless and thereby tally with the truth.

HUANG-LONG: (d. 1069). Chan Master Pu-jue of Mount Huang-long. Alias Hui-nan, founder of a sub-sect of the Lin-ji School. Famous for its 'three gates'. Eventually transmitted to Japan by the monk Yosai.

HUI-NENG: (d. 713). Sixth and last Chan Patriarch, after whom the transmission of the Mind flourished all over China. Disciple of Hong-ren at the Dong-chan Monastery, Huang-mei Prefecture. Hui-neng's main teaching was to indicate the non-abiding mind' which is pure and clean and fundamentally beyond 'birth and death', as hinted at in his famous *gatha:* 'In essence Bodhi has no trunk, the bright mirror no chest-stand.' However, he had no choice but to teach his disciples to 'purify their minds' by ridding themselves of all dualistic thoughts which alone lead to 'birth and death'. He is wrongly held to have rejected the use of sutras and traditional methods of repentance and reform, which view is not supported by his *Altar Sutra* of Tan-jing. After appearing at the Bao-lin Monastery, his teaching became known throughout China. His two main successors were Huai-rang and Xing-si.

HUI-WEN: (n.d.). A Chan Master in the Northern Qi Dynasty (550–78) who founded the Tian-tai School after reading Nagarjuna's *Madhyamika Shastra* and realising his enlightenment. The Tian-tai School was later consolidated by Zhi-yi.

HUI-YUAN: (d. 417). Founder of the Pure Land School in China and the 'White Lotus Association' on Mount Lu in Jiangxi.

JI ZU SHAN: The 'Cock's Foot Mountain' in Dali Prefecture, Yunnan Province. Site of the Ying-xiang Monastery where Master Xu-yun was Abbot for several years. It was one of the first temples restored by Xu-yun, famous for being the *bodhimandala* of Mahakasyapa in China.

JIU HUA SHAN: The *bodhimandala* of Kshitigarbha Bodhisattva in China, situated in Anhui Province.

JNANABHAISAJYA: An India *Tripitaka* Master who visited Cao-xi district in 502, bringing with him a bo-sapling which he planted by the altar previously set up by Gunabhadra, predicting that a 'flesh and blood' bodhisattva would later be ordained there.

KARMA: (Chin. Ye): The law of cause and effect (Chin. Yin-guo), or the understanding that actions and thoughts create a necessary response and due retribution.

KARMADANA (Chin. Wei-na): The duty distributor or manager of duties in a temple.

KASAYA, THE FIVE (Chin. Wu-zhuo): The five *kasaya* or periods of turbidity, chaos and decay: (1) the *kalpa* or aeon in decay when it suffers deterioration and gives rise to the ensuing forms; (2) Deterioration of views, egotism arising, etc.; (3) the passions and delusions or desire, anger and stupidity, pride and doubt prevail; (4) Human misery increases and happiness decreases; (5) Human life diminishes to ten years.

KLESA (Chin. Fan-nao): *Klesavarana* or conative hindrance, the affliction of passion, be it worry, anxiety, desire, fear, etc., and whatever causes it. Usually referred to in conjunction with *jneya-varana* or cognitive hindrance, the mind clinging to its own power of acting and formulating.

KSANA (Chin. Chan-na): An instant, a measure of time, equal to one seventy-fifth of a second.

KSANTI (Chin. Chan-ti): Patience, endurance. The third *para-mita* or perfection. At its highest it is *anutpattikadharma-ksanti*, perfect rest in the imperturbable reality underlying phenomenal activity, synonymous with insight into the inherent emptiness of conditioned things.

KSITIGARBHA BODHISATTVA (Chin. Di-zang): Lt. 'Earth-store' Bodhisattva. He is said to have vowed to help liberate all living beings between the *parinirvana* of Shakyamuni Buddha and the coming of Maitreya. Depicted in iconography as a monk with a pilgrim's staff in his right hand, holding a pearl in his left hand. One of the eight *dhyani-bodhisattvas*. His vows even extended to the idea of entering the 'hells' and darkest realms out of compassion. According to tradition, his compassionate vows extend not only to the human and animal realms, but even to every blade of grass.

LAKSANA (Chin. Xiang): Form, appearance, characteristic marks of phenomena.

LANKAVATARA SUTRA (Chin. Leng-jia-jing): Said to have been expounded by the Buddha on Grdhrakuta Peak of 'Vulture Peak' in Lanka, the modern-day Sri Lanka. It teaches the 'Mind Only' doctrine, closely linked with the Chan School. There are four Chinese translations: Dharmaraksha's (412–33); Gunabhad-ra's (443); Bodhiruci's (513) and Siksananda's (700–4). The first has now been lost.

LIN-JI: (d. 866). Master Yi-xuan, founder of the Lin-ji Chan School at the monastery in Zhenzhou, Hebei Province. Disciple of Huang-bo and teacher of many enlightened successors. His teaching is famous for its 'three shouts', each serving a different purpose, its 'shining wisdom', and its 'three mystic sentences' used to foster a correct understanding of the 'host' and 'guest', subject and object, so as to realise one's undivided whole or Bodhi. Lin-ji was a strict disciplinarian and he has been misjudged for instructing his disciples not to cling to 'impure Buddhas' created by their discriminating minds. Modern people sometimes forget that Buddha also warned his followers not to cling to things and Lin-ji's 'true man of no title' is precisely the enlightened nature which the Buddha said was inexpressible and indescribable. Master Xu-yun also revived the Lin-ji teaching.

MA-ZU (709–88). Chan Master Dao-yi of Jiangxi, alias Ma-zu or 'Ancestor horse'. Eminent successor of Huai-rang and teacher of Bai-zhang. Famous for his 'Chan shouts' and fierce teaching which consisted of direct pointing to the Mind. Died on Mount Shi-men.

MADHYAMIKA (Chin. Zhong-guan-pai): The Madhyamika doctrine; one of the two main Mahayana schools in India. Wrongly called 'sophistic nihilism' in modern dictionaries, its founder, Nagarjuna, rather taught the interdependence of all phenomena in the interest of a 'middle way' which avoids both naive realism and nihilism. He only denied that relative knowledge can be applied to the real nature of things, he did not deny that there is an ultimate reality. The Madhyamika is based on three shastras, translated in China by Kumarajiva. These are: the *Madhyamika Shastra* (409); the *Sata Shastra* (404) and the *Dvadasanikaya Shastra* (408).

MAHAKASYAPA (Chin. Ma-ha-jia-she): One of the ten main disciples of the Buddha. A Brahmin of Magadha who became the First Patriarch of the Chan tradition in India according to Chinese records. He is credited with supervising the first compilation of the Buddha's sutras or sermons.

MAHAPARINIRVANA SUTRA (Chin. Da-ban-nie-pan-jing): Said to have been the last sutra expounded by the Buddha. Its title means the great, or final entrance of the Buddha into nirvana. Translated into Chinese by Dharmaraksa in 423, it teaches the 'Four Nirvana Virtues' which are True Eternity; True Bliss; True Personality and True Purity.

MAHASTHAMPRAPTA (Chin. Da-shi-zhi-pu-sa): One of the 'Three Holy Ones' of the Pure Land School. He appears on the right of Amitabha Buddha, representing wisdom, with Avalokitesvara on the right, symbolising compassion.

MAHAYANA (Chin. Da-cheng): The 'Large Vehicle' or 'Complete Teaching' of the Northern School. It teaches universal salvation which it inculcates through the Bodhisattva training.

MAITREYA (Chin. Mi-li): A Bodhisattva said to be living in the Tushita-heaven and the Buddhist Messiah who is to appear 5,000 years after the *nirvana* of Shakyamuni Buddha.

MANJUSRI (Chin. Wen-shu): A bodhisattva who symbolises the wisdom aspect of mind. He often appears in iconography as the left-hand assistant of Shakyamuni Buddha, seated on a lion. His sacred mountain is Wu-tai.

MANTRA (Chin. Zhen-yan): A mystic syllable, word or verse which is recited to still the mind and harness certain energies. Some mantras have specific purposes such as healing, besides being used as direct aids in quest of enlightenment.

MARA (Chin. Mo-gui): Personification of demonic influences, but on a deeper level, understood in terms of psycho-spiritual energy, which by no means denies the objective reality of possession, evil manifestations, etc.

NIDANAS, THE TWELVE (Chin. Ni-ta-na): The twelve links in the chain of dependent-origination or conditioned existence; These are: ignorance, conception, consciousness, name and form, the six sense organs, contact, sensation, craving, grasping, existence, birth, old age and death.

NIRMANAKAYA (Chin. Hua-shen): Understood in two different ways: (1) As a variant of *rupakaya* or transformation bodies of ordinary individuals; (2) As a special 'transformation-body' assumed by Buddhas and Bodhisattvas in order to help liberate living beings. Samantabhadra, for instance, is said to have appeared as a courtesan in order to help liberate living beings. Manjusri is said to appear in all sorts of guises in order to help pilgrims going to his holy mountain of Wu-tai.

NIRVANA (Chin. Nie-pan): Complete liberation from conditioned existence, cessation of rebirth and entry into bliss. It really means the 'blowing out' of the fires of ignorance which create nescience or the sense of a separate conditioned existence.

PANG-YUN (d. 811) Alias Dao-xuan. A famous lay-Buddhist and Chan adept who threw all his cash in the river and took up a simple life making bamboo ware and growing hemp. He called on famous Masters like Shi-tou and Ma-zu and realised complete enlightenment. His family were also Chan adepts and well versed in the transmission of the Mind, It was Pang-yun who coined the saying that 'supernatural power and its wonderful function are to be found in fetching water, chopping wood'.

PARAMITAS, THE SIX (Chin. Po-lou-mi): The six means of reaching the 'other shore' of enlightenment; sometimes 'the six perfections': (1) *dana* (almsgiving); (2) *sila* (discipline); (3) *ksanti* (patience); (4) *virya* (zeal, progress); (5) *dhyana* (meditation, stillness); (6) *prajna* (wisdom).

PITAKA (Chin. Zang): Means 'basket', 'store' or 'receptable'. The Chinese *Tripitaka* or 'Three baskets' are made up of the *Vinaya* texts, *sutras* and *shastras*.

PRAJNA (Chin. Pan-ru): The fundamental wisdom inherent in all men; the wisdom of non-duality.

PRAJNAPARAMITA SUTRA (Chin. Pan-ru-po-lou-mi-tou-jing): Actually a number of sutras which elucidate the teaching of emptiness (*sunyata*). The oldest version is the *Astasahasrika*, the earliest Chinese translation being Lokaraksa's made in 172. The *Mahaprajnaparamita Sutra* or longer version was translated by Xuan-zhuang in the seventh century, comprising 600 chuan (rolls) in 120 volumes. Shorter versions like the *Vajracchedika* and *Hrdaya* have been of immense value, being a condensation of the wisdom teaching in a handy form (see Bibliography).

PRATYEKA BUDDHA (Chin. Pi-chi-fu): Originally meant one who had awakened to the 'chain of causation' but it now usually means one who lives a solitary life and pursues self-enlightenment only. Considered inferior to those who cultivate the Bodhisattva career.

PU-TUO: The sacred island near Ningbo, Zhejiang Province. The Bodhimandala of Avalokitesvara or Guan-yin.

PURE LAND SCHOOL (Chin. Jing-tu-zong): Founded in China by Master Hui-yuan (d. 417). Its adherents seek salvation through faith in Amitabha Buddha aided by single-minded recitation of mantras and visualisation techniques. This method has the same effect as the *hua-tou* techniques used by Chan practitioners and Master Xu-yun also taught this practice.

QING: An instrument used by Chinese Buddhists, either a stone chime or small bell. The former is used to rouse people from meditation, the latter is used when chanting sutras, mantras, etc.

RUPA (Chin. Se): Form, matter.

SADDHARMA PUNDARIKA SUTRA (Chin. Miao-fa-lian-hua-jing): the *Lotus Sutra*. A sutra in which the Buddha introduced the idea of there being only 'One Vehicle' *(Ekayana)* and in which it was explained that the Hinayana methods were but an expedient means used to prepare followers for an understanding of the One Dharma-nature. Three Chinese versions exist: Dharmaraksha's (285); Kumarajiva's (400) and the joint translation by Jnanagupta and Dharmagupta (601).

SAMADHI (Chin. Ding; San-mei): A state of mental and spiritual imperturbability, the outcome of a successful meditation but not the meditation itself. It is free of disturbance from phenomenal activity.

SAMANTABHADRA (Chin. Pu-xian): A Bodhisattva who symbolises the fundamental law, *dhyana* and the practice of all the Buddhas. Famous for his 'ten vows'. Appears in the Gandavyuha portion of the Avatamsaka Sutra, His *bodhimandala* is Mount Emei in Sichuan.

SAMBHOGAKAYA (Chin. Bao-shen). Lit. 'reward body'. It means the body of bliss or enjoyment won by a Buddha as the fruit of past labours while still a bodhisattva.

SAMSARA (Chin. Sheng-se): The Chinese term is literally 'birth and death' but the Indian one means 'faring on' in conditioned existence, suffering birth, life, death and rebirth in an endless round.

SANGHA (Chin. Seng-ja): The Buddhist Order of monks and nuns.

SELF-NATURE; SELF-MIND (Chin. Zi-xing; Zi-xin): The Chan teaching consists of 'direct pointing to the mind for perception of self-nature and attainment of Buddhahood'. Here, the terms 'self-nature' and 'self-mind' mean the inherent *Bodhi*-nature, not the 'ego-self' associated with the body of four elements. It means the 'Self of all', the *Dharmata* or Dharma-nature. In the *Nirvana Sutra* the Buddha spoke of the 'Great Self'. This can only be perceived by wiping out the ego-illusion.

SRAVAKA (Chin. Sheng-wen): Lit. 'Sound-hearer.' A Hinayana follower who hears the Buddha's teaching, puts it into practice, but lacks bodhisattva-wisdom and compassion.

STUPA (Chin. Tu-pa): A reliquary, usually bell-shaped, in which the ashes of monks or holy people are placed for veneration.

SUNYA (Chin. Kong): Emptiness, inherent emptiness. A term used by the Buddha to point to the inherent emptiness of phenomenal things. To prevent clinging to this very term, he also spoke of the 'voidness of the void' or 'emptiness of emptiness' *(kong-kong)*.

SUPREME VEHICLE (Chin. Shang-cheng): The Supreme reality as taught by the Buddha. Sometimes used for the Mahayana but especially the Chan School which teaches outright cognisance of he *Dharmakaya* or Buddha-body.

SURANGAMA SUTRA (Chin. Leng-yan-jing): Translated by Paramiti in 705 at the Zhi-zhi Monastery, Canton. It explains the underlying cause of delusion and how to transmute the 'store consciousness' into the 'great mirror-wisdom', thus sublimating sense organs, sense objects and sense-data.

TATHAGATA (Chin. Ru-lai): Title of the Buddha, meaning 'he who comes thus', manifesting the 'suchness' as do all Buddhas.

TIAN-TAI (SCHOOL): Mount Tian-tai in Taizhou Prefecture in Zhejiang Province. Famous as the centre of Tian-tai Buddhism which based its practices on the *Lotus, Mahaparinirvana* and *Mahaprajnaparamita Sutras*, and Nagarjuna's *Madhyamika Shas-*

tra. Its methods aim at unlocking all the secrets of phenomena by means of its 'triple combined insight', a variant of *Samatha-vipasyana* meditation. It had begun with Master Hui-wen of the Northern Qi Dynasty (550–78) but was later consolidated on Mount Tian-tai by Master Zhi-yi, who wrote many commentaries.

TRIKAYA (Chin. San-shen): The 'three bodies of a Buddha': the *Nirmanakaya* or transformation body; the *Sambhogakaya* or reward body; and the *Dharmakaya*, or essential body.

TRUE WORD SCHOOL (Chin. Zhen-yan Zong): It utilises mantras, *dharani*, etc., similar to Tibetan Buddhist practices. Introduced to China by Amoghavajra in about 733.

UPASAKA: UPASIKA (Chin. Jing-xin-nan/Jin-shan-nu): Male and female lay disciples respectively. They observe the first five precepts, which are: not to kill; not to steal; not to commit adultery; not to lie; and not to take intoxicants.

VAIROCANA (Chin. Pi-lu-she-na): Vairocana symbolises the *Dharmakaya* or essential body of the Buddha, the ground of all things. Figures in the *Avatamsaka Sutra* and *Brahmajala Sutra*. His land is described as one of 'eternally tranquil light'.

VAJRACCHEDIKA SUTRA (Chin. Jin-gang-jing): A concise resumé of the Buddha's teachings on *sunyata* and *prajna*, emptiness and wisdom. Very popular with the Chan schools. Kumaraji-va's translation is the most well known.

VIMALAKIRTI (Chin. Wei-mu-chi): A renowned layman of Vai-sali in India who appeared in order to help the Buddha teach the 'non-dual Dharma'. His name means 'spotless reputation'. The *Vimalakirti Sutra* has been very popular in the Far East. *Vimala-kirti* rebuked those who mistakenly fettered others with the Hinayana teaching if the latter could awaken to the broad, *Mahayana*-mind. He stressed the 'non-abiding mind' which is beyond all compare.

VINAYA SCHOOL (Chin. Lu-zong): the Discipline School. Founded in China by Master Dao-xuan (596–667). The *Vinaya* texts comprise one of the 'three baskets' or portions of the *Tripi-taka* and provide the rules and regulations for monastic life.

VIRYA (Chin. Pi-li-ye): The fourth *paramita* – zeal, energetic progress along the way, strength of devotion.

WEN-SHU (see Manjusri).

WU: As in 'Jie-wu' it means awakening, enlightenment. Not to be confused with another term pronounced 'wu', which means 'nothing', 'no', 'not', – the void aspect of mind.

WU-TAI-SHAN: The 'Five Peaked Mountain' sacred to Manjusri, situated in Shansi Province. The famous Xian-tong and Pusa-ding Monasteries are located there. Manjusri is said to appear in all sorts of guises to aid pilgrims who go to his holy peak.

XIAN-SHOU: One of the five Hua-yan Patriarchs, also called Fa-zang. A prolific commentator on the *Avatamsaka Sutra*. As a term of respect he was called 'Xian-shou' or 'Wise-head'. The Emperor gave him the title 'Dharma-Master Guo-yi' or 'First in the Realm'.

XING-SI: (d. 471): Chan Master Xing-si of the Qing-yuan Mountain. Disciple of Hui-neng and teacher of Shi-tou. His school and body successors came to be known as the 'Qing-yuan' lineage.

XUAN-ZANG: (d. 664). An eminent Tang Dynasty monk who journeyed to India in 629 to acquire original sutras. He travelled via central Asia and Afghanistan. After returning to China in 645 with 657 Indian scriptures, he eventually translated 1,300 fascicles of work in Chinese, also penning his 'Record of the Journey to the West' (Xi Yu Ji).

YANG-SHAN: (814–90): Alias Chan Master Hui-ji, co-founder of the Gui-yang Chan School. Taught on Mount Yang near Yuan-zhou, Jiangxi Province. See Gui-shan.

YIN-GUANG (1861–1940): An eminent Pure Land adept whose teachings are still followed in the Far East today.

YOGACARA SCHOOL (Chin. Yu-jia Zong): The Idealist School, based on the Vijnanavada system. Founded in India by Asanga and introduced to China by Amoghavajra, a Singhalese of Brahmin descent. It utilises mantras, *dharani*, visualisation, etc., as in Tibetan Buddhism.

YONG-JIA (665–713): Master Xuan-jue of Yong-jia. An eminent

Tian-tai and Chan adept, famous for his 'Song of Enlightenment' or 'Zheng Dao Ge'. Known as the 'overnight enlightened one' after calling on Hui-neng at Cao-xi. Wrote many commentaries on Tian-tai and Chan practice.

YONG-MING (904–75): Alias Yan-shou. An eminent Chan Master and prolific commentator, He also taught Pure Land Buddhism and is one of the Nine Patriarchs of this school. He compiled his voluminous 'Zong Jing Lu' (Source-Mirror Record) to explain the complementary nature of all methods of practice.

YONG-ZHENG: Emperor of the early Qing Dynasty (reigned 1723–35) who was famous for holding 'Chan weeks' or periods of meditation at the imperial palace. Chan Master Tian Hui-che of the Gao-min Monastery in Yangzhou realised his awakening there.

YUN-MEN: (d. 949). Chan Master Wen-yan of the Yun-men Monastery, Shaozhou district, Guangdong Province. Founder of the Yun-men Chan School. Disciple of Mu-zhou and Xue-feng, teacher of Shou-chu and many other enlightened successors. Famous for his 'one word teaching' and 'three gates'.

ZHAO-ZHOU: (778–897). Chan Master Cong-shen of the Guan-yin Monastery in Zhao-zhou, Hebei Province. Disciple of Nan-quan, teacher of many outstanding followers. Famous for his gong-an 'Wu'.

ZHEN-RU: See Bhutatathata.

ZHEN-RU MONASTERY: Famous monastery on Mount Yun-ju in Jiangxi Province. Well known in the Tang and Song dynasties as a centre of the Cao-dong School. The last monastery to be restored by Master Xu-yun.

BIBLIOGRAPHY

Material Specifically Dealing with Xu-yun's Teaching

Further material giving Xu-yun's teaching can be found in: *Chan & Zen Teaching, Series I*. Translated by Upasaka Lu K'uan-Yu (Charles Luk). Rider, 1960. Century-Hutchinson reprint, 1987. This material comprises: *The Prerequisites of Chan Training; The Chan Training; Daily Lectures at Two Chan Weeks; The Master's Arrival at Cao-xi*.

These are extracts from *Xu-yun He-shang Nian-pu* and *Xu-yun He-shang Fa-hui*. The present volume contains one of the *Chan Weeks* included in the above, and also *The Master's Arrival at Cao-xi*. Readers interested in practising Buddhism are urged to digest the rest of the Master's teaching contained in the titles listed above. Upasaka Lu was a lay-disciple of Master Xu-yun and the latter personally encouraged him to undertake translations for Western people. See below for details of the two supplementary Chan and Zen Volumes.

Titles of Related Interest

Blofeld, John, *The Zen Teaching of Huang Po* (Buddhist Society, London, 1968).

The Zen Teaching of Hui Hai (Buddhist Publishing Group, Leicester, 1987).

Chang, Garma, *The Buddhist Teaching of Totality* (Pennsylvania State University Press, 1971).

Cleary, Jonathan, *Zen Dawn: Early Zen Texts From Tun Huang* (Shambhala, 1986).

Evans-Wentz, W. Y., *The Tibetan Book of the Dead* (Oxford University Press, 1960).

Kapleau, Philip, *The Three Pillars of Zen* (Tokyo, 1965).

Luk, Charles, *Chan and Zen Teaching, Series 1* (Century-Hutchinson (Rider), 1987).

Chan and Zen Teaching, Series 2 (Century-Hutchinson (Rider), 1987).

Chan and Zen Teaching, Series 3 (Century-Hutchinson (Rider), 1987).

Practical Buddhism (Rider, 1971).

Secrets of Chinese Meditation (Rider, 1964).

The Surangama Sutra (Rider, 1973).

The Transmission of the Mind (Rider, 1974).

The Vimalakirti Sutra (Routledge/Shambhala, 1972).

Schloegl, Irmgard, *The Wisdom of the Zen Masters* (London, 1975).
Soothill and Hodous, *A Dictionary of Chinese Buddhist Terms* (Kegan, Paul, Trench & Trubner; Cheng Wen Reprint, Taiwan, 1975).
Suzuki, D. T. *Essays in Zen Buddhism, Series 1* (Rider, 1980).
Essays in Zen Buddhism, Series 2 (Rider, 1980).
Essays in Zen Buddhism, Series 3 (Rider, 1980).
The Lankavatara Sutra (Trans.). Routledge, 1973.
Yuan and Walker, *Grass Mountain: A Seven-Day Intensive in Chan Training with Master Nan Huai-Chin* (Weiser, 1986).

CHINESE SOURCES
Works Relating to Xu Yun

虛雲和尚法彙　　岑學呂

(1) Xu Yen He Shang Fa Hui (Xu Yun's Discourses & Dharma Words). Ed. Cen Xue Lu. Chung Hua Buddhist Publishing House, 1961.

虛雲和尚年譜　　岑學呂

(2) Xu Yun He Shang Nian Pu (Xu Yun's Autobiography). Ed. Cen Xue Lu. Jia Tun Printing, Hong Kong. Reprint 1981.

Contemporary Sources of Note

禪與道概論　　南懷瑾

(1) Chan Yu Dao Gai Lun.　　Nan Huai Qin.
Lao Gu Publishing Co. Taibei, 1968.

習禪錄影　　南懷瑾

(2) Xi Chan Yu Lin.　　Nan Huai Qin.
Lao Gu Publishing Co., Taibei, 1976.

Classical Sources

景德傳燈錄　　道原

(1) Jing De Chuan Deng Lu.　　Ed. Dao Yuan.
(TSD 51, no 2076)

五 燈 會 元

(2) Wu Deng Hui Yuan.
Xin Wen Feng Printing House, 1984.

普 濟

Ed. Pu Ji.

從 容 錄

(3) Cong Rong Lu.
(TSD 48, no. 2004)

宏 智 正 覺

Hong Zhi Zhend Jue.

憨 山 大 師

(4) Han Shan Da Shi Meng Yu Ji.
(Dai Nihon Zoko-zokyo 2, 32, 2–5)

夢 遊 集

Chinese Sutras

法 華 經

(1) Fa Hua Jing. (TSD 9., no. 262).

金 剛 經

(2) Jin Gang Jing. (TSD. 18, no. 866).

楞 嚴 經

(3) Leng Yan Jing. (TSD. 19, no. 945).

維 摩 經

(4) Wei Mo Jing. (TSD. 14, no. 475).

圓 覺 經

(5) Yuan Jue Jing. (TSD. 17, no. 842).

Dictionaries

佛 學 大 辭 典

(1) Fo Xue Da Zi Dian. Xin Wen Feng Printing Co. Taibei, 1969.

漢 英 佛 學 大 辭 典

(2) Han Ying Fo Xue Da Zi Dian. Cheng Wen Publishing Co. Taibei, 1975.